DAVID BOWIE
A CHRONOLOGY

DAVID BOWIE
A CHRONOLOGY

Kevin Cann

VERMILION
London Melbourne Sydney Auckland Johannesburg

Vermilion and Company
An imprint of the Hutchinson Publishing Group
17–21 Conway Street, London W1P 6JD

Hutchinson Group (Australia) Pty Ltd
30–32 Cremorne Street, Richmond South, Victoria 3121
PO Box 151, Broadway, New South Wales 2007
Hutchinson Group (NZ) Ltd
32–34 View Road, PO Box 40–086, Glenfield, Auckland 10
Hutchinson Group (SA) Pty Ltd
PO Box 337, Bergvlei 2012, South Africa

First published 1983
© Kevin Cann 1983
Phototypeset in Linotron Times by
Input Typesetting Ltd, London

Printed in Great Britain by The Anchor Press Ltd
and bound by Wm Brendon & Sons Ltd,
both of Tiptree, Essex

British Library Cataloguing in Publication Data

Cann, Kevin
  David Bowie.
  1. Bowie, David
  I. Title
  784.5′0092′4   ML420.B754
  ISBN 0 09 153831 9

This book is dedicated to Joe
and the actor
and with much love and respect to
Thelma and Brian Cann

Contents

ACKNOWLEDGEMENTS

Ken Pitt (without whom . . .) and Tony Visconti.
The *Beckenham Journal/Bromley Times*, Liz Clark, George Tremlett, Ray Stevenson, Alan Yentob, Brian Lane and Bromley Technical High School, Peter Noone, Julian Meldrum (BM Archives), Capital Radio, David and Gina (*Starzone*), Gille and Rita (Bowie Bureau), Ann Gayle, Francis Plomp, Ann Pasker (MGM) and Stuart Grundy (BBC Publications). Thanks also to Corinne Schwab, and to Ruth Evans and Susan Hill.

Jesper Muller, Peter Bernsdorf, Nolene Atkinson, Michael Grote, Geraldine Stroud, Dianne and David, Barbara Carpenter, Kamiko Kajiwara, Mark Adams, Ulrike Burger, Gloria Cimino, Bob Skeens, Kevin Macan-Lind, Alassin, Simon and Melanie, Ian Dale and Marcus.

RCA London/New York, Jill Barry, Gill Smith (Decca) and Bruce Dunbar (Bewlay Bros).

Preface

A chronology is a series of events arranged according to their dates. David Robert Jones is an event: a Londoner who became one of the most original and inexhaustible talents of today's music scene. This book doesn't seek to explain his talent, too many have tried already. It is designed to simply and clearly put bald facts in order.

The book is divided into two sections to define the early days in David's life, which neatly tie up as the first twenty-five years, and the last decade from 1972. I hope it will, above all, underline the sheer guts and determination that the young Bowie obviously showed, and perseverance against false starts and disappointments. His faith in himself and his ability to adapt, remodel, discard and improve has made him the individual he is.

It may also highlight the many musicians, friends and associates David encountered in his career, show his old environments and become, perhaps, a scrapbook of events and trivia that I hope will give some idea of what happened, in what order and thus, why.

I have checked all dates printed, but early shows and events are occasionally covered with a general title and a rough date as many of these are uncertain. Dates were researched from January 1978. Thanks must be extended to David's fans worldwide who were an invaluable source of information.

Finally there are many people who have given much time and help to this project and I have tried to credit everyone involved, but to all of them I would like to say thank you again. This is as much their book, their anecdotes and part of their lives as it is mine.

Kevin Cann, 1983

The Jones Family

8 January 1947
David Robert Jones born just after midnight at 40 Stansfield Road, Brixton, London SW9.
Father: Haywood Stenton Jones.
Born: 21 November 1912 at 41 Sepulchre Gate, Doncaster.
One daughter from previous marriage, Annette Jones.
Mother: Margaret Mary Burns.
Born: In 1914 in Tunbridge Wells, Kent.
One son from previous marriage, Terry.

11 August 1947
Mrs Jones's divorce becomes absolute on the grounds of her husband's adultery.

12 September 1947
Haywood Jones and Margaret Burns marry in Brixton.
After David they had no more children.

Little is known of David Bowie's early life. He was happy, healthy and well liked locally. He attended infant school in Streatham Hill; his first memory is of the puddle he left there on the first day! His route to school often took him past Brixton Prison; he remembers being told that men were locked up there and never being able to understand why.

The South Lambeth district was a working-class redevelopment area during David's childhood. London was still recovering from the Blitz and the general hardship left an impression. Some children in his school had no shoes though David later recalled that he was never left wanting for anything.

His father, the son of a shoe manufacturer, was a well-mannered and bespectacled Yorkshireman. Haywood Jones first married Hilda Louise Sullivan from Kilburn in 1933. They had one child, Annette, born in 1935. During the Second World War Haywood Jones served in the Eighth Army in North Africa, returning to London after the war. His first marriage had broken up and by 1946 he was living at 40 Stansfield Road, Brixton, London SW9, with Margaret Burns. She also had a child from a previous marriage, a son, Terry, born in 1939.

David was born on 8 January 1947 at home in Brixton. His parents married on 12 September that year. His father was thirty-four and his mother, who was Jewish, thirty-three. Stansfield Road was to be their home for the next eight years. His father worked for Dr Barnardo's at 32 Burton Street, London WC1, close to Kings Cross Station. His mother took part-time work as an usherette in a Brixton cinema.

David's stepsister Annette has never fully been in the picture. David later said that she disappeared to Egypt with a millionaire businessman and lost touch with her family after that. It is probable that Annette remained in the custody of Hilda Jones, and contact was lost that way. It is not known whether Annette ever stayed at or visited Stansfield Road.

Terry, however, figures prominently in David's life. As children the two spent a lot of time together despite the age difference of eight years. When David was eight years old and Terry sixteen, they were both sent to their uncle's farmhouse in Yorkshire. David was then at boarding school near Doncaster. His parents scrimped and saved to send him. Terry helped his uncle (their father's brother) on the farm, which was basically livestock, sheep and cattle. The slower pace of life there left little impression on the youngsters and the initial excitement of living on a farm was soon replaced with homesickness.

Terry was the most important influence on the young David Jones. David would later evoke those years in songs like 'The Bewlay Brothers' on 'Hunky Dory'. Terry introduced David to writers like Jack Kerouac and Allen Ginsberg, and jazz musicians like King Curtis and Eric Dolphy. Later, while David was attending secondary school, Terry was travelling the world as a merchant seaman, often away for months at a time. It was a great event for David when he returned.

During the mid- to late sixties, Terry was committed to a local asylum where he still is today. David has always acknowledged the streak of madness in his family, and Terry's illness devastated him. When David and Angie, his wife, were living at Haddon Hall they would pack a lunch and clean laundry and regularly visit Terry. David later said that Terry never really responded. 'He would just lay on the lawn and look at the sky, never said a word,' David said in 1972.

Many of the songs on 'The Man Who Sold the World' LP from 1971, particularly 'All the Madmen', were about David coming to terms with this.

His father died in August 1969, but the sadness of that time was buffered by David's first successful single, 'Space Oddity' and his success in the Malta and Italian Song Festivals that same month. But David was greatly upset: he had been very close to his father, to the extent of having his finances managed by him until his twenty-first birthday. David registered his father's death and handled all the funeral arrangements. Later that year the family home at 4 Plaistow Grove was sold, David moving to Haddon Hall with Angie, and his mother into a flat in nearby Beckenham. David furnished both homes in his favourite style at that time, Art Nouveau.

1952–54
Attends an infant school in Streatham Hill, South Lambeth.

Summer 1955
David and Terry move to uncle's farmhouse in Yorkshire.

1955–57
David attends boarding school near Doncaster.

David's first musical impression was formed around this time when he saw a cousin dancing to Elvis Presley's 'Hound Dog'. He was amazed at the effect the record had on her. The first record he ever owned was Fats Domino's 'Blueberry Hill' (which was one of the first tracks featured in his first major film *The Man Who Fell to Earth*). But neither of these two stars made any real initial impact on Davy Jones. That particular honour fell to Little Richard. 'I never showed any particular leanings towards anything much, until I hit about nine or ten, and then I fell in love with the Little Richard Band. I never heard anything that lived in such bright colours in the air. It really just painted the whole room for me,' David was later to say on the 20/20 Show (USA) in 1981.

June/July 1957
David and Terry return to London, to a new home at 4 Plaistow Grove, Sundridge Park, Bromley, Kent. Mr and Mrs Jones had moved in some months before to prepare for the boys' return. The house

stands next to Sundridge Park station and nestles behind The Crown public house in Plaistow Lane. Like many of its time it had a bath in the kitchen.

September 1957
David spends his final year at junior school at Burnt Ash Junior Mixed School, Rangefield Road, Bromley.

Plaistow Grove

Plaistow Grove, Bromley is a haunt for the Bowie tourist. David lived in number four on and off between 1957 and 1969. The house is terraced and has since been modernized. All of its rooms are small, and it has a tiny front and back garden. David's bedroom was at the rear of the house, overlooking the back of the pub.

Although his links with the house have been severed some thirteen years now, post for David still finds its way there and the present occupants are quite used to fans pointing camera lenses at their front door. It's hard to believe, looking at the size of David's old bedroom, that it once housed an elementary studio: reel-to-reel tape recorders linked by microphones for overdubs. The house also occasionally gives up clues to its famous old occupant; the present owners found an early self-portrait on the back of their cupboards while decorating.

The residents of Plaistow Grove are generally very aware of the boy who used to play in the street. Many actually knew David well and have anecdotes to offer. One of the best is a good indication of how hard he found life in the music business. After one early disappointment in his teens he climbed onto the roof of his house and scattered all his records off the top in despair.

Mrs Pollard, one of Plaistow Grove's oldest residents, used to make David bread puddings in the early days when his records weren't selling. David, in 1980, remembered her kindness and sent her a signed photograph while he was appearing on Broadway in *The Elephant Man*. While on a visit to the UK in late 1978, David went to see his old home in Bromley, but stayed firmly in the car, too shy to knock on the front door.

July 1958
Burnt Ash Junior School.

15

September 1958
David starts his secondary schooling at Bromley Technical High
School, Oakley Road, Keston, an all-boys school in peaceful surround-
ings. It was not long before he turned quite rebellious, and began
taking more interest in his R & B groups out of school than schoolwork
itself. His mother became particularly concerned about his change in
attitude. Arguments between the two were frequent and Mr Jones
would often have to intervene.

Bromley Technical
High School

Now known as Ravenswood School for Boys, Bromley Technical High School is little changed. David and the school's other famous pupil, Peter Frampton, the face of 1968 and before that lead singer with The Herd, are well remembered. David has never returned to the school since leaving in July 1963 and his old music teacher, Brian Lane, now head of the upper school, is the only member of staff remaining who was there in David's day.

Many rumours and stories of David's life at Bromley Tech. have emerged. Most are confused. It is true that David and school never really gelled. He preferred Jazz and Rhythm and Blues to schoolbooks and homework, although this never affected his attendance which was always good. By his third year in class 3A, art was his main subject. He was well liked at school but apart from a close group of friends he kept himself to himself. Never at any time did the school find it necessary to expel him as has sometimes been claimed in the press. Sometimes, however, the colour of his hair would change, 'It was probably only food dye or something removable,' Mr Lane told me. 'The next day he would put the colour right when asked to.' That year, 1962, his school report referred to him as a 'complete showman'.

David's closest school friend was George Underwood, with whom he still keeps in touch today. George was equally keen on art and music and they both formed groups around the same time, George's being George and the Dragons and David's being The Kon-Rads.

In May of 1963, Peter Frampton's father (David's art master) organized a concert to raise money for a projected cricket pavilion. George and the Dragons got top billing. Peter Frampton, then of The Little Ravens, was also in the show. David did play though his name didn't appear in the programme. After a fight of the previous year George and David's friendship had become firmer than ever, and on George's invitation David joined the group for the evening.

17

David had made one of his earliest-known appearances with his own group the previous summer at a school fete arranged by the PTA. The resulting concert caused such a commotion amongst the schoolboy audience that the plug was pulled and the power cut off. No one explained to David at the time what happened.

David was also a keen sprinter at school and his sports coach of the time recalled he had above average ability as a hurdler. David generally spent his time well at school, occasionally attending school trips, like the week to Exmouth in the Easter holidays of 1961 where he attempted to win a table-tennis competition.

He never really held much interest in the type of music taught to him by Mr Lane, though he, like all the other boys, was taught the basics. David was taking lessons for the saxophone outside school. 'He was once asked to tell the class about his group and the type of music they played and he stood up and gave a very memorable account of the regular shows he was giving at the Chislehurst Caves in Kent,' Mr Lane said. Probably more interest was shown in Mr Frampton's art classes.

David left school in July 1963 with 'O' levels in art and woodwork. It was agreed that he could leave school a week early so that he could start a job in commercial art, where he was hired as 'junior visualizer'.

1959
David's mother buys him a saxophone for Christmas because he had shown such enthusiasm for the white plastic one he had been practising on for months beforehand, after having been given a Little Richard single which he learned by heart and covered with his early groups.

The family home at this time also housed an old upright piano which David tinkered with.

8 January 1960
David Robert Jones is thirteen.

1960
David finds the telephone number of jazz saxophonist Ronnie Ross and arranges lessons. Tapes were said to have been made during some of these sessions, the earliest known with David.

1962 Spring Term
After a fight between David and best friend George Underwood, David was taken to Farnborough Hospital where both his eyes were

18

operated upon. He was retained for further treatment on his left pupil which has remained permanently dilated ever since. The medical term for this condition is aniscoria. The fight was over George's girlfriend whom David had been making a play for. The friendship was repaired although David was to lose three months from his fourth school year.

Summer 1962
David and his group play at the school PTA fete on the steps of the school. The performance of Shadows's numbers running well over time and causing much commotion amongst the gathered schoolboys, was stopped when the power was cut off.

The Kon-Rads
David's first official group, made up of a five-piece unit and billed as a 'vocal and instrumental best group'. The five even had suits made up. No tapes are known to have been made.

December 1963
The Kon-Rads never produced their own material, cover versions being their repertoire. The Christmas of 1963 saw a small-scale publicity campaign; they sent cheaply printed Christmas cards to friends and interesting people: the sax player's name . . . Dave Jay!

David would later tell friends that during his schooldays, at weekends, he would travel up to Trafalgar Square to try and talk with the beatniks about Burroughs, Kerouac and the Beat movement. He would pester them so much that they would chase him away! This was inspired by his brother, Terry, who gave David a copy of *On The Road* by Jack Kerouac.

May 1963
The Bromley Technical High School pageant arranged by Mr Frampton and featuring George and The Dragons with Davy Jones on saxophone. Also on the bill young Peter Frampton with The Little Ravens, named after the school badge ensign. The school show was to raise money for the sports pavilion which now stands at the bottom of Ravenswood games fields. There were two performances, one in the afternoon for the pupils and one in the evening for the parents. George and The Dragons went down well. Peter Frampton recalled that David had now become the school hero: 'He brought the house down.' The show generally was a great success and raised the amazing sum (in 1963) of £50. This pageant has often been mistaken for the school's Christmas

end-of-term concert, but was a quite separate and unique event.

1962–3 were formative years for David. George Underwood and he became the class mods, often travelling to Eel Pie Island near Richmond, and the AA Athletic Ground and the Crawdaddy clubs in Richmond on Friday nights to see groups like Gary Farr and The T Bones and Jeff Beck's three-piece group (prior to The Yardbirds) The Tridents. During a Capital Radio interview in 1979, David recalled that they would often travel back to Sundridge Park Station on the milk train. They never rode scooters!

July 1963

Leaves Bromley Tech. with 'O' levels in art and woodwork. Arranges with the school to leave a week early to start work as a 'junior visualizer' at a commercial art company.

David's first and only full-time employment was at a London-based advertising agency, The Design Group Limited. He worked there for less than six months. In the evenings he was still playing saxophone and this, he later admitted, did not mix with his job. After a row at work he decided that music was his vocation, though he was still unsure exactly how to proceed.

Late 1963

Makes the change from jazz to 'pop'. Legend has it that about this time he met three lads in a barber's shop in Bromely High Street while waiting for a haircut. Robert Allen (drums), Roger Bluck (lead guitar) and Frank Howard (bass), previously known as The Hooker Brothers, joined David and George Underwood and became The King Bees.

April 1964

John Bloom, millionaire and business tycoon, receives a letter from Davy Jones asking for financial help for The King Bees. Bloom, impressed by his nerve and style contacts a friend, Leslie Conn, in the music business who in turn sends David a telegram with a phone number. Through this came their first engagement, a wedding anniversary party at Jack Isow's Jack of Clubs in Brewer Street, Soho. Although their loud R & B went down badly they managed to get £100 for the gig and interest from Conn. Their set for the show only lasted for two numbers, after which Conn had to pull David to one side and ask him to stop. Davy Jones then burst into tears.

20

The King Bees
The King Bees were David's first real attempt at breaking into the music business. Though not under contract, Leslie Conn managed their affairs and negotiated a contract with Decca who issued their only single on the Vocallion Pop label. Early shows were at the Marquee, Café des Artistes and the Round House plus a series of university dates.

5 June 1964
First single released 'Liza Jane'/'Louie Louie Go Home'. Davy Jones with The King Bees (Vocallion Pop). 3,500 copies were issued.

Les Conn
Born in Stamford Hill, East London, Leslie Conn was The King Bees' manager for a few months in mid-'64. As well as the recording deal with Vocallion Pop he arranged a BBC television spot to promote his first single 'Liza Jane', David's first ever TV appearance. Conn thought that David, even then, showed all the signs of becoming a big star and knew that it would be better in the long run for David not to sign any long-term commitment. David and Les Conn parted on good terms, David going on to join his next band, The Manish Boys, and Conn continuing as a talent scout for Dick James Music. He abandoned his association with Bowie because, it is said, he did not feel ready to manage a talent that he perceived as potentially major.

Music publisher Dick James, when presented with David and Marc Bolan late in 1964, promptly ordered Les Conn to, 'Get those long-haired gits out of my office!' To aid an erratic income Bolan and Bowie decorated Conn's office more than once. Their friendship formed its earnest links then.

September 1964
'You're Holding Me Down'/'I've Gotta' single released by The King Bees and George Underwood, without Davy Jones (Coral).

It has been claimed by David that he occasionally backed Sonny Boy Williamson who would often be booked for long engagements around this time at the Marquee. The Stones would also often work with him.

12 November 1964
Appears on BBC I with fellow long-haired friends (mainly from The King Bees and The Manish Boys and heads a plea for 'The prevention

of cruelty to long-haired men'. At seventeen it is his earliest known television interview, with Cliff Michelmore.

Luminaries of 'the prevention of cruelty to long-haired men' campaign included David Sutch (later to become Screaming Lord Sutch) and Jimmy Page of Led Zeppelin, who used to session for both groups at the time.

Late 1964

The King Bees join forces with David's new group, The Manish Boys. Originally The Band Seven their name changed on David's advice. David would often travel to see the up and coming Rolling Stones play, mostly at the Marquee. David's taste in fashion then was heavily influenced by Jagger and The Manish Boys name was similarly drawn from an old Muddy Waters song.

At one time David was playing in both The King Bees and The Manish Boys, the groups briefly joining together to create what one local reporter terms, 'the Medway sound'.

The Manish Boys consisted of David Jones (vocals, auto sax), John Edward (lead guitar), Paul Rodriguez (tenor sax, trumpet), Wilf Byrne (baritone sax), Bob Solly (keyboards), John Watson (bass) and John Whitehead (drums). Their billing would often be Davy Jones and The Manish Boys as well as just The Manish Boys. This proved disastrous for the group. When their first single was released furious rows ensued between David and the other members of the group as to who should receive top billing.

January 1965

'Restless'/'Take My Tip' single released by Kenny Miller (Stateside). The first song sale for David and also the first of his own compositions he was to record. David's song being introduced to Miller by record producer, Shel Talmy.

3 March 1965

As a publicity stunt David is interviewed at home by the *Daily Mirror*, published the next day with the headline: 'Row Over Davy's Hair'.

Davy, who comes from Bromley, Kent, said: 'I've said that I have no intention of having my hair cut. Mr Langford has left the matter open till Friday (5 March 65) in case I change my mind . . . but I won't.' Mr Langford, thirty-nine, said: 'Kids today just don't want this long hair business anymore.'

5 March 1965
'I Pity the Fool'/'Take My Tip' single released by The Manish Boys, the B-side being written by David (Parlophone). Session guitarist for these tracks was Jimmy Page. The single was credited to The Manish Boys which upset David who had become used to an individual credit. This and other problems led to the group's demise.

David and group reprieved by producer Barry Langford for the Monday evening live TV broadcast of 'Gadzooks! It's all happening'. Davy's reaction: 'I want to prove that the length of my hair doesn't matter. It's the performance that counts.' Langford said, 'For his own sake, Davy should have a haircut.'

8 March 1965
Appears on 'Gadzooks! It's all happening' with The Manish Boys performing 'I Pity the Fool'. Makes the papers by refusing to cut his hair for the BBC. A compromise was made, however, at the eleventh hour. Barry Langford agreed to let them perform under the condition that any complaints would lose their fee to charity. No complaints were received.

Mid-1965
The Manish Boys disband having supported Gerry and The Pacemakers, The Kinks and Gene Pitney on tour.

David joins forces with three new musicians from Thanet in Kent, Dennis Taylor (lead guitar), Graham Rivens (bass guitar), and Phil Lancaster (drums). The group was loosely managed by ex-Moody Blues roadie Ralph Horton. Publicity was arranged by another friend, Gaby Sturmer. The new group became known as The Lower Third.

June/July 1965
The Lower Third play their first gigs along the south coast, including the Bournemouth Pavilion and Seaside Club.

31 July 1965
Davy Jones and The Lower Third support Johnny Kidd and The Pirates at the Ventnor Winter Gardens, Isle of Wight. (Kidd died the following year, October 1966.)

WINTER GARDENS

VENTNOR

Saturday, July 31st

JOHNNY KIDD
and the PIRATES

plus DAVY JONES and the LOWER THIRD

and **NEIL ANDERSEN**

Late Coaches to and from Cowes, Ryde, Newport

8 – 11-30   Fully Licensed   Admission **7/6**

Next Saturday : **THE PRETTY THINGS ! !**

20 August 1965

'You've Got a Habit of Leaving'/'Baby Loves That Way' single released by Davy Jones (*and* The Lower Third, but the band were not credited on the label) (Parlophone). Both tracks were written by David who had started to become a serious songwriter. Produced by Shel Talmy, 'You've Got a Habit of Leaving' was reputedly the first track that David ever demoed in a recording studio. A press release issued at the time of the single's release by Martin Ross at EMI featured this short interview with David.

What do Davy and his new group think of their partnership? Says Davy: 'We like each other's ideas. We have the same policies and fit rather well together. All of us like to keep to ourselves and we like things rather than people.'

Late 1965

Tony Hatch signs David to record for Pye Records and produces David's music himself. Hatch later said that David was one of the first singer/songwriters to emerge. Their collaboration was not commercially successful although David planned with Hatch in 1966 to produce a musical called *Kids on the Roof*. The musical was to have an 18th-century setting and be rather like *Oliver*. Another project David was then working on was for a television series called 'Peacock's Farm' about a young man called Peacock who runs a boutique. Although 'Peacock's Farm' never materialized, the musical became the spine of material included on his first LP, 'David Bowie' for Decca, and accounts for the album's high-production feel.

September 1965
David and The Lower Third appear at the Marquee for afternoon shows.

1965
The Lower Third played many London and provincial gigs. London shows were mostly Marquee-based where they had begun to gain a following. In September 1965, on Ralph Horton's advice, Kenneth Pitt, a manager and publicist, wandered down to one of their Sunday afternoon shows at the Marquee to see if Davy Jones was as good as Horton had said. He was impressed and a meeting was arranged at Horton's flat in Warwick Square. David's career was now demanding more time and experienced guidance. It was decided later that Ken Pitt should take over as David's manager. The Lower Third, David later said, 'were booed off every gig we did', the afternoon shows evidently coming about because of their high-volume sound that the Marquee management thought appropriate only for afternoon gigs.

31 December 1965
Davy Jones and The Lower Third play their only concert date outside the UK at the Golf-Drouot club in Paris. This was also David's first trip abroad and his last live date as Davy Jones.

During a live phone-in on French radio in 1977 David was reminded of that show when Henri Leproux, owner of the Golf-Drouot, rang in . . .

HENRI LEPROUX: *Je voudrais demander à David s'il se souvient qu'il est passé le 31 Décembre 1965 dans un club à Paris, et qu'il a donné quatre concerts accompagné par les Lowaires Tseurdes . . .*
JEAN-BERNARD: *It's very funny, it's a very old friend of mine we've got on the phone right now, called Henri Leproux, et qui est le dir . . . c'est un très vieil ami à moi qu'on a au téléphone, qui est directeur du Golf-Drouot . . .*
DAVID: Ah, ah, ah, bravo!

JEAN-BERNARD: *Il voudrait demander s'il se souvient qu'il est passé à Paris le 31 Décembre 1965 au Golf-Drouot. Do you remember that?*

DAVID: I remember Golf-Drouot very well indeed. It's the first place that I tried out . . . I think you remember the sound we were trying out, something which was pretty much like a kind of punk thing?

JEAN-BERNARD: *Il demande à Henri s'il se souvient, à l'époque il essayait de mettre au point quelque chose avec son groupe qui s'appelait le Loweurr*
. . .

DAVID: Lower Third!

HENRI LEPROUX: *Bien sûr, j'me souviens très bien! D'alleurs il avait obtenu un très gros succès. Nous ne le connaissions pas en France, à l'époque, mais on savait déjà, à l'avance, qu'il allait devenir une très grosse vedetta, et j'en profite pour le féliciter pour sa très grande carrière!*

JEAN-BERNARD: *OK. He wants to say that he knew at the time, that's twelve years ago that you would be very big, and he wants to . . . how do you say . . . 'féliciter'?*

DAVID: Well . . . I . . . I . . . would like to say myself that his club was very inspirational for me, it really was, because we were trying out, at that time what we considered was fairly exciting music, and we had a chance to play somewhere, and he let us work there.

January 1966

On a trip to the USA, Ken Pitt cabled David from New York to say that a new group called The Monkees had been formed for television with a lead singer called Davy Jones. On Pitt's return David announced that he was now David Bowie. The name was evidently chosen as a reference to the Bowie knife, a twelve-inch blade.

Although David has used the professional stage name of Bowie since January 1966, he has never officially changed it through deed-poll and is technically still David Jones. All legal documents are signed by him under that name.

Ken Pitt had taken to the USA an acetate copy of 'Rubber Band', already letting prospective record company executives know about the new boy genius he had discovered. Pitt was then describing David as 'someone rather special'.

14 January 1966

'Can't Help Thinking About Me'/'And I Say to Myself' single released by David Bowie and The Lower Third (Pye).

David dropped a promo copy of this record into Paul McCartney's recording studio in Soho Square to little effect. The press release issued to promote the single 'Can't Help Thinking About Me' had David saying, 'If the record is a hit, that's all right, but I really want to become established.'

Davie Jones is back in his locker.....

at the bottom of the sea. And instead we have DAVID BOWIE, a 19 year old singer discovered by Tony Hatch. Why David Bowie? "There are too many Davie Jones's" David explains. "David Jones is my real name and when I first turned professional two years ago and my pirate-like character was just right at that time, and the name fitted in with the image I wanted to give myself."

Looking at DAVID BOWIE it would be difficult to recognise under that smart exterior the somewhat controversial and angry young singer who styled himself after his famous namesake. Gone are the outlandish clothes, the long hair and the "wild" appearance and instead we find a quiet, talented vocalist and song writer – DAVID BOWIE.

His debut disc has been written by himself and tells the story of a young man leaving home. Most of David's lyrics are taken from his own experiences of city life – a theme about which he is well qualified to write since he has attempted 'to make his own way' since he was sixteen.

CAN'T HELP THINKIN' ABOUT ME
c w And I Say to Myself   Pye 7N 17020

11 February 1966
David Bowie and The Lower Third appear at the Marquee supported by Boz and The Sidewinders. Ronnie Ross and Rod Stewart were also playing at the Marquee that month.

28 February 1966
Interviewed by *Disc* and *Music Echo*. Headlined 'From Dave', it was a rare interview. For many years David and his management found it very difficult to achieve press coverage.

'Caroline' was David's fan club secretary in 1966, actually a pseudonym for Ralph Horton. Glossy fan club postcards were issued featuring a photo of David in a recording studio, singing in a military jacket. David's first fan club was run by two girls who lived in Plaistow Grove.

Late February 1966
The Lower Third disband after a long tour. The group by now had built up quite a solid London following, but the pressures of life on the road were too much for a couple of the members. The group had travelled in an old ambulance that David had acquired from the local council very cheaply. It was often parked and slept in overnight near the Marquee. When the group disbanded it was dumped at a local garage and eventually resold to a commercial traveller.

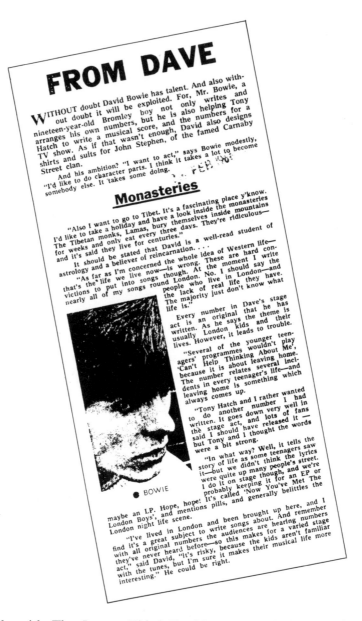

FROM DAVE

WITHOUT doubt David Bowie has talent. And also without doubt it will be exploited. For, Mr. Bowie, a nineteen-year-old Bromley boy not only writes and arranges his own numbers, but he is also helping Tony Hatch to write a musical score, and the numbers for a TV show. As if that wasn't enough, David also designs shirts and suits for John Stephen, of the famed Carnaby Street clan.

And his ambition? "I want to act," says Bowie modestly, "I'd like to do character parts. I think it takes a lot to become somebody else. It takes some doing.

Monasteries

"Also I want to go to Tibet. It's a fascinating place y'know. I'd like to take a holiday and have a look inside the monasteries The Tibetan monks, Lamas, bury themselves inside mountains for weeks and only eat every three days. They're ridiculous— and it's said they live for centuries."

It should be stated that David is a well-read student of astrology and a believer of reincarnation. . . .

"As far as I'm concerned the whole idea of Western life— that's the life we live now—is wrong. These are hard convictions to put into songs though. At the moment I write nearly all of my songs round London. No. I should say the people who live in London—and the lack of real life they have. The majority just don't know what life is."

Every number in Dave's stage act is an original that he has written. As he says the theme is usually London kids and their lives. However, it leads to trouble.

"Several of the younger teenagers' programmes wouldn't play 'Can't Help Thinking About Me', because it is about leaving home. The number relates several incidents in every teenager's life—and leaving home is something which always comes up.

"Tony Hatch and I rather wanted to do another number I had written. It goes down very well in the stage act, and lots of fans said I should have released it — but Tony and I thought the words were a bit strong.

"In what way? Well, it tells the story of life as some teenagers saw it—but we didn't think the lyrics were quite up many people's street. I do it on stage though, and we're probably keeping it for an EP or maybe an LP. Hope, hope! It's called 'Now You've Met The London Boys', and mentions pills, and generally belittles the London night life scene.

"I've lived in London and been brought up here, and I find it's a great subject to write songs about. And remember with all original numbers the audiences are hearing numbers they've never heard before—so this makes for a varied stage act," said David, "it's risky, because the kids aren't familiar with the tunes, but I'm sure it makes their musical life more interesting." He could be right.

● BOWIE

While with The Lower Third David wrote and demoed (amongst others) 'Love You Till Tuesday'. An acetate on the EMI label exists of 'Love You Till Tuesday'/'Over the Wall We Go', the B-side being a song that David would frequently use with The Lower Third in his live set. Neither of these versions has ever been released.

David as Mod

Mod culture was the single biggest influence on Bowie during his teens. In various degrees it spanned nearly five years of his life and played an almost apprenticeship-type role for his professional life.

Like most mods he experimented with pills and amphetamines but that was never important to him.

A song he was to record in 1967 probably best describes his feelings for those days. 'The London Boys' was almost a late lament on mod culture and definitely incisive. He has admitted that basically he just wanted to be 'a part of what was going on and trendy' just like most people, jumping from one tinny band to the next. 'Everyone on the scene wanted to be the next Elvis,' he said in 1972.

Clothes were clearly important to him. In 1976 he said: 'I lived out of the dustbins on the backstreets of Carnaby.'

All of his early recorded material is now available on one rerelease or another, making redundant the need to buy dodgy counterfeits.

1 April 1966
'Do Anything You Say'/'Good Morning Girl' single released as David Bowie. Produced by Tony Hatch, it was his first solo release (Pye).

April 1966
Signs a five-year contract with Kenneth Pitt. Around this time David and The Lower Third were rehearsing up to eight hours a day to prepare for a tour.

Although now a singer, David was still billed with The Buzz (the group that followed The Lower Third). The band was really only a backing for him from this point.

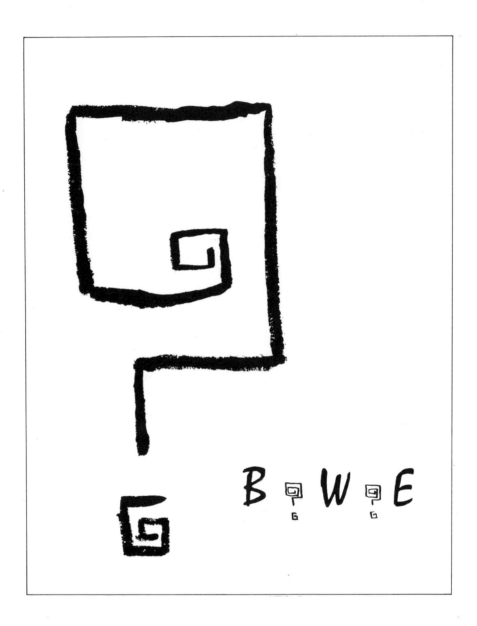

May 1966
'Can't Help Thinking About Me'/'And I Say to Myself' single released
in the US (Warner Brothers Records).

A Press release was issued:

David Bowie must be one of the most talented stars on the pop scene today. It is not enough just to be able to sing nowadays, most of the top artistes compose and sometimes act as well and David is no exception.

Not only did his first record get to No. 34 in the hit parade but it was his own composition. 'I compose all the time,' he said. 'Sometimes I sit down and think out a song and other times they just come to me.'

You might think that David, still only twenty, wouldn't have time to do anything else but he is a disc jockey at the famous Marquee Club in Soho where he has his own show called the 'Bowie Showboat'.

David Bowie is a solo artist but he is backed by his group The Buzz. Their record, 'Can't Help Thinking About Me' was released in the US and was the 'Cashbox' best bet, so it may do as well there as it has done here. David said he would quite like to go to the States but his main ambition as far as travel is concerned is to go to Tibet. Why Tibet? 'I don't know, I'd just like all those mountains and the monasteries and priests, I know I'd find it fascinating.' As an expert in astrology and a believer in reincarnation, his desire to visit Tibet is perhaps not so surprising.

June 1966

The 'Bowie Showboat' at the Marquee. David, with a now substantial local following would arrange Sunday afternoon shows with the sponsorship of the pirate radio station, Radio London. Friends would travel down from Bromley every week and his mother was in regular attendance, sitting at the front in her straw hat. Around this time David Bowie and The Buzz played support to The Hi-Numbers, later to become The Who, impressing Radio London enough to sponsor six more Sunday afternoon shows for broadcast in August.

David Bowie and The Buzz with Long John Baldry and Bluesology, which featured young Elton John on keyboards, play the Shoreline Club at Bognor.

15 July 1966

David Bowie and The Buzz play the Loughton Youth Club, Essex.

July 1966
For a Radio London feature on acts at the Marquee Club, David, appearing with The Buzz, was interviewed up on stage, his earliest radio interview.

And now a young British boy whose career will surely develop him into one of the bigger names in the show-biz field. He's a great attraction here at the Marquee and his name is David Bowie.
David, you're working with a backing group, The Buzz, have you always been with them?
D.B. As David Bowie, yes. I've always been with them, for about six months.
Why do you say as David Bowie?
D.B. I was someone else before that.
This is what, your second record and it's a song you wrote.
D.B. Yes, I write most of the stuff I record, the A-sides and the B-sides.
I understand there are plans for something much more ambitious.
D.B. At the moment I'm concentrating on a musical with my A&R man Tony Hatch.
Now is this going to be a pop-type musical or a straight musical?
D.B. Not at all, it's going to be perfectly legit.
Well surely, writing this is going to take up a lot of your time for the next few years?
D.B. Um humm, yes.
Do you still think you'll be able to carry on and continue your pop career?
D.B. Uh, I hope so, I'd like to get into cabaret obviously.
Well, how would you change your act?
D.B. I have one or two ideas on that as well.
Which you're not going to expand upon?
D.B. (laughs) No.
You don't see yourself as another Tommy Steele?
D.B. Not at all, no.
Just the first original David Bowie.
D.B. I hope so.
Well, thank you very much David for talking with us here on stage at the Marquee. This is David Bowie and The Buzz with David's latest single release 'I Dig Everything', David Bowie . . .

12 August 1966
David Bowie and The Buzz appear at the Latin Quarter, Leicester.

13 August 1966
The Boston Gliderdrome.

Ken Pitt

In late 1965 it had become apparent to Ralph Horton, as it had been to Les Conn, that David was a demanding talent requiring an experienced manager. It was David's good fortune that Horton knew such a person, Ken Pitt, who had been involved with the music business since the early fifties, when he interviewed stars in America for the embryonic *New Musical Express*.

Pitt was born and educated in London, studying fine art at the Slade for a time and later going into commercial art, advertising and then publicity. This led him into the music business. During the fifties he became good friends with Frank Sinatra.

In 1964, Pitt was chosen by Bob Dylan's manager, Albert Grossman, to help launch Dylan's name in Europe, where he was little known. He was, by then, also managing other acts including Crispian St Peters, Manfred Mann and The Kinks.

Ken Pitt's first sight of the young Bowie (then Jones) was on stage at the Marquee, watching him perform a set that included covers of songs like 'When You Walk Through a Storm', plus early versions of his own songs. From that short set, Pitt realized his potential.

Today, Ken Pitt is still sought after by young musicians who want to be managed by one of the best. He is still actively present in the music business, most of his activities today concentrated in America, working with Rod McEwan amongst others. He is a very friendly and cultured man and very proud of his association with David Bowie. There is no doubt that without Ken Pitt's insight and intelligence David's career could have taken a very different course.

David's interest in the theatre was definitely broadened while under Pitt's management. Before they met, David had never been to any legitimate theatre and Pitt put that right, taking David along to most of the major London shows of the time, including *Where the Rainbow*

Ends and even to see Cliff Richard in pantomime at the London Palladium as well as things like Roy Dotrice's one-man show.

19 August 1966
'I Dig Everything'/'I'm Not Losing Sleep' single released by David Bowie (Pye). Lower Third and other backing musicians uncredited.

21 August 1966
Starts first of six Sunday afternoon shows at the Marquee known as the 'Bowie Showboat' recorded and broadcast by Radio London. During the first David gave another interview from the stage. The idea around the 'Showboat' was to provide a mixed package of groups and records, mostly of David's own choice, and was in some ways a more formal version of the Arts Lab that he was to work on in Beckenham three years later. The shows generally added to his cult status.

Late 1966
Pye Records release David from contract after no great success is achieved with his three single records. Now without a recording company and an album's worth of new songs, Ken Pitt had the task of finding Bowie a new record company. Decca were setting up a new label called Deram. David Bowie and Cat Stevens were the first signings. Only one of them was to prove successful for the label.

About this time David met up with three new musicians, Dek Fearnley (bassist and producer), John Eager (drummer) and Derek Boyes (organist). All three are now out of the music business and work mainly in offices. To augment the line-up of Bowie, Fearnley, Eager and Boyes, John 'Hutch' Hutchinson was elected into the group after being given David's number by Marquee club owner, Harold Pendleton. 'And that's how I joined The Buzz, the group David had then. I think David liked my Swedish clothes,' Hutchinson said later. This was the start of a sporadic working relationship that continued through Feathers mime company until the 1973 world tour.

September 1966
Starts work recording new songs for Deram.

November/December 1966
Occasional recording sessions for LP preparations.

2 December 1966
'Rubber Band'/'London Boys' single released, David's first for Deram. Produced by Mike Vernon it featured David on guitar and saxophones.

December 1966
Advanced £350 for arrangements for Decca. After pressure from Ken Pitt and his father, David starts preparations for a cabaret act. It was to be an extravagant production with dancing, singing and elaborate props, including a cut-out of Paul McCartney. Much to Pitt's amusement David bumped into McCartney walking down Baker Street when carrying this on his way to an audition. The cabaret idea was dropped when a club owner told him the show was just 'too good!' Informed sources remain evasive about this project.

8 January 1967
David celebrates his twentieth birthday.

30 January 1967
'Over the Wall We Go'/'Everyday of My Life' single released by Oscar (Reaction). The singer later changed his name to Paul Nicholas. The A-side, written by David, featured Bowie on backing vocals.

February 1967
Recording finished on David's first LP.

14 April 1967
'The Laughing Gnome'/'The Gospel According to Tony Day' single released featuring 'chipmunk' vocals by Ken Pitt and Paul Buckmaster (Deram). The first of an occasional series of Marquee appearances with Fearnley, Eager and Boyes.

Around mid-1967 music publisher Geoffrey Heath asked David if he would write lyrics to a Claude François tune that he had recently acquired called 'Comme d'Habitude'. David wrote a new lyric for the French song and it was agreed that the song would be David's new single. The French publisher, however, had never heard of David Bowie and wanted someone established to record it in English. David's demo version was cut over the top of Claude François's original and is still in Ken Pitt's possession. The song was eventually rewritten as 'My Way' by Paul Anka at the request of Frank Sinatra who was unaware of David's version.

April 1967
'David Bowie' LP released in the US without two of the tracks which appeared in the UK version in June: 'We are Hungry Men' and 'Maids of Bond Street'.

May 1967
Signs contract with Decca Records to produce an LP. David was the first UK performer without a hit single ever to be signed for an album.

During this period he occasionally attended the Dance Centre, Floral Street, London WC2.

Is introduced to Tony Visconti by Ken Pitt in the offices of Denny Cordell, who signed David to Deram. David and Tony Visconti become firm friends, David often spending evenings at Tony's flat at 108 Lexham Gardens, London W8 with Marc Bolan. 'David and Marc used to come around, listen to records and jam at least twice a week for several months,' Tony later told me. Beach Boy records were often played, but Buddha was the main topic of conversation, David still unsure of how far to pursue this religion. Visconti remembers that even in 1967 David was also impressed by Andy Warhol.

2 June 1967
First LP released titled 'David Bowie' produced by Mike Vernon (Deram). The LP featured fourteen of Bowie's songs, and was mostly put together with a 'musical production' in mind. The LP did little commercially for David's career. It did, however, get a fair piece of airplay and also supplied the basic soundtrack for the film that Ken Pitt was to make around him.

With the LP came a complimentary song book, now a very rare item, issued by Essex Music.

7 July 1967
'The Laughing Gnome'/'If I were a Rich Man' single released by Ronnie Hilton (HMV Pop).

Comparisons between David and Anthony Newley, by whom David was deeply influenced at the time (and who had also been involved with Ken Pitt on the production of 'The Small World of Sammy Lee') were made with his first LP release. David later said, 'I considered Newley to be an "A-1" English artist.' Newley said, 'Bowie used to write very "Anthony Newley" type songs, and we had the same song publisher, David Platz. Maybe that's why he sounded like me at times.'

DAVID BOWIE   "LOVE YOU TILL TUESDAY"   DM 135
                         (RELEASED ON JULY 14)   DERAM

          DAVID BOWIE IS A REMARKABLY TALENTED
YOUNG RECORDING STAR AND IT LOOKS AS THOUGH HE'S HEADED
TOWARDS A WELL-DESERVED HIT WITH THE CHARMING "LOVE YOU
TILL TUESDAY"

          THERE'S
SONG AND DAVID'S FINE LYRI
SPARKLING TWO-WAY SIDE O
AND FULL OF DAVID'S FLAIR
TILL TUESDAY" JUST STAND
PLACING.

          DAVID
CURRENTLY FLOURISHING ON
RELEASED DERAM LP "DAVID
CRITICS AND PUBLIC ALIKE

          HE
FOURTEEN TRACKS ON THE
MATERIAL FOR FUTURE
TEMPTING FILM OFFERS.

NEW Decca group releases

DAVID BOWIE   "RUBBER BAND"   DM 107*
                       (RELEASED ON DECEMBER 2)   DERAM

          DAVID BOWIE IS A BRIGHT AND ORIGINAL NEW
STAR WHO LOOKS SET TO MAKE HIS MARK ON THE DISC SCENE WITH
THIS FIRST DERAM RELEASE.

          "RUBBER BAND" IS A BALLAD OF LOST LOVE--IT'S
ORIGINAL IN PRODUCTION, UNIQUE IN PRESENTATION AND WAS
WRITTEN BY DAVID.

          THERE'S A NEAT OFF-BEAT APPROACH TO THE
LYRICS THAT TOUCH ON SUCH TOPICS AS GARDEN TEA PARTIES,
WAXED MOUSTACHES AND THE FIRST WORLD WAR. YET THE UNDER-
LYING SENTIMENT REFLECTS THE IDEALS AND HUMOUR OF THIS
LONDON-BORN SINGER.

          DAVID IS 18-YEARS OLD, HE STUDIED ART AT
BROMLEY ART SCHOOL BEFORE DRIFTING TOWARDS A MUSICAL CAREER
THAT ENCOMPASSED THE GROUP SCENE AND STINTS IN PARIS AND
LONDON.

          NOW DAVID LIVES WITH HIS FAMILY IN KENT,
WORKS HARD ON A CABARET ACT AND HAS HIGH HOPES THAT
"RUBBER BAND" WILL ADVANCE HIS AMBITIONS. PERSONALLY WE
DON'T THINK HE'LL HAVE MUCH DIFFICULTY IN ACHIEVING THEM!

          (FLIPSIDE: "THE LONDON BOYS")

'David Bowie' released 2 June 1967 (Deram DML 1007)

Side One
Uncle Arthur (Bowie)
Sell Me a Coat (Bowie)
Rubber Band (Bowie)
Love You Till Tuesday (Bowie)
There is a Happy Land (Bowie)
We are Hungry Men (Bowie)
When I Live My Dream (Bowie)

Side Two
Little Bombardier (Bowie)
Silly Boy Blue (Bowie)
Come and Buy My Toys (Bowie)
Join the Gang (Bowie)
She's Got Medals (Bowie)
Maids of Bond Street (Bowie)
Please Mr Gravedigger (Bowie)

Produced by Mike Vernon

Arranged by Dek Fearnley and David Bowie

David Bowie (vocal, guitar, saxophones)
Dek Fearnley (bass)
Derek Boyes (organ)
John Eager (drums)
unknown session musicians

The cover photograph was taken by Gerald Fearnley, Dek's brother.

14 July 1967

'Love You Till Tuesday'/'Did You Ever Have a Dream' single released, an earlier version of the LP track and used as the theme for the film of the same name (Deram). Alternative versions of most tracks were cut during the sessions for the LP. One recently adopted by bootleggers was a version of 'When I Live My Dream' down tempo and simply titled 'My Dream'. This track was originally destined for legitimate single release at the time.

David meets Lindsay Kemp in a fringe theatre in Covent Garden. David, with an increasing interest in mime and theatre, strikes up an immediate friendship with Kemp and begins to attend his classes.

Lindsay Kemp

Probably the most important influence on Bowie's career, Lindsay Kemp was the first true 'generalist' David was to meet.

A highly-talented Scot, Kemp is descended from William Kemp, Shakespeare's clown at the Globe Theatre. With a list of credentials that range from film production, painting and poetry, to classic dance and most successfully, mime, he is a former pupil of the Bradford Theatre School. He also trained with Marcel Marceau and has appeared in films by Fellini and John Cassavetes.

Accounts of the meeting conflict. David recalls: 'Lindsay was holding a one-man show and he played one of my numbers during the interval. So we met up backstage and he asked me to write more music for his shows, and I said I would if he would lead me into the mysteries of mime. So I became his pupil. He was the master and I was the student. I was into ballet and mime and I got into the company and wrote some of the plays with him, and I realized that Lindsay Kemp was a living Pierrot. Everything in his life was tragic and dramatic and straight theatrical. So the stage was, for him, just an extension of his own life.'

Whatever happened, the two gelled immediately and David started a short period of training in mime and dance under Kemp's guidance. This culminated in a short run with Kemp's company in *Pierrot in Turquoise*.

After the first night in Oxford, the show then moved to Cumberland, to a theatre owned by Nicky Seker, a patron of Kemp's. The troupe travelled in an old coach. David had by then become used to rather better standards. Both Kemp and Bowie have great admiration for the other's talents.

Time has perhaps exaggerated their work together. Apart from fifteen or so performances of *Pierrot In Turquoise* they only worked together on two other productions: a controversial Scottish TV appearance in February 1970 with Angie, and Kemp's production for the *Ziggy Stardust* show at the Rainbow in 1972.

Today, Kemp is living and working in Italy where he is regularly invited to make television appearances. He considers Rome now to be his home. His most recent work in the UK was his inspired contribution to BBC 2's 'The Cruel Garden' screened just before Christmas 1982. Although these days they rarely meet further collaboration is a possibility.

Kemp has directed one film of his own, *Lindsay Kemp's Circus*.

The following extract is taken from an interview conducted by Gilles Verlant for Belgian TV in 1981 where Lindsay Kemp was asked about his earliest association with Bowie:

G.V. *You once taught David Bowie mime and dance, how did that happen?*
L.K. Oh, I once heard him on the radio singing something and it sounded as if it could have been me singing, if I had had that kind of voice. My voice, of course, is my body, but if I had a voice that came from my chest, it might have sounded something like David Bowie. In other words, I identified myself with David Bowie like I identified myself with Picasso and with Jean Genet, which was how I came to do *Flowers*. It was a voice that attracted me like a siren. I was Ulysses, attracted by the song of Sertee. It was inevitable that we came together, we found each other and we began to work together. My memory is absolutely terrible, I don't remember the exact details.
G.V. *You said at one time, that you brought beauty into rock, what did you mean by that?*
L.K. What I meant was I brought David Bowie a visual beauty that he didn't have before. David worked with my company for three or four years and at the beginning, like any new love, you want everyone to notice, 'Who's that lady I saw you with last night', or 'Who was that *man* I saw you with last night', you know. It's very important, especially for me, that they notice what I am wearing or who I am in love with, the dancer has no secrets. But they didn't mention him, they didn't mention his voice, they didn't mention the way he looked. So I picked up a tin of spray paint, it was red paint that we sprayed the furniture with and I sprayed his hair. And then they said, 'Hey, who was that man I saw you with last night!'
G.V. *You produced the 1972 version of Ziggy Stardust on stage . . .?*
L.K. I was overwhelmed by the sudden, well it wasn't sudden success, it's just that I was living in Scotland and Bowie had been in London for six months and it was extraordinary. In six months he had become acclaimed and had been booked into the Rainbow Theatre, which holds about 6,000 people and he asked me to direct that show, *Ziggy Stardust* at the Rainbow, which later went to New York. A lot of those songs we wrote for each other. It was the first time they started to talk about 'Gay rock', God knows what they meant by that!

September 1967
At this time, with an ever increasing interest in Buddhism, David would spend afternoons in Hampstead with lama monk, Chimi Youngdong Rimpoche. Chimi was one of four monks who fled from Communist China, the other three setting up a monastery in Scotland with other monks from Vietnam and China. In an interview for George Tremlett for a press release David explained his visits to Chimi.

I just sit there, asking questions, and he usually answers them with another question. In fact, he's teaching me to find my own solution . . . to meditate . . . you can't show people what Buddhism is . . . you can only show them the way towards it . . . it's really a process of self-discovery . . . of discovering truth.

David also spoke of his attitude to wealth.

'Material things just don't interest me. I have one good suit in case I have to go anywhere important, but I don't want a car, and I live with my parents. I'm not interested in clothes at all, really.

September 1967
'Love is Always' single released (Palette). A-side lyrics by David and recorded by Dee Dee from Belgium. The single was released in Belgium only. Music by Albimoor and Glround.

15 September 1967
'Silver Treetop School for Boys'/'I've Lost a Friend and Found a Lover' single released by The Slender Party. The A-side was written by David (Polydor).

30 September 1967
Fab 208 magazine photo session.

10 November 1967
Appears on 'Fan Club', a Dutch television pop show.

2 December 1967
'Silver Treetop School for Boys'/'Sugar Chocolate Machine' single released by The Beatstalkers, A-side written by David (CBS). The group originally recorded for Decca, the connection with Bowie being Ken Pitt who also managed The Beatstalkers.

18 December 1967

'Top Gear' BBC radio performance recorded by David with Tony Visconti as the musical director for the show. David sang five songs for the session including 'Silly Boy Blue', Steve Peregrine Took of Tyrannosaurus Rex adding backing vocals for that track, 'Karma Man', 'Let Me Sleep Beside You', 'In the Heat of the Morning' and 'When I'm Five' ('When I'm five I will wash my face and hands all by myself, when I'm five, I chew and spit tobacco like my Grandpa Jones, when I'm five, I am only four and five is far away'). Tony Visconti said that session was 'magical'. Billing for the broadcast was David Bowie and The Tony Visconti Orchestra.

Tony Visconti was born in Brooklyn, New York and attended a school for musically-gifted children, playing his first gig there in a school band at the age of twelve.

In his late teens, Visconti was signed to a New York publisher called Howard Richmond and was sent to London where he became an apprentice to Denny Cordell at Decca. 'For six months I sat by Denny's side in the studio every day and watched how patient he was, how he'd coax people to do things they didn't want to do and I learnt about some of the technicalities of the job. It eventually came time for me to actually produce something myself,' Visconti later said of his first months in England.

Visconti's career has been wide and varied apart from his work with David. Another early talent he helped develop was Marc Bolan and Tyrannosaurus Rex, whom he first saw performing in the Middle Earth club in 1968.

Visconti's first meeting with David was later described to *Record Mirror* reporter, James Parade:

At the time, David was on Deram. One day the Deram man called me into his office and said, 'We've got this young man David Bowie and no one quite knows what to do with him. You seem to be the expert on weird people. I'd like you to meet him.' I remember the first time we met he was, and still is, the complete Englishman. He played me 'Space Oddity' which he was convinced was a hit, but I thought it was just so corny. It was the week of the space walk and he'd obviously copied the idea from that. Anyway, I didn't like it, so he did it with Gus Dudgeon and you know the rest. I think the tracks we did together must've been what finally got him chucked off the Deram label. They were really awful.

David and Tony Visconti have worked together on and off ever since. Visconti has produced and coproduced nine of David's LPs to date and despite occasional differences they have remained good friends.

As well as producing other artists like Hazel O'Connor and writing arrangements for, among others, Paul McCartney, Visconti keeps himself busy at his recording studio Good Earth in Soho. He released one LP of his own in 1977 called 'Inventory' (Mercury).

28 December 1967
After approximately one month's training, David makes his first appearance with Lindsay Kemp in the mime production *Pierrot In Turquoise* at the Oxford New Theatre.

1967–68 also saw David attempt to work as a model but his scruffiness hindered him. Other part-time work included a spell at a friend's litho print shop near Russell Square, doing odd-jobs to earn a few pounds.

'The good thing about that arrangement,' Ken Pitt told me, 'was if we had a job in for David, we would just call and he would be able to come immediately.'

By late 1967 David had grown away from his Dylan lookalike period and tidied up considerably.

David at this time, found himself with plenty of spare time. Ken Pitt recalled that most of this was spent in Soho coffee bars drinking gallons of coffee and never paying for any of it. He became a well-known local character. He would often stop in at Ken Pitt's Curzon Street office to 'bother the girls'. They would often slip off to have a cup of coffee with him. 'He was always drinking coffee, coffee and cigarettes, coffee and cigarettes!'

3–5 January 1968
Appears in *Pierrot In Turquoise* at the Rose Hill Theatre, Cumberland. Inclusive fee for the three performances, £40.

January 1968
Returns to London for auditions at the BBC for a play called *The Pistol Shot*. Although it was the first time that he had danced a minuet he took to it straight away and got the part. The play was recorded later that month at the television centre, Shepherds Bush.

8 January 1968
David's twenty-first birthday.

30 January 1968
The Pistol Shot broadcast. Also in the play was Hermione Farthingale, with whom he fell in love and lived with for a year.

5–16 March 1968
Appears in *Pierrot In Turquoise* at the Mercury Theatre, Notting Hill Gate, London W11.

22 March 1968
'Silly Boy Blue'/'One Minute Women' single released by Billy Fury. A-side written by David (Parlophone).

25–30 March 1968
Appears in *Pierrot In Turquoise* at the Intimate Theatre, Palmers Green, north London. David's last performance with the company though he was to work with Kemp again on two other projects over the next four years. Kemp said that David and Hermione 'walked hand in hand out of my life'.

April 1968
'Deborah'/'Child Star' single released by Tyrannosaurus Rex (Regal Zonophone). A-side featuring David on handclaps!

Since the death of Marc Bolan in 1977 many rumours have emerged about recordings that have featured both artists, mainly Bolan tracks that David guested on. Most are wildly inaccurate, as has been verified by Bolan's producer of the time, Tony Visconti, who cannot even remember David attending any of the T. Rex sessions. David's contribution on 'Deborah', however, was mentioned by Bolan more than once, so this rumour may be open to conjecture.

18 April 1968
'London Bye Ta Ta'/'In the Heat of the Morning' demo recorded by David for Decca. 'London Bye Ta Ta' was never released officially, this version being very different from the later 'Spiders' version recorded in the early seventies. This recording had a similar feel to other material released on the '67 'David Bowie' LP.

Marc Bolan

Marc Bolan's name has cropped up alongside David's on many occasions, the two wandering in and out of each other's early careers up to Bolan's death in 1977.

Bolan was born Marc Feld in Hackney, London in 1948. At times his career seemed to run parallel with David's. As a smart mod his first main contact in the business was also Les Conn.

Bolan was very successful as a model but music was his main love. It is very difficult to accurately chart a brief Bolan history. Even Bolan himself changed accounts of events in interviews.

At times David was definitely under Bolan's influence and at one point in the late sixties, the two were virtually living out of each other's pockets. David even took a demo cut of 'Space Oddity' for the scrutiny of Bolan, David returning to tell Pitt later that Marc says, 'It's gonna be a hit Davy.'

Although they did come to know one another very well, they still maintained a distance, something David made apparent when interviewed by Michael Watts for *Melody Maker* in 1972. Reflecting on the Tyrannosaurus Rex tour of 1969, David said: 'We'd sit at opposite ends of the room, just looking at each other. It was a very kinda moody thing, I suppose, on an infantile level. We were just terribly polite to each other all the time. I'd never say we were in competition to each other 'cause we're at different ends of the spectrum. We might just have happened in the same period.'

The press built up a great but artificial rivalry between the two. Although Bolan was to have a greater singles success in the UK, David was to take the much richer international market. Bolan never caught in America the way David did.

Their only filmed appearance together was made on 9 September 1977 in Manchester for Bolan's 'Marc' TV show. David appeared as a special guest singing 'Heroes' for the first time in the UK and then jamming to finish off the programme on 'Standing Next To You', a hastily-arranged number that disintegrated before the first chorus when Bolan slipped off the stage and broke down laughing.

A week later, Bolan, driven by his girlfriend Gloria Jones, died when their car hit a tree in Barnes, south London. He was buried on 20 September at The Chapel, Golders Green, north London.

Summer 1968
Works as an extra in *The Virgin Soldiers*, the film adaptation of the Leslie Thomas book. All the filming was done on location at Ascot and he was on set for about two weeks.

Other auditions were also attempted during the late sixties, for leading roles in *Sunday Bloody Sunday* and *Triple Echo*. He had no success. Appears in a short pilot TV commercial for Lyons Maid, advertising their new ice cream 'Luv'. The sequence was filmed partly on a bus and partly on stage and featured David on the soundtrack.

In the late sixties David would often be asked to make personal appearances for charity events. One, around '68/'69, was at Brands Hatch where he drove down with his parents to make a special appearance. David's father rarely attended any of these performances even though he took a very firm interest in his son's career generally.

3 June 1968
Presents in mime, a short play at the Royal Festival Hall. The piece is set to the soundtrack of 'Silly Boy Blue', which has an anti-communist theme. It provoked an American in the audience to stand up and shout, 'No politics!' The reaction, as Ken Pitt was to tell me, cheered David at the time. 'David was quite pleased actually, he was glad to get any crowd reaction at the time.' The Whit-Monday show was headed by Tyrannosaurus Rex and Roy Harper and hosted by John Peel. Later David was to refer to the mime piece for 'Silly Boy Blue' as 'Yet-San and the Eagle'.

By the summer of 1968, David was well into his next project, a mixed-media group called Feathers. He moved into a small flat with Hermione Farthingale in Clairville Grove in Chelsea. In an adjoining room slept John Hutchinson, the bass player from Hull and member of Feathers. The flat was to be their home for nearly a year.

The mixed-media troupe comprised Hermione, John 'Hutch' Hutchinson and David. All three would attempt a combination of music, prose, dance and poetry mostly using material that has never been presented since. As with most of David's ventures a lot of recordings were made, some finding their way on to acetate but most staying in the possession of Ken Pitt. Feathers was a working project for less than four months and was not a commercial success. 'I got the impression,' says Pitt, 'that Feathers was just designed to get Hermione involved with something; he was very keen on her then.'

A bootleg of one of Feathers' songs has recently surfaced. 'The Ching-A-Ling Song' was taken from the only Feathers' acetate in circulation. There is also a live version of this song, again on a single.

The first few shows by Feathers featured guitarist Tony Hill and not Hutch. Tony Hill left the group to join Tide, a group David was later to support on a couple of occasions.

21 June 1968
'Rain Coloured Roses'/'Everything is You' single released by The Beatstalkers (CBS). The B-side was written by David who was also on backing vocals with Tony Head, for which they both received £9.

September 1968
Appearances this month with Feathers included shows at the Middle Earth club (on the bill with Flame) and at the Wigmore Hall where the trio supported The Strawbs. These shows are their earliest known appearances.

Photographer Ray Stevenson's first meeting with David was in the dressing room at Middle Earth. A few days after that meeting, while on a separate commission in Clairville Grove, Stevenson by chance ran in to David again, David inviting him up for a chat and beginning a friendship that was to last through Feathers, the Arts Lab and Hype. Ray Stevenson was one of the only photographers at that time who was photographing David and Feathers's appearances with any regularity.

Late 1968
Occasional recording sessions with Feathers made at Soho's Trident studios with Tony Visconti producing.

17 November 1968
Feathers appear at the Country Club, Hampstead, north London. Featured on the same bill were The Third Ear Band and Doris Henderson.

6 December 1968
Feathers appear at the Arts Lab, Drury Lane. David was later to label this arts lab as 'pretentious'.

7 December 1968
Feathers appear at Sussex University.

December 1968
David would always stay at home with his family over Christmas. This was to be the last they were to share together in Plaistow Grove.

1968 was a year for David to experiment with as many different ideas as possible to gain artistic flexibility. Early 1968 saw a shift in style from the moody Dylan period. He tidied his appearance. No records were released this year and Ken Pitt would despair when the projects he put to David foundered. A more productive year was to follow.

11 January 1969
'Little Boy'/'When I'm Five' single released by The Beatstalkers (CBS). B-side written by David.

Early 1969
Feathers at the Round House playing support to The Who and The Scaffold. This was the first time Angie Barnet saw David, quite a while before they were introduced later in the year.

In late 1968 a German television producer approached Ken Pitt with an interest in Bowie. His idea was to produce a film to showcase David's talents and the idea immediately interested Pitt. In February 1969 filming began in Greenwich for the production of a 30-minute television show, but before the project was complete, the German backers dropped out and Pitt was left to put £7,000 of his own money in to see the filming through. The film was almost totally made up of songs from the Deram LP though it also included a new song especially written for the promotional video *Space Oddity* and a piece of mime called *The Mask*, adapted from a traditional mime.

Filming was completed after about two weeks and has never been entirely publicly screened, although sections were occasionally used by the BBC (who turned the film down when it was originally offered).

Angela Barnet

Mary Angela Barnet was born in Xeros, Cyprus in the summer of 1950. Her father, George Barnet, although of English parentage, was an American, as was her mother, Helene Marie, who originally came from Poland. Angie had one elder brother.

She spent most of her schooldays away from home in boarding schools in Europe and America, eventually going to Kingston Polytechnic in London.

At nineteen she met and fell in love with David who had not long before finished with Hermione Farthingale. They were quietly married in Bromley on 20 March 1970 in front of only a handful of guests. Right from the start the two planned an open relationship, Angie realizing and accepting that she alone could not hold his total interest. David was likewise happy to let his wife see whoever she wanted. It was agreed that David's career would take priority and Angie's would follow. It could be said that their relationship was a success, the confines and pressures of fame being the real root of the split. Whatever the reason, nearly ten years later on 8 February 1980, David and Angela's divorce became final, David having custody of their son Joe (as Zowie had become known) and Angie getting a settlement of £30,000. Angie has since written a book of their life together and has started to seriously build her career as a model and poet/performer. She is now living in California.

8 February 1969
'When I Live My Dream' scene shot at Hampstead Heath, London. The scene also included Feathers and it was the last time the three were to work together complete. A small section of this piece was featured on the Arena 'My Way' documentary on BBC 2 in 1979.

11 February 1969

David and John Hutchinson appear at Sussex University as a duo, the last Feathers show. According to Ken Pitt the audience was virtually unmoved although it was a remarkable performance. By now David and Hutch had developed a two-man comedy act as a filler between songs, David using Hutch as the stooge. This performance was only fulfilled out of obligation, Feathers really finishing when Hermione decided to leave both the group and David.

The break up of this relationship led David to write two songs that were later to appear on his first Mercury LP 'David Bowie': 'Letter to Hermione' and 'An Occasional Dream'. They are two of the most candid and affectionate songs that he has written to date.

David later said of his love for Hermione, 'We had a perfect love – so perfect that it burned out in two years. We were too close, thought alike and spent all the time in a room sitting on the corner of a bed. She was a brilliant dancer, and I was a struggling musician.' David moved out of Clairville Grove and back to Manchester Street.

1969

David's first attempts at acting were designed by Ken Pitt and David himself to attain a greater knowledge of appearance and presentation, not only for acting's sake but performance generally.

Ken Pitt, forever busy trying to instil new and interesting projects for his artist, managed to arrange a part for David in a Negus–Fancey film *The Image*, directed by Michael Armstrong. It featured David as 'The Boy', an image haunting an inspired artist. The boy first appears at the window, nose squashed against the glass. He then appears in the hallway and the artist turns on him punching him in the face and stomach, then hitting him with a bronze bust. The boy is now apparently dead and the artist returns to his masterpiece to study his work (which is of David, arms outstretched for sympathy). Not unexpectedly the boy once again appears behind the artist, who then tries to escape.

Finally the boy is stabbed repeatedly by the artist and ends up sliding slowly down the bannister, crumpling up at the foot of the stairs. Finding that the boy still is not dead the artist again pounces and savagely finishes him off, then collapses with exhaustion.

Realizing that he has destroyed the image of his painting, he rips the painting off the easel and apparently starts to destroy the picture and the film finishes.

The painting, incidentally, survived the artist's attack and to this day hangs in Ken Pitt's hallway, David's arms outstretched to all visitors. No copies of this film are known to exist.

Michael Armstrong had become friendly with David while preparing what he hoped would be his first film *A Floral Tale* for which he hoped to commission David (whose work he very much admired) to provide the soundtrack. It was through trying to sell *A Floral Tale* that he was offered *The Image*, which became his first film. Armstrong's reflection of the film's production? 'It was fourteen minutes long, black and white, shot in two and a half days and starred David. The film was originally meant to be a ghost story with a twist at the end, however, we ended up with seven and a half minutes of screen time which meant that when I cut it, I had to make it arty with flashbacks and forwards to extend it. It must be the only film in history to grow twice as long in the cutting room.'

At one point Armstrong considered David to play the supporting role of the killer in his film *The Haunted House of Horror*. David's musical commitments meant the part went to Julian Barnes.

(Seven pieces of music for *A Floral Tale* were prepared by David and remain unreleased and in the possession of Michael Armstrong.)

22 February 1969
David plays support to Tyrannosaurus Rex at the Manchester Free Trade Hall, the first show of a short concert tour.

23 February 1969
Plays support at the Bristol Colston Hall.

1 March 1969
Plays support at the Liverpool Harmonic.

8 March 1969
Plays support at the Brighton Dome.

Mid 1969
David and Angie are introduced by Calvin Mark Lee at a press conference being held for the group King Crimson at London's Speakeasy. Support act for the night was Donovan. Signs new recording contract with Mercury Records in London – the only company to show interest in 'Space Oddity'. Signing conducted by Lou Reizner.

Summer 1969
With a growing interest in the idea of an arts lab David and *International Times* journalist, Mary Finnigan, start their own, the Beckenham Arts Lab at the Three Tuns pub in Beckenham High Street. David had, by now, moved into Mary's home in Foxgrove Road.

The Beckenham Arts Lab

The Beckenham Arts Lab in a back room in the Three Tuns pub in Beckenham High Street, was an idea that David had wanted to put into practice since he first came into contact with the Arts Lab run by American Jim Haynes in Drury Lane. David's intentions for the Lab were quite clear: he would create an alternative environment to feature new and developing artists, providing a simple showcase for them. In theory, the Lab was a great idea. A little slow in setting off it eventually gained a good local reaction. As time progressed, however, most of the audience were just turning up to see David perform his set. The Arts Lab was cofounded by *International Times* journalist Mary Finnigan with whom David was living at the time. Her role was that of Arts Lab administrator, which basically meant that she handled the paperwork. David was the artistic director. Many of the people who performed at the Lab were local to Beckenham. Others included Steve Harley, producer and performer Ricki Sylvan, Mick Ronson, Keith Christmas and many of David's friends including Tony Visconti.

'I had little to do with the Arts Lab,' Visconti recalled to me. 'I sang a set of my own songs once, my friend, Tucker Zimmerman, sang a set and I accompanied him on bass. I also accompanied David several times, alone and with Mick Ronson and John Cambridge on drums (The Hype). Keith Christmas and Dave Cousin are the only other artistes of merit I can remember from the Arts Lab. David and us, his trio, reciprocated by playing at David Cousins' Arts Lab in Southall for one gig, in a pub called the White Lion.'

The Lab ran for little over six months, interest as well as finances running low which even led David to write to a few well-known people with requests for financial help, including John Peel. The Arts Lab was a Sunday evening club, its only outside function being the Beckenham Free Festival.

Today the Three Tuns pub is drastically different. The interior was redesigned in the mid-seventies and the back room that housed the Lab is now a buffet bar. The staff are hard-pressed to recall David Bowie's involvement with the pub, but it is not hard to find a regular who remembers.

David speaking on the Beckenham Arts Lab, September 1969 to Chris Welch of *Melody Maker*:

I run an arts lab which is my chief occupation. It's in Beckenham and I think it's the best in the country. There isn't one pseud involved. All the people are real – like labourers or bank clerks. It started out as a folk club, arts labs generally have such a bad reputation as pseud places.

There's a lot of talent in the green belt and there is a load of tripe in Drury Lane. I think the arts lab movement is extremely important and should take over from the youth club concept as a social service.

The people who come are completely pacifist and we get a lot of cooperation from the police in our area. They are more than helpful. Respect breeds respect. We've got a few greasers who come and a few skinheads who are just as enthusiastic.

We started our lab a few months ago with poets and artists who just came along. It's got bigger and bigger and now we have our own light show and sculptures, etcetera. And I never knew there were so many sitar players in Beckenham.

Mary Finnigan interviewed David for *International Times* in July 1969:

Part of my motivation in doing a hit parade number is to promote the arts labs along with it, but without elitist attitudes. Arts labs should be for everyone not just the so-called turned-on minority. We need energy from all directions, heads and skinheads alike.

Here we are in Beckenham with a group of people creating their own momentum without the slightest concern for attitudes, tradition or preordained moralities. It's alive, healthy and new and it matters to me more than anything else.

11 July 1969
'Space Oddity'/'Wild Eyed Boy from Freecloud' single released (Philips). Most of the initial pressings were in mono. The record took two months to make the top ten in August 1969 (highest chart position No. 5). David was then greeted home at Plaistow Grove with a banner proclaiming 'Local Boy Makes Good' placed by a neighbour. Session musicians received a fee of £9 for work on the track. This was Rick Wakeman's first work with David.

July 1969

David and Ken Pitt leave the UK for David to perform at the Malta Song Festival at the Hilton Hotel. David won singing 'When I Live My Dream'. All the contestants went on to Italy where David won again.

5 August 1969

David arrives at Heathrow Airport with Ken Pitt, and heads home for Bromley. He later phones Ken Pitt to tell him that his father had died that evening of lobar pneumonia, aged fifty-seven.

7 August 1969

David informs the Bromley and Chislehurst Registry Office of his father's death and handles the funeral arrangements. Arts Lab Commitments are cancelled for a few weeks.

Mid-August 1969

After the death of his father, David and Angie decide to move into Plaistow Grove to help David's mother.

David was to keep his own bedroom in Plaistow Grove until the house was sold in late 1969.

Late 1969

David's drummer, John Cambridge, a childhood friend of guitarist Mick Ronson from Hull, Yorkshire introduces David and Tony Visconti to Ronson for the first time. Ronson had recently done some session work on Michael Chapman's 'Fully Qualified Survivor' LP.

David featured on John Peel's 'Top Gear' radio show, the first appearance of new group concept, The Hype, and the first time David had appeared with Mick Ronson. The BBC show, by all accounts, was not good, being completely unrehearsed and was quickly forgotten by all involved.

The Hype were a tongue-in-cheek reaction to David's sudden rise to fame via 'Space Oddity'. The Hype featured David on guitar and vocals, Mick Ronson on guitar, Tony Visconti on bass and ex-Junior Eyes' drummer, John Cambridge.

'The Hype' as a name, was suggested to David by Ray Stevenson.

Mick Ronson was born in Hull, Yorkshire into the Mormon faith. After playing around in various R & B groups in his town he formed his own group, The Rats. This group also featured both Trevor Bolder and Woody Woodmansey, who eventually became David's Spiders backing group.

NEWS SPIN

Philips Records · Stanhope House · Stanhope Place · London · W2

PHILIPS

"SPACE ODDITY IS THE FIRST SINGLE I REALLY WANTED TO RELEASE"

So says David Bowie, one of the most creative young men in today's music

David Bowie is known on the pop scene. He is known for the songs he writes and for the way in which he sings them. He is known because he writes powerful songs, songs he believes in, and because he performs them with love and care and with a freshness that belies all the work he has put into them.

His first Philips single "Space Oddity" b/w "Wild Eyed Boy From Freecloud", is released on July 11th on BF1801. It was produced by Gus Dudgeon.

David Bowie was born in London in 1947. At fifteen he didn't attend school often; he played tenor sax in a modern jazz group and worked up an interest in Buddhism. At sixteen he went into an advertising agency and worked as a commercial artist. He re-read "On The Road" and formed a progressive blues group.

At seventeen he was involved with more groups but he was frustrated with amplifiers and went solo .... back into Buddhism.

At nineteen/twenty his first L.P. appeared .... completely and devoted most of his time to the ....

At twenty-one he acted, wrote and produce .... his own mime, music and mixed media trio. H..............

Now he is solo again and is making an L.P. .... recent activities was the founding of an Art................

JULY 1969

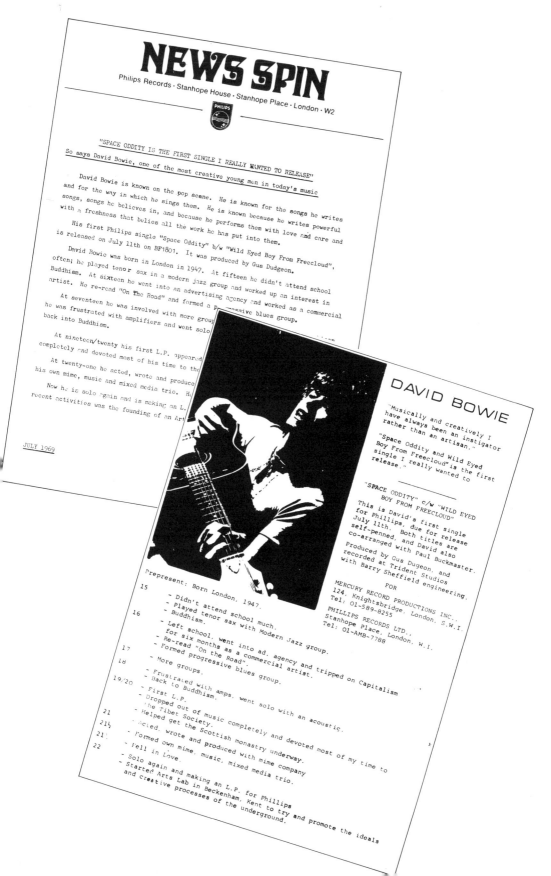

DAVID BOWIE

"Musically and creatively I have always been an instigator rather than an artisan."

"**Space** Oddity and Wild Eyed Boy From Freecloud" is the first single I really wanted to release."

"**SPACE ODDITY**" c/w "WILD EYED BOY FROM FREECLOUD"

This is David's first single for Phillips, due for release July 11th. Both titles are self-penned, and David also co-arranged with Paul Buckmaster. Produced by Gus Dugeon, and recorded at Trident Studios with Barry Sheffield engineering.

FOR

MERCURY RECORD PRODUCTIONS INC.,
124, Knightsbridge, London, S.W.1.
Tel: 01-589-8255

PHILLIPS RECORDS LTD.,
Stanhope Place, London, W.1.
Tel: 01-AMB-7788

Represent: Born London, 1947.

15	– Didn't attend school much.
	– Played tenor sax with Modern Jazz group.
16	– Buddhism.
	– Left school, went into ad. agency and tripped on Capitalism for six months as a commercial artist.
	– Re-read "On the Road".
17	– Formed progressive blues group.
18	– More groups.
	– Frustrated with amps, went solo with an acoustic.
19/20	– Back to Buddhism.
	– First L.P.
	– Dropped out of music completely and devoted most of my time to the Tibet Society.
21	– Helped get the Scottish monastry underway.
21½	– Acted, wrote and produced with mime company
21¾	– Formed own mime, music, mixed media trio.
22	– Fell in Love.
	– Solo again and making an L.P. for Phillips
	– Started Arts Lab in Beckenham, Kent to try and promote the ideals and creative processes of the underground.

Ronson was introduced to David in late 1969 by John Cambridge. The two immediately struck up a friendship and Ronson moved down to Beckenham.

With David retired and temporarily out of action in 1973 the time was right for Tony DeFries, who managed both David and Ronson, to launch Ronson with all the energy and build up the occasion apparently suited. Unfortunately for Ronson the whole thing became a huge embarrassment for him and most of the shows of the tour were soon forgotten by all involved.

After the release of two solo LPs, 'Slaughter on Tenth Avenue' and 'Play Don't Worry', Ronson made appearances with Mott the Hoople, leaving Hoople with Ian Hunter shortly after to form the Hunter–Ronson Band which has been an on/off project ever since.

In late 1975 Ronson surprisingly turned up on Bob Dylan's 'Rolling Thunder Revue' tour, one of the guitarists in a huge entourage for that tour.

Since then, his work has been very sporadic. He was on Roger McGuin's 'Cardiff Rose' LP and has worked occasionally with Annette Peacock. For whatever reason (and it is always claimed to be managerial problems), virtually all of Ronson's UK appearances for the last five years have been cancelled at the last moment.

Although Ronson still has a flat in London most of his time is spent in the US, and in recent years he has been remarkably quiet. It was rumoured that David had asked Ronson to tour with him in 1976. Ronson has refused to confirm this.

Whatever Ronson's reasons for not contributing to the music scene lately, he definitely made an impact on British music history as one of the most interesting guitarists of the seventies.

Summer 1969

The Beckenham Free Festival. This was to be a very successful day for David and the highpoint of his arts lab activities. Held at the Croydon Road recreation ground, over 5,000 people turned up. David was congratulated by the chief of police and the mayor. Tony Visconti said, 'David and The Hype (Mick, John Cambridge and myself) played the Beckenham Free Festival for about one and a half hours. It consisted of the songs from the 'Space Oddity' LP and 'Madame George' by Van Morrison and several others I can't remember. We did 'Space Oddity' in a reggae version. To commemorate the event David wrote 'Memory of a Free Festival', later released as a single.

This was David's reaction to the festival a few weeks after the event:

56

It was a very unusual kind of festival because it was all local people. No big names or anything, the idea was just to use people from the area who never got a chance to be seen by more than a hundred people because they only do tiny clubs and this day they were playing to over five thousand people, which was great! And they went down very well, maybe the quality was kind of dodgy but the enthusiasm was tremendous.

General Arts Lab shows continued, including performances by Ron Geeson, Bridget St John, a poetry-reading session from Lionel Bart and for one of the Arts Lab's summer highlights, a performance by David and Peter Frampton. Frampton was then a hot property as lead singer with The Herd.

2 October 1969
'Space Oddity' enters the UK top twenty.

During the week of the American space walk 'Space Oddity' was not included in the BBC's official play list, being considered to be in bad taste. This may account for the slow movement of the single in the charts.

October 1969
David appears in Wolverhampton, doing a complete mime session and travelling to the venue with Angie and Ray Stevenson in the Fiat left to David in his father's will.

8–26 October 1969
Rolling Stones's manager, Andrew Loog Oldham, books David to do a 15-minute mime act as support to his new group, Humble Pie. David, tired of mime and with a recent hit single decides to put on a straight acoustic set, much to Oldham's chagrin. The first show was at Coventry Theatre, then recently opened. The tour was a strange showcase for David's twenty-minute acoustic set, and was followed by an incredibly loud set by Humble Pie. That first night though, was a great success. The rest of the tour (except for the last dates in London) were rather less successful. David bravely carried on, putting up with heckling and having to dodge lighted cigarettes. The bad reception damaged an already shy talent and a chance at becoming a major success was lost. It was two years before he felt happy enough to embark on a major tour again.

Also on the bill for the tour was Dave Edmunds's Love Sculpture.

19 October 1969
Plays support to Humble Pie at Rebecca's in Birmingham.

26 October 1969
London Royal Festival Hall, last night as support to Humble Pie.

Late October 1969
Supports Herman's Hermits and The Troggs at the Sunderland Empire.

David's earnings, after expenses, for this month £1,000. Big business at last.

David has always been a collector of just about anything that takes his fancy, whether it be glassware, old cars, photographs, books or antiques. He became quite well known to Beckenham antique dealers.

Mrs Anne Gayle of Pepys's Antiques in Kelsey Road, Beckenham which opened in 1969, says that the young Bowie, with Angie, would often wander around the shop browsing and asking advice. David once invited her to Haddon Hall for an opinion on an Art Deco polar bear he had acquired.

DISC & MUSIC ECHO OCTOBER 25th, 1969

On hearing a new LP called 'David Bowie', someone remarked: 'Well it's very nice, but do you think he's a lasting talent?'

The answer is Yes. Not just on the strength of this album but merely because 'Space Oddity' is not the be all and end all of his talents, and because David Bowie has been around writing some very good songs for the past four years. Unheralded, and to a great extent, unnoticed, except by the Bowie believers and devotees.

This album then is David Bowie NOW. As he has always been. David is a very social writer. He does not exactly make blatant social comments, but rather uses social diseases and the rather frightening atmosphere we all live in as a back-drop to his songs.

'David Bowie' took six months to write. 'This has been a good writing period for me and I'm very pleased with the outcome. I just hope everyone else is too' says Bowie.

The album is out at the beginning of next month. On it David has arranged all the tracks, and is helped along in some almost semi-classical sounds by Juniors' Eyes.

The atmosphere of the album IS rather doomy and un-nerving, but Bowie's point comes across like a latter-day Dylan. It is an album a lot of people are going to expect a lot from. I don't think they'll be disappointed.

Here David goes through the tracks:-
Space Oddity: 'This is slightly longer than the single. The sad thing about the record was that not all the copies were in stereo. This is definitely a stereo sound and you lost a lot of impact on the single. This is how it's supposed to sound.'
Unwashed and Somewhat Slightly Dazed:
'This is a rather weird little song I wrote because one day when I was very scruffy I got a lot of funny stares from people in the street. The lyrics are what you hear – about a boy whose girlfriend thinks he is socially inferior. I thought it was rather funny really.'
Letter To Hermione:
'I once wrote a letter I never sent to Hermione, who was a dancer with the Lindsay Kemp mime company. I thought I'd record it instead and send her the record. I think she's in Greenwich Village now.'

Most collections were little more than flirtations and after two or three weeks he would become interested in something else, the best example of this being an interest in Man Ray photographs which were a 'passion' for less than a fortnight.

More serious collections were in glassware, especially Lalique and Galle from France, Art Deco and Art Nouveau objects of every kind, unusual furniture, *Eagle* comics and books.

Today, apart from a vast collection of books, he just collects passport stamps. Most acquisitions from the past are now scattered in the possession of old friends or simply lost.

4 November 1969
'David Bowie' LP released (Philips), later to be reissued by RCA as 'Space Oddity'. US counterpart released about the same time titled 'Man of Words, Man of Music', and featuring a less original sleeve

---

Cygnet Committee: (9 minutes 30 seconds). 'I wanted this track out as a single but nobody else thought it was a good idea. Well it is a bit long I suppose. It's basically three separate points of view about the more militant section of the hippie movement. The movement was a great ideal but something's gone wrong with it now. I'm not really attacking it but pointing out that the militants have still got to be helped as people-human beings – even if they are going about things all the wrong way.'
Janine: 'Mmm. This is a bit hard to explain without sounding nasty. It was written about my old mate George and is about a girl he used to go out with. It's how I thought he *should* see her.'
Occasional Dream: 'This is another reflection of Hermione who I was very hung up about.'
Wild Eyed Boy From Freecloud: 'I must say I seem to say most things the long way round – I suppose that's why a lot of my numbers are very involved and long. The Wild Eyed Boy lives on a mountain and has developed a beautiful way of life. He loves the mountain and the mountain loves him. I suppose in a way he's rather a prophet figure.

'The villagers disapprove of the things he has to say and they decide to hang him. He gives up to his fate, but the mountain tries to help him by killing the village.

'So in fact everything the boy says is taken the wrong way – both by those who fear him AND those who love him, and try to assist.'
God Knows I'm Good:
'Communication has taken away so much from our lives that now it's almost totally involved in machines rather than ordinary human beings. There's nobody to talk your troubles over with these days, so this track is about a woman who steals a can of stew, which she desperately needs but can't afford, from a supermarket and gets caught.

'The machines look on "shrieking on the counter" and "spitting by my shoulder".'
Memory Of A Free Festival: 'Well we go out on an air of optimism, which I believe in. Things WILL get better. I wrote this after the Beckenham festival when I was very happy.'

59

than the UK version. When the LP was reissued by RCA a 'filler' track was removed called 'Don't Sit Down', this being just a short jam ending rather abruptly after about twenty seconds.

7 November 1969
Begins a nine-day tour of Scotland as part of the LP promotion. The first show in Perth left him rather startled when, for the first time, he was screamed at! Generally though, this tour did little to encourage him to continue live work away from London. Interviewed over the telephone from Perth by Gordon Coxhill for the *NME*.

19 November 1969
Plays at the Brighton Dome.

20 November 1969
'An Evening with David Bowie' at the Purcell Room in the Royal Festival Hall. The show was arranged by David's then constant companion Calvin Mark Lee, head of Mercury Records (UK). Ken Pitt had to make last-minute booking changes when it was realized that no one had paid for the show. David arranged a backing group especially for that evening. The group were friends from Beckenham called Copus. A lot of the audience were friends from Bromley and Beckenham and staff from Mercury and Philips. By all accounts, David was magnificent that evening but none of the press had showed up. Someone had forgotten to send out invitations and so an excellent show had been wasted. Thus Calvin Lee (who ran the European offices of Mercury Records) was suddenly very much out of favour. David was furious.

Support group for the evening were Juniors' Eyes.

'David Bowie' released 4 November 1969 (Philips SBL7912)

Side One	*Side Two*
Space Oddity (Bowie)	Janine (Bowie)
Unwashed and Somewhat Slightly Dazed (Bowie)	An Occasional Dream (Bowie)
Letter to Hermione (Bowie)	The Wild Eyed Boy from Freecloud (Bowie)
Cygnet Committee (Bowie)	God Knows I'm Good (Bowie)
	Memory of a Free Festival (Bowie)

Produced by Tony Visconti
Arranged by David Bowie and Tony Visconti
('Space Oddity' track arranged by David Bowie and Paul Buckmaster and produced by Gus Dudgeon)

David Bowie (vocals, 12-string guitar, Stylophone, Kalimba, Rosedale
  electric chord organ)
Keith Christmas/Mick Wayne/Tim Renwick (guitars)
Honk/Tony Visconti/Herbie Flowers (bass)
John Cambridge/Terry Cox (drums)
Tim Renwick/Tony Visconti (flutes, recorders)
Rick Wakeman (mellotron, electric harpsichord)
Paul Buckmaster (cello)
Benny Marshall and friends (harmonica)

Ken Scott, David's later producer on 'Hunky Dory', 'Ziggy Stardust',
'Aladdin Sane' and 'Pin-Ups', began his association with David as an
engineer on 'Space Oddity'.

'Don't Dig Too Deep, Pleads Oddity David Bowie' by Gordon Coxhill, published in the *NME*, 15 November 1969.

It looked like a piece of master planning, but it wasn't. It looked like a monster hit, and it was. David Bowie's 'Space Oddity', inspired by a visit to the film *2001*, was released just as the world was staying up all night to watch the moon landing.

Like the modest, self-effacing young man he is, David passed the credit on to his record company, but as it was written last November, he can hardly disown his amazing foresight!

'Put it down to luck,' he said over the phone from Perth where he was about to start a short tour of the Haggisland. 'I really am amazed at the success of the record, even though I had confidence in it.

'I've been the male equivalent of a dumb blonde for a few years, and I was beginning to despair of people accepting me for my music.

'It may be fine for a male model to be told he's a great looking guy but that doesn't help a singer much, especially now that the pretty boy personality cult seems to be on the way out.

'I dearly want to be recognized as a writer, but I would ask them not to go too deeply into my songs. As likely as not, there's nothing there but the words and music you hear at one listening.'

Although David made a good impression on the recent Humble Pie tour, he maintains he is a songwriter first, and even denies he is a good performer.

'It was my first tour and I never stopped being surprised the concerts even went on. It appeared so badly organized to me, but I suppose everybody knew what they were doing.

'For me, it was nothing near an artistic success, mainly because I was limited to a twenty minute spot, and I ended up accompanying myself after a mix-up.

'I was very pleased to see that "Space Oddity" went down well, I thought the audience would miss the orchestral backing which was on the record.

'I throw myself on the mercy of the audience, and I really need them to respond to me. If they don't I'm lost. I'm determined to be an entertainer, clubs, cabaret, concerts, the lot.'

November 1969
David and Angie move into new lodgings in Station Road, Beckenham.
The new house was an old Victorian building called Haddon Hall.

Haddon Hall

A marvellously named, red-bricked Victorian town house became David and Angie's home for just over three years. They had the ground floor flat at Haddon Hall, 42 Southend Road, Beckenham, Kent.

The house was first seen by David and Angie in late 1969 when they were both living rather uncomfortably in Plaistow Grove. They both immediately fell in love with the house and Angie charmed the landlord into leasing the property to them.

With David and Angie moved Tony Visconti, his girlfriend Liz, and a couple of other friends including Roger Fry, their Australian roadie. The Spiders also lived in Haddon Hall for a while, practising in the basement (which had been converted into a studio by Tony and David) and sleeping on the landing. Also in residence was David's cocker spaniel from Plaistow Grove.

It was originally hoped that Haddon Hall would become a productive paradise, a place where David, Tony and Mick Ronson could create inspirational work. That this didn't quite come off in the early stages was partly because of personal troubles David had at the time.

Haddon Hall eventually proved to be a good place for David to work and 1971 was a prolific year for him. He learned to play and compose on the piano, having been given a grand piano by a generous neighbour. There are many tapes in circulation of the songs he worked on during this time, though most have escaped mass bootlegging.

As fame grew in 192, the 'curiosity shop' home of Art Nouveau, paintings, books and musical instruments became increasingly difficult to live in. Quite often David and Angie would return home and find fans sitting out in the garden or on the wall, hoping for a chat or an autograph. They decided to move out and rented a small place in Maida Vale. Haddon Hall today no longer exists. If you wander down Station Road today you will be confronted with, ironically, forty-two new flats.

In 1976, the Haddon Hall landlord, Mr Salter, sued David for unpaid back rent and damage to his property. David had painted his bedroom ceiling pink with large silver rings, the general colour scheme for the house being blue. Incidentally, David had also failed to pay his rates bill for the last quarter of 1972, that bill catching up with him while on tour here in 1978.

Many master tapes, test pressings and demo discs exist of early front-room sessions, several owned by Ken Pitt. Tony Visconti watched over the general studio recordings of both released and unreleased material. David has always had a habit of leaving material behind him when he moves on. Recently an old friend of David's found twelve uncatalogued mid-60s demo discs.

November 1969
David is awarded the Ivor Novello award from the Songwriters' Guild of Great Britain for the most original song of the year, 'Space Oddity'. The show was cabled out from The Talk of the Town to the US and also to Australia. He was mobbed on arrival that night.

30 November 1969
Is presented to Princess Margaret at the 'Save Rave' charity concert at the London Palladium, alongside Dusty Springfield, Marmalade, The Mojos, Tiny Tim and The Settlers.

December 1969
Angie spends Christmas at home in Xeros; David with his mother in her new flat and later at home at Haddon Hall. David proposes to Angie by post and during a telephone conversation plays her a demo copy of a song written for her, 'The Prettiest Star'.

Early in the New Year Angie returns to London, met by David at Heathrow Airport.

From Purcell Room to Palladium, from Zen Buddhism to Art Nouveau. Tim Hughes and Trevor Richardson break down the prismatic personality of Britain's Pop phenomenon, David Bowie.

It's a bitterly cold December afternoon. David is rehearsing a 'Save The Children' charity show at the Palladium. He is going solo with acoustic guitar – wisely dispensing with the pit orchestra hastily assembled for the Royal Occasion.

Princess Margaret and Peter Sellers will be there. There's a hassle over the sound equipment. The management seem unable to produce a supplementary mike for his guitar. Justifiably he's upset with having to make do with one.

The gigantic white safety curtain drops in. Isolated in a single spot, against mammoth projections of the Apollo Space Shot, David performs 'Space Oddity'. It's spectacularly effective and contrasts strongly with the tatty presentation of the rest of the show.

Afterwards David sits quietly with us in the stalls. A strapping Radio I DJ introduces a stunningly bad parade of groups and soloists. He cracks a stream of excruciating gags and occasionally opens his dress shirt to reveal an expanse of rotating stomach flesh. Dusty arrives to rehearse in a trim suede trouser suit. She assumes control of the rehearsal. Out go the pit orchestra. In come her own sixteen session men, sound balancers, backing girls and extra amplifiers. All of us including David, are suitably impressed by her dazzling professionalism.

Another scene, another place. The concrete halls of the South Bank are filling up as the electronic A summons the cultured to an evening's serious entertainment. Half an hour later the serried ranks of the sober suited may be seen on the Queen Elizabeth Hall monitor gravely grooving to the refined sonorities of a Haydn string quartet. Who would imagine that next door in the Purcell Room, Juniors' Eyes are belting out the big sound, warming up a very different audience for the appearance of David Bowie.

The concert is to launch his new LP released by Philips. The publicity says simply that it is given by 'David Bowie and Friends'. It is clear that this refers as much to the audience as to the performers. For David is not a pop star in the conventional sense. He is a very switched-on creative young man, rightly admired by the discerning for his talent and known only to the masses for his guaranteed-success single 'Space Oddity'.

In the interval the two audiences surge together for drinks and two cultures mingle strangely, the orthodox and the freaked-out. They view each other's appearance, whether bizarre or commonplace, with mixed feelings ranging from amused tolerance to confused mistrust.

But all are curiously united by the same artistic experience, whose expression alters with the vagaries of time and taste, but whose roots are constant. Oddly enough the Bowie band looks more baroque than the Haydn mob.

After the interval David at last appears. Perched on a stool he begins with some quiet reflective songs, accompanying himself with acoustic guitar. Some friends join him and the sounds become more involved. Finally, Juniors' Eyes plugs in and suddenly there's a really hard sound and one can scarcely believe that its centre is the slight pre-Raphaelite figure who first appeared. The range is incredible. But he says of himself, 'I've been grown up for too long.'

He could never do a whole programme of unrelenting rock and roll, as many groups do. His creativity needs more than one outlet and he has too much to express for one medium. His background is unusually varied – art school, tenor sax with Ronnie Ross's modern jazz group, poetry, mime with Lindsay Kemp, films. And even now he feels that he hasn't really begun to tap all his resources. Mixed media fascinates him and for a time he worked with a dancer and a folk singer. He has started writing a musical based on the life story of 'Someone whom everyone's mum and dad loves'.

His heroes are rather surprising – George Formby, Nat Jackley, Gracie Fields, Albert Modley – until one realizes his admiration for the artist as an entertainer. Modern influences are Jacques Brel, Dylan, Tony Newley, John Lennon and Tiny Tim.

The car breaks down. It's raining and we arrive late to take the photos. The house is a stunning and monstrous folly of a place in deepest Beckenham. Light on. Door open. No sign of David. He's just popped down to the shops for paraffin and meat for the night's stew.

David takes us on a conducted tour of his mansion – ramshackled yet strangely beautiful in its decay. Sweeping staircases. Huge stained-glass windows. Moulded ceilings. Carved and tiled fireplaces. Liberty print blocks. Art Deco lamps. William Morris screens. There is an almost child-like excitement about the way he pounces on each new treasure. It's infectious.

'We have only been here a month and we've hardly started yet. There is so much to do and it's the wrong time of the year.' We wonder if he doesn't get professional help. 'No. It's my first real place and I want to do it by myself. I'm just getting someone to do the ceilings. Isn't the garden wonderful? It's full of birds and animals.' Later outside in the failing light during the photo session squirrels leap through the branches and a fox careers across the lawn.

David is a refreshing change from so many of the inarticulate and untalented charlatans currently littering the world of pop. He doesn't think they have anything to contribute, though the public are not taken in for long. Unlike them he has something to say because he has bothered to think about himself, about what he wants to do and how he should do it and about life. He hasn't come up with any startlingly original philosophy but he differs from the herd in having a rather philosophical attitude to work and life.

Kerouac made a deep impression on him at an early age and he was genuinely affected by his recent death. He was a practising Buddhist for some time and the discipline of meditation has made him reflective. His outlook is, however, tempered by the exigencies of living in a Western capitalist society and he lacks the mindless realism of so many of his contemporaries. Money is useful. Every bloody hippy wants money to do their own non-capitalistic thing. 'Money means that I can afford to furnish my new house as I want.' He's not really materialistic – just practical.

The same attitude is seen towards relationships. 'I am a loner. I don't feel the need for conventional relationships. The few friends I have belong to the period before the success of "Space Oddity". I was madly in love last year but the gigs got in the way. One needs food.

I'm not really part of "the Scene". It leaves me cold. I just do what I have to. For instance I want to write songs. At the moment the best way of having them performed is to do them myself. But being a performer gets in the way and I look forward to the day when other people will come along and want to use my material. I have this Arts Lab at Beckenham where there's a lot going on. But I exercise a tight control over it. I have to. Free expression often means chaos, and in any case they need a leader. I don't want to be a leader – after all who wants to be a cause? It's not cliquey like most of these joints. There's hippies and skinheads and nice young people who don't fit into any category. They just come along and if they have something to offer they do it.'

It's the midnight hour and the taxi drops us somewhere behind Oxford Street. We plunge down a red stairwell. This is the 'Speakeasy' – the club for Top Pop People. David is doing the late-night spot. Someone takes our coats and we make our way to the bar. The drinks are very expensive. The lighting is so murkily subtle that it is almost impossible to make out the features of the person standing next to us. We are dimly aware of the other inhabitants. A sprinkling of boys in bone-tight velvet pants held up by redundant broad leather belts whose heavy ornate buckles force one's eyes to midriff level. Hordes of girls with deader than dead-pan faces stand in predatory clusters – these are the notorious groupies – 'the Scene's' attendant Furies. They outnumber the boys four to one. It's just not David's scene. The disco stops and a single spot stabs it's way through layers of multicoloured light show. It's David's turn. Perched precariously on two boxes – a luminous elfin face surrounded by an aureole of blond curls – he looks very vulnerable. He works hard. Numbers from the LP . . . Jacques Brel. Some bawdy poems by Mason Williams. Buzz the Fuzz. Throughout the act there is a spattering of blasé applause. Groupies parade. People keep right on talking. No one seems involved. The reaction is disturbingly muted. It's all over and David joins us at the bar. The elfin face looks puzzled. 'I can't believe it. The manager says I got a good reception. If that's what happens when they like you – what happens when they hate you?' A marauding groupie gropes him in the crush. 'Who was it? I ought to get a fee for that.'

8 January 1970
David plays a solo set at the Speakeasy on his twenty-third birthday.

30 January 1970
Plays the Johnston Hall, Aberdeen University.

3 February 1970
David and The Hype play the Marquee, sharing the bill (and the drummer, John Cambridge) with Juniors' Eyes.

14 February 1970
Voted 'Brightest Hope' in the *Disc and Music Echo* poll for 1970 (the award was later given to Ken Pitt by David). The award ceremony was held at the Cafe Royal, Regent Street.

28 February 1970
Hype support The Tide at the Basildon Arts Centre, introduced as David's 'New Electric Group'.

Late February 1970
The Hype 'bomb' at the Round House. The event was special because of the costumes put together for the show by Angela and Tony Visconti's girlfriend. The show was an unbilled support to Country Joe McDonald. Each member of the group dressed up in a different costume: David as 'Rainbowman', Tony as 'Hypeman', Mick Ronson as 'Gangsterman' and John Cambridge as 'Cowboyman'. The only person there to show any real enthusiasm, according to David, was Marc Bolan, the rest of the audience seemingly baffled.

Early 1970
'The Zig-Zag Festival' LP released including one track by David, 'Space Oddity' (US – Mercury SRD–2–29).

February 1970
David and Angie appear with Lindsay Kemp on 'Cairngorm Ski Night', a special made for Grampian TV. The show turned out to be controversial. 'We showed a little too much tits and ass for Scottish TV' Kemp later recalled. The 'Cairngorm Ski Night' tape has since been wiped by Grampian.

During their stay with Kemp in Edinburgh, they slept down on his floor. It was the first time Angie had met Kemp. She later studied dance and movement with him.

6 March 1970
The Hype play at Hull University, in Mick Ronson's home town. 'The Prettiest Star'/'Conversation Piece' single released, A-side featuring Marc Bolan on guitar and most of Hype (Mercury). The master tapes to this version of 'The Prettiest Star' were mysteriously stolen from the basement of Haddon Hall. The publishing rights to the song were given to Ken Pitt by David as a present. The next single, which was released a full eight months after 'Space Oddity', was originally going to be 'London Bye Ta Ta' but was changed, unbeknown to Ken Pitt, to the 'The Prettiest Star' at the eleventh hour.

'Conversation Piece' was later rerecorded by The Spiders but remains unreleased by RCA.

7 March 1970
Hype play at the Regent Street Polytechnic.

12 March 1970
Hype play at the Royal Festival Hall.

March 1970
'The World of David Bowie' LP released, a reissue of the 1967 LP 'David Bowie' (Decca).

Mid-March 1970
David interviewed for *Melody Maker* by Raymond Telford (published 28 March 1970):

All my songs are very personal and I combine this with an exaggeration so the meaning is clearly brought home to the listener. A lot of my compositions are very much fantasy tales. I like Marc Bolan's songs very much because I think he obviously feels the same way.

During the interview David spoke of Hype and it's future:

Although we're all happy with the set up, I can't see it becoming a permanent thing. I want to retain Hype and myself as two separate working units whereby we can retain our own identities.

19 March 1970

The afternoon was spent in Kensington Antique Market where Angie was to choose her wedding dress and David a pair of black satin trousers. The evening was spent with Angie and an artist friend, Clare Shlastone.

20 March 1970

After oversleeping all three race to reach Bromley from Clare's Bloomsbury flat. Half an hour late they arrive at the Registry Office in Beckenham Lane, to find David's mother waiting on the steps. There were only four people at the ceremony, the wedding rings being an exchange of Peruvian bangles sent to Angie by her brother. After posing for press and personal photographs, the party wandered across the road to the nearby Swan and Mitre pub for a drink. Later that afternoon they had a party at Haddon Hall.

30 March 1970

Hype appear at the Star Hotel, London Road, Croydon, supported by another local group, Ugly Room.

26 June 1970

'Memory of a Free Festival Pt I'/'Memory of a Free Festival Pt 2' single released. David's third single release for Mercury. The single commemorated the Free Festival in Beckenham David had organized the previous summer with Mary Finnigan. The song was also the first Bowie record that featured David's new drummer, Mick 'Woody' Woodmansey, a friend of Mick Ronson's from Hull.

August 1970

'Oh Baby'/'Universal Love' single released by Dib Cochrane and The Earwigs, better known to you and I as Marc Bolan and friends (Bell). The recording did not feature David in any way. This is Tony Visconti's account:

It was myself, Marc Bolan, Mick Ronson and John Cambridge. I am not sure if Steve Took or Mickey Finn played on it. This was a period when Marc became very jealous of David and David stayed away from him. The only time they ever recorded together was on 'The Prettiest Star'. Marc came to the session for an hour, played his solo and left promptly. The atmosphere was very heavy. The only other time they played together was on that television programme of Marc's. There was always a lot of talk about recording together, but I can assure you, it never happened.

November 17th, 1970
Haddon Hall

Mr. Bob Grace
Chrysalis Music Ltd
308/396 Oxford Street
London W1

Dear Bob

I was born in Brixton and went to some Schools thereabout and studied
Art. Then I went into an Advertising Agency which I didn't like very
much. Then I left and joined some Rock 'n' Roll Bands playing
Saxophone and I sang some which nobody liked very much.

As I was already a Beatnik, I had to be a Hippie and I was very heavy
and wrote a lot of songs on some beaches and some people liked them.
Then I recorded 'Space Oddity' and made some money and spent it which
everybody liked.

Now I am 24 and I am married and I am not at all heavy and I'm still
writing and my wife is pregnant which I like very much. (Roger still
lives with us).

LOVE DaVID

News From The Philips Group London

DAVID BOWIE CONTINUES HIS THEME OF "MAN VERSUS MACHINE"

"Memory Of A Free Festival" released on June 26

Ever since his astounding record "Space Oddity", David
Bowie has been hailed as one of the biggest assets British
music has.

He won a special Ivor Novello Award For Originality from
the Song Writers Guild Of Great Britain for "Space Oddity" last
year, at which time his first Philips album was released.

Recently, David has been working with lead guitarist Mick
Ronson, drummer Michael Woodmansey and record producer/bass
player Tony Visconti who are now David's backing group.

Together, they have re-recorded one of the tracks from the
LP for release as a single.

"Memory Of A Free Festival" continues David's theme of "man
versus machine" with superb results, and is released on the
Mercury label on June 26.

With the compliments of:

JUNE 1970

Nick Massey,
Press Relations Officer,
PHILIPS GROUP RECORDS.

Summer 1970

Work started on 'The Man Who Sold the World' which was to be David's last Mercury album. Apart from the complete 'The Width of a Circle', the only other material given to Tony Visconti and Mick Ronson was chord changes and song titles. The songs were interpreted and recorded in David's absence with David adding words later with the final mix. David later called the album 'a nightmare' and complained about a lot of personal problems at the time.

David is introduced to a young lawyer called Tony DeFries, an acquaintance of Tony Visconti. David, at that time, considered his affairs to be in quite a mess and DeFries promised to get him out of his old contract with Ken Pitt. There was never any animosity between David and Pitt and the break gave David a chance to redirect his ideas. David remains firm friends with Pitt, often arriving on his doorstep unannounced.

October 1970

'Ragazzo Solo, Ragazza Sola'/'Wild Eyed Boy from Freecloud' single released in Italy. The A-side was an Italian version of 'Space Oddity' with a remix of the backing track and new Italian lyrics written by Mogol. Mercury records sent someone down to Trident studios to teach David the new Italian lyrics. The B-side was the same as the UK version featuring Paul Buckmaster on cello (Italy–Philips).

November 1970

'Ragazzo Solo, Ragazza Sola'/'Sheila' single released by The Computers, A-side music written by David. This single was released almost simultaneously in Italy with David's own Italian version. Both sank without trace. The Computers were an Italian duo (Italy–Numero Uno). The rough translation of 'Ragazzo Solo, Ragazza Sola' is 'Lonely Girl, Lonely Boy'.

November 1970

'The Man Who Sold the World' LP released in the US, nearly six months before the UK release because he was signed to Mercury Records in Chicago, not to Philips in London which the previous LP and single had been released on.

Late 1970
The Stockport Sixth Form union presentation of David Bowie, Barclay James Harvest and High Tide at the Poco-a-Poco club. Entrance was 50p.

David attended the first UK shows of Phillip Glass at the Royal College of Art, (also attended by Eno) beginning David's firm interest in the artist.

December 1970
'All the Madmen'/'All the Madmen' single released in the US only (Mercury).

Although the only painting David did during the few years he lived in Haddon Hall was on the woodwork, at Christmas he carved an engraving for a Christmas card for close friends and acquaintances.

Early 1971
'Dimension of Miracles' LP released including one track by David, 'The Width of a Circle' (UK – Mercury 6641–006).

January 1971
David prepares for forthcoming tour of the US. Mick Ronson and Woody Woodmansey return to Hull. Tony Visconti, generally disillusioned and upset by the bad feeling created by the LP, moves out of Haddon Hall to set up home with Mary Hopkin.

17 January 1971
'Holy Holy'/'Black Country Rock' single released (Mercury).

Just before his trip to the US, David left a demo tape with producer Mickie Most, of a song called 'Oh, You Pretty Things'.

20 January 1971
Appears on Granada Television singing 'Holy, Holy' wearing a frock and playing acoustic guitar.

27 January 1971
David leaves for New York. Official live work is ruled out because of

work permit problems. He did play some unofficial college dates, calling them musical 'discussions' and there are tapes in circulation of some of these acoustic sets. Stays at the midtown Holiday Inn. Goes to a Greenwich Village club to see the late Tim Hardin.

Radio station visits were also made during the trip including an interview on KSAN–FM, San Francisco, explaining to the DJ that, 'My last LP was, very simply, a collection of reminiscences about my experiences as a shaven-headed transvestite.'

While in Texas during the tour, David and one of his celebrated Mr Fish dresses caught the attention of one of the local 'rednecks', as David later explained to Russell Harty in an interview in 1973.

R.H. *Have people attacked you, physically, ever?*
D.B. A couple of times, yeah.
R.H. *What happened then?*
D.B. I ran.
R.H. *Where did that happen?*
D.B. That was in America. Somebody . . . do you want to know why? In Texas I was approached by a man who had a lorry. You see, in Texas the gentleman has a rifle attached to the inside of his car or something like that, and somebody threatened me with his rifle which was very scaring because he really didn't care very much.
R.H. *What did he say to you when he threatened you?*
D.B. Well, a lot of swearing went on as well. 'If it wasn't against the law, I'd blow your head off' . . . kind of thing. It was just like a film . . . a very bad film actually . . . a very boring film.

February 1971
Rodney Bigenheimer, then working for Mercury Records in PR, became David's guide and friend during David's stay in Hollywood. With David's encouragement, Bigenheimer opened his famous English Disco, a place that even Elvis Presley was to visit out of curiosity. The club regularly played David's records. It closed in 1975 though Bigenheimer still maintains his popular weekly radio show for KROQ in Pasadena, California. Every year on David's birthday Bigenheimer has a 'Bowie Salute', inviting guests and fans into the studio to chat and play rare records.

20 March 1971
Disc and Music Echo interview published.

On 14 February 1970 David Bowie was voted *Disc*'s brightest hope that year. Now, one year and 34 days later, we find out what went wrong. David and his lady live in a beautiful Victorian house which even has turrets on the roof and a gallery running around the first floor inside the house. It overlooks a kind of banqueting hall. There's also a huge garden, the domain of a very lazy King Charles spaniel.

Spread out on the floor of one room were numerous tapes from an album to be released here in April, called 'The Man Who Sold the World'. It's already selling well in the States where Three Dog Night have covered three of the tracks. Bowie also has material for a new album he is working on and demos of songs he has sold to other artists.

Peter Noone's next solo single, 'Oh, You Pretty Things' was written by Bowie, as were other tracks bought by producer Mickie Most, a song for the Sir Douglas Quintet and one for Gene Vincent.

'It's funny how I suddenly seem to have taken off as a songwriter. But this is what living down here has done for me. I'm wrapped up in my friends and include them in my songs. One of my songs "Rupert the Riley" is about the car.

'I became disillusioned after "Space Oddity". The album was released at the same time and did absolutely nothing. No one even bothered to review it and I'm personally convinced that some of the tracks were really good. I just decided to leave London and come to live down here.

'In fact, the only thing that gave me faith again was being asked to go across to America. If I'm into making it in records, I'll have to go and live there.'

A frenzied search of the house for a copy of the new LP was fruitless but David talked about the talent of the two musicians who played on it. They are Mick Ronson and Woody Woodmansey, from a blues band in Hull. Although they felt they could make it if they teamed up as a permanent band, they returned to their group at home.

Although he has strong feelings about politics, he never includes them in his numbers.

'Britain just doesn't know what revolution is. The people should be fighting against the Common Market but they won't until it's too late.'

It was getting late, and it seemed only fitting that the accelerator should fall out of the car as David drove me to the station.

The first American visit was very important for many reasons. For years America had been a 'Myth land' for David (to quote from his own words), this trip firing his imagination greatly. The results of that visit can easily be detected in the following two LPs. The visit also broke ground for him so he knew what demands to expect on a full tour.

Late February 1971

David returns from America. Mickie Most contacts him to tell him that his song is to be recorded for a solo performance by Peter Noone of Herman's Hermits. David attends the sessions playing piano on

'Oh, You Pretty Things', 'Right on Mother' and two other Bowie tracks that were also recorded at these sessions.

Peter Noone said of David at the time, 'My view is that David Bowie is the best writer in Britain at the moment . . . certainly the best since Lennon and McCartney, and in fairness you don't hear so much of them nowadays.'

In 1983 Peter Noone spoke to me of Bowie:

It was my first solo record and David played piano on it. I was probably his biggest fan then. He's kind of an inspiration, David Bowie, to people in show business, because he managed to maintain his role as a rock 'n' roll singer and all the other things he does. He never made two albums that were similar, he never became an all-round family entertainer, he got to do movies and a Broadway play.

Of the session for 'Oh, You Pretty Things', Noone said:

When we recorded that, David had some trouble playing it through completely, so we recorded it in three sections. There were actually three breaks in that piano track, something that Mickie Most helped to arrange.

April 1971
'The Man Who Sold the World' LP released. The famous dress cover featured David sporting his Gabriel Rossetti look and the back cover featured him wearing a black beret. The cover was taken in Haddon Hall.

The Hype broke up as soon as 'The Man Who Sold the World' was completed.

Although the 'dress cover' is the most collectable of David's records, the Dutch version of this Mercury release comes in a close second. The whole LP cover folds open to create a circle with David in beret in the centre and on the cover, flicking the earth away with his half hand, half eagle body (Mercury 633 8041). The US cover was much less distinguished, being a cartoon drawing of a cowboy taken from Mick Wellars's 'Metropolist' painting. This was thought to be safer than a picture of a man in a dress!

'The Man Who Sold the World' album released April 1971 (Mercury 6338041)

Side One
The Width of a Circle (Bowie)
All the Madmen (Bowie)
Black Country Rock (Bowie)
After All (Bowie)

Side Two
Running Gun Blues (Bowie)
Saviour Machine (Bowie)
She Shook Me Cold (Bowie)
The Man Who Sold the World
  (Bowie)
The Supermen (Bowie)

Produced by Tony Visconti

David Bowie (guitar, vocals)
Mick Ronson (guitar)
Tony Visconti (electric bass, piano, guitar)
Mick Woodmansey (drums)
Ralph Mace (Moog synthesizer)

23 April 1971
Interviewed at Chrysalis music publishers' offices by George Tremlett to promote new LP.

30 April 1971
'Oh, You Pretty Things'/'Together Forever' single released by Peter Noone. A-side written by David who also sings back-up vocals. The recording of the single was the first time the two artists had met. Also featured on the recording are Herbie Flowers and Clem Cattini.
    David had originally written 'Oh, You Pretty Things' with Leon Russell in mind.

Early 1971
Meets art student Freddi Burretti in a London club. Though a lot more fashion conscious than musical, David encourages Freddi to sing and helps him put a group together called Arnold Corns with Freddi adopting the name Rudi Valentino.

April 1971
David telephones Mick Ronson and Woody Woodmansey asking them to return to Beckenham to start work on a new LP, also informing them of Tony Visconti's departure and the need for a bass player. Ronson and Woodmansey return with friend and bass guitarist, Trevor Bolder. All three were to live with David and Angie in Haddon Hall for the next few months, sleeping on the landing.

Most of the time was spent working, recording two 'very up' LPs. During this time Tony DeFries had sorted out contractual problems and had begun negotiations with RCA records, the success of 'Oh, You Pretty Things' proving an important incentive for RCA.

Hunky Dory was finished by the end of April but, by this time, David was prepared for the recording of the follow-up LP, this also being recorded at Trident studios. After the recording of Hunky Dory David offered Rick Wakeman a permanent place in his backing group, but was turned down because of Wakeman's session commitments.

Arnold Corns

Rudi Valentino (lead vocals), David Bowie (guitar and lead vocals), Mark Carr Pritchard (guitar), Mick Ronson (guitar), Trevor Bolder (bass) and Woody Woodmansey (drums).

The group's original concept included two of Freddi's friends from Dulwich College though it was really David's own group that provided the Arnold Corns musical backdrop. David wrote a number of songs with Freddi in mind, these turning out to be the blueprint for David's 'Ziggy Stardust' LP. The overall musical contribution Freddi Burretti made to the Arnold Corns project was minimal, his only recorded vocal work being 'Man in the Middle', the rest featuring David exclusively on vocals. At one point an LP was planned with the working title of 'Looking for Rudi'.

Only three tracks ever emerged from the various sessions, 'Man in the Middle', 'Hang Onto Yourself' and 'Moonage Daydream'.

During the summer of 1971 David and Freddi turned up in dresses for an interview in a Carnaby Street pub, not unnaturally turning the heads of the regulars. David was to say about Burretti, 'I believe that Rudi will be the first male to appear on the cover of *Vogue* magazine. I believe that The Rolling Stones are finished and that Arnold Corns will be the next Stones, if we must make a comparison at all.'

Arnold Corns made no impact at all and it was Burretti's real worth as clothes designer and tailor that proved most influential. All of the outfits used on the 'Ziggy' tour were designed and made by Freddi. The job was almost full time and Angie would often lend a hand along with Freddi's girlfriend, Daniella, and other friends from Dulwich College.

Burretti now lives in Italy.

Mid-1971

In between various commitments with David, Mick Ronson set up his own group project, Ronno. This was basically an extension of Ronson's earlier group The Rats and featured Ronson on guitar, Trevor Bolder on bass, Mick Woodmansey on drums and Benny Marshall on lead vocals and harmonica. Ronno made only one single, 'The Fourth Hour of My Sleep' and barely had time to establish itself as a group when David again called on their services as session musicians.

The Rats had released two singles, 'Got to See My Baby' and 'Spoonful', but were little known outside of Hull.

On a visit to London in one of his splendid but unreliable Riley cars, David stalled outside Lewisham police station. David accidentally left the car in gear and while he was cranking the engine it lurched forward, sinking the starting handle into his leg and narrowly missing an artery. He was taken to Lewisham hospital and remained there for nearly a week.

DeFries around this time was still spending a lot of time and energy trying to interest the record labels in New York. CBS and RCA both showed some interest, CBS eventually dropping out of the bidding when it was considered by them that DeFries was asking too much. However, RCA man Dennis Katz raved about David as soon as he heard the acetate and thus David signed to RCA.

7 May 1971

'Hang Onto Yourself'/'Moonage Daydream' single released by Arnold Corns, produced and written by David who is also featured on lead vocals and guitar (B & C).

28 May 1971

Duncan Zowie Haywood Bowie born in Bromley hospital, Blyth Road. David was at home listening to a Neil Young LP when the phone rang with the news. Later that day David wrote 'Kooks' to commemorate the event, performing it for the first time the following week on John Peel's radio show.

5 June 1971

David and friends appear on John Peel's 'In Concert' BBC radio show. The whole appearance was as much to entertain David as it was to entertain the audience and was David sort of filling the lull before the storm.

The show was mainly used to showcase the 'Hunky Dory' LP material and featured David, Mick Ronson, Mark Pritchard, Trevor Bolder, Mick Woodmansey, Jeff Alexander, Dana Gillespie and old school friend George Underwood.

The songs featured on the show were, 'Queen Bitch', 'Bombers', 'Supermen', 'Looking for a Friend', 'Almost Grown', 'Kooks', 'Song for Bob Dylan' and 'It Ain't Easy'.

The show has been kept for posterity on a bootleg album 'Ziggy 2'.

JOHN PEEL, COMMENTING ON THE SUNDAY EVENING 'IN CONCERT' RADIO RECORDING AT LONDON'S PARIS STUDIOS. PUBLISHED IN *SOUNDS* JUNE 1971

With David you can never be too sure what's going to happen. This time he'd arrived with an entire circus. Geoffrey Alexander was there, for example, because he lived in the same road as David and likes to sing and that's as good a reason as any. All the songs were David's except for Chuck Berry's 'Almost Grown' and Mick Ronson, Mick Woodmansey and Trevor Bolder of Ronno were playing on most of them – as was Mark Carr-Pritchard of Arnold Corns. They started with 'Queen Bitch', which will be on the next David Bowie LP and so will 'Bombers'. 'Supermen' was on the last one, 'The Man Who Sold the World', which was very good and very much overlooked. Also overlooked has been the Arnold Corns's single 'Moonage Daydream', which David wrote and produced. Their next one will be 'Looking for a Friend', so David sang that next before going on to 'Almost Grown'.

Last Sunday David became a father. He seemed uncertain about the baby's name, saying he preferred to let a name develop round the evolving personality. At the moment he's Zowie Bowie, which is a good start.

His father had written a new song specially in celebration and that's called 'Kooks', and he did that one by himself.

If you have the first Tyrannosaurus Rex LP, or David's 'Space Oddity' LP, or the 'Gentle Giant' LP, then you have in your home an example of the painting of George Underwood. George, it turns out, is a Dylan freak, so David wrote him a special song which he, George, sang next and which may also be a single. It's called logically enough, 'Song for Bob Dylan', at least,it is at the moment. You may have seen or heard of Dana Gillespie before. Anyway, it was her turn next. David says that she is a very good songwriter, but she didn't sing any of her own songs, which was a pity. She has a better voice than I'd imagined too – really good. She sang David's song 'Andy Warhol', which is going to be another single. The programme ended with just about everybody singing 'It Ain't Easy'.

---

20 June 1971

David plays an acoustic set with harmonica at dawn at the Glastonbury Fayre, evidently turning in a marvellous performance. The complete live tapes are still unreleased and owned by Jake Riviera. David was later to contribute a studio track to the 'Glastonbury–Revelations' LP.

Late June 1971
Work started on new LP 'Ziggy Stardust', recording being completed within two weeks. At this time, David's backing group were still playing with a view to working independently from David and were calling themselves Ronno. Plans for an LP and tour of their own with David's help were soon forgotten as David's career started to take precedence.

2–28 August 1971
Andy Warhol's *Pork* at the Round House.

Pork

This Andy Warhol production was very important for David and the cast of *Pork* became the spine of his Mainman organization. *Pork* hit the London news as soon as it arrived. The opening night was 2 August 1971. The cast featured a host of Warholian unknowns including Kathy Dorritie (Cherry Vanilla), Wayne County, Anthony Zanetta, Leee Black Childers, Gerri Miller and Jamie de Carlo Andrews.

The play, directed by Tony Ingrassia (another name later associated with Mainman and Bowie), was based on conversation tapes supplied by Warhol. (David once asked Ingrassia for permission to use extracts of some of the tapes in his stage act. Ingrassia refused.)

While David was appearing at Hampstead's Country Club with Mick Ronson, Cherry Vanilla and Leee Childers walked through the audience and David asked them to take a bow. Friendship was immediately struck and Vanilla encouraged David to come to see the play at the Round House. With Angie, Mick Ronson and Dana Gillespie, David went and fell in love with the production. From then on David pursued the actors, realizing the potential for publicity and making valuable contacts with the New York underground.

David also attended the final night on 28 August, venturing backstage with his entourage and then following the cast on to the Hard Rock Cafe for drinks. After rather overstaying his welcome there he went on to his favourite club, the Sombrero, where he met Tony Zanetta to talk. The following day, on Angie's invitation, Zanetta travelled down to Haddon Hall and listened to David's music and his plans for the future. At the end of the day David promised to look Zanetta up the next time he was in New York.

Four members of the *Pork* company went on to fill key roles within the Mainman organization. Cherry Vanilla became David's press agent, Tony Zanetta David's personal assistant, Leee Black Childers, official tour photographer and Jamie Andrews, general administration.

August 1971

David and Mick Ronson as a duo play the Hampstead Country Club, the set consisting of songs like 'It Ain't Easy', 'Amsterdam', 'Andy Warhol', 'Song for Bob Dylan' and 'The Supermen'. On some of the numbers, like 'Oh, You Pretty Things', Rick Wakeman would accompany them on piano.

David said at the time, 'It's very exciting for me to work in a duo format. Not being a musician, as such, it is hard for me to cope on stage on my own.'

At one time, David had decided to collect together Egyptian costumes and jewellery for a stage concept he was putting together. Apart from a photo publicity session to compliment the look, David decided to drop the idea when the Tutankhamen exhibition of the summer of 1971 created national headlines, typically shying away from any claims to be 'cashing in'.

28 August 1971

Attends the final performance of *Pork* at the Round House. From a backstage party, David and entourage go on to the Hard Rock Cafe with the cast for drinks.

September/October 1971

David and group appear on a short concert tour of Holland, Belgium and France.

September 1971

David and group play the Borough Assembly Hall, Aylesbury. The show was filmed but this has been lost by Mainman.

Late 1971

David, Angie and Tony DeFries go to New York to sign a contract with RCA Records. David and Angie stay at the Plaza Hotel and see Elvis Presley at a Madison Square Gardens concert.

Although a meeting with Presley could have been arranged David preferred not to. Much later in David's career, Elvis showed interest in one of David's songs, 'Golden Years' but did not record it before his death the following year.

David made the most of his visit to New York, looking up Tony Zanetta who looked after them during their stay. He met both Iggy Pop and Lou Reed at an RCA party, but the trip was most notable for his meeting Andy Warhol.

David had already written and recorded the song 'Andy Warhol', taking a copy of it with him to give to Warhol at the Factory in New York.

After a few minutes of uncomfortable silence, David played the song, Warhol listened carefully then got up and left the room without saying a word. After a few minutes he returned again saying, 'That was great, thank you.' He then switched on his own tape recorder and started taking Polaroid photographs of David, peeling each one off carefully and laying it down on the table.

Speech between the two was still nonexistent after well over an hour. Warhol's friends there began to talk amongst themselves when suddenly Warhol noticed David's crocodile shoes and went, in David's words, 'Bonkers about them! I'd forgotten that he used to be a shoe designer before he was a commercial artist.' The silence was thus broken and conversation developed, but David later left knowing little more about the man than before he arrived.

October 1971
'Eight Line Poem'/'Bombers' single released as a promotion disc in America (RCA).

15 October 1971
'Walnut Whirl'/'Right on Mother' single released by Peter Noone, B-side written by David who is also featured on the session (RAK).

November 1971
'Hunky Dory' LP released in the US (RCA). 'Changes'/'Andy Warhol' single released in the US (RCA).

Late 1971
David, Angie, Zowie, Woody Woodmansey and Mick Ronson spend a week in Cyprus, David's second visit there with Angie. During the flight home the plane travelled through a violent storm and when they reached Heathrow airport David had decided that he would not fly again.

17 December 1971
'Hunky Dory' LP released. The album, completed earlier in the year, reflected David's immediate reaction to America, especially the people he had encountered (RCA).

25 December 1971

Disc and Music Echo, 'Hunky Dory' review published titled, 'Forget the "Spacey" David and Enjoy This Offering':

As one of our more talented eccentrics, it's to be hoped that his songs will have as much success for himself as they have for other people. He has included 'Oh, You Pretty Things' with an arrangement not too different from Peter Noone's. However, his voice makes the difference, being sharper and more effective. He has used Rick Wakeman on piano, not being too confident of his own ability in that field, and the musicians from the abortive group he tried to get off the ground a few months ago. They seem to have reached the right understanding of Bowie's songs, but unless they get radio airing and Bowie doesn't take them out in concert, he may well lose out again.

'Hunky Dory' album released 17 December 1971 (RCA SF8244)

Side One
Changes (Bowie)
Oh, You Pretty Things (Bowie)
Eight Line Poem (Bowie)
Life on Mars (Bowie)
Kooks (Bowie)
Quicksand (Bowie)

Side Two
Fill Your Heart (Rose, Williams)
Andy Warhol (Bowie)
Song for Bob Dylan (Bowie)
Queen Bitch (Bowie)
The Bewlay Brothers (Bowie)

Produced by Ken Scott (assisted by the actor)

David Bowie (vocal, guitar, alto and tenor sax, piano)
Mick Ronson (guitar)
Trevor Bolder (bass and trumpet)
Rick Wakeman (piano)
Mick 'Woody' Woodmansey (drums)

'Hunky Dory' – 'I'm going to be huge, and it's quite frightening in a way because I know that when I reach my peak and it's time for me to be brought down, it will be with a bump!'

Steeleye Span bass guitarist Rick Kemp rehearsed with David's embryonic Spiders at one time but DeFries thought that Kemp was not right, image-wise, for the group.

Kemp was introduced to David via Mick Ronson who had worked with Kemp on Michael Chapman's 'Fully Qualified Survivor' LP. Through Kemp, David was later asked to contribute saxophone on a Steeleye Span track.

January 1972

This was a busy month, mostly spent at Haddon Hall entertaining a train of journalists. Every paper and magazine seemed to want to run a feature on him. 'Hunky Dory' had created a lot of interest in him amongst the music press and the general word in the press was that the follow-up LP was going to be even better. Early in the month he chopped off his long hair himself in favour of a trim 'mod' cut especially for the cover session photographs for 'Ziggy Stardust', taken by Brian Ward in Heddon Street, just off Regent Street.

7 January 1972

'Changes'/'Andy Warhol' single released, David's first single release for RCA. Sales for the single were not good though interest in his career was still growing. 'Changes' was even chosen as Tony Blackburn's record of the week!

11 January 1972

John Peel session (BBC Radio I).

January 1972

Plays a 'warm up' *Ziggy* show at the Borough Assembly Hall, Aylesbury in preparation for the Lancaster Festival. David had always been fond of the old Assembly Hall in Aylesbury and was sad when he played at the nearby Friars Hall five years later with Iggy Pop to find that the old hall had been turned into a furniture store.

19 January 1972

Rehearsal week. David and The Spiders rehearse at the Royal Ballroom in Tottenham High Road. (The name 'The Spiders' developed during the first UK tour, provided by the LP title).

22 January 1972

Melody Maker interview published. David declares, 'I'm gay,' later saying to another reporter that, 'It was probably the best thing I've ever said.'

February 1972

Bowie interviewed for *Melody Maker*.

I'd done a lot of pills ever since I was a kid. Thirteen or fourteen. But the first time I got stoned on grass was with John Paul Jones of Led Zeppelin many, many years ago, when he was still a bass player on Herman's Hermits records. We'd been talking to Ramblin' Jack Elliott somewhere and Jonesy said to me, 'Come over and I'll turn you onto grass.'

I thought about it and said, 'Sure, I'll give it a whirl.' We went over to his flat, he had a huge room, with nothing in it except this huge vast Hammond organ, right next door to the police department. I had done cocaine before but never grass. I don't know why it should have happened in that order, probably because I knew a couple of merchant seamen who used to bring it back from the docks. I had been doing coke with them. And they loathed grass. So I watched in wonder while Jonesy rolled these three fat joints. And we got stoned on all of them. I became incredibly high and it turned into an in-fucking-credible hunger. I ate two loaves of bread. Then the telephone rang. Jonesy said, 'Go and answer that for me, will you?' So I went downstairs to answer the phone and kept on walking right out into the street. I never went back. I just got intensely fascinated with the cracks in the pavement.

3 February 1972
David and new three-piece line-up play at the Lancaster Arts Festival, Roland Kirk also on the bill.

8 February 1972
'Old Grey Whistle Test' television recording.
'Five Years', 'Queen Bitch' and the only recently broadcast 'Oh, You Pretty Things'.

10 February 1972
First major UK tour starts at the Toby Jug, Tolworth, London.

11 February 1972
High Wycombe Town Hall, Bucks.

12 February 1972
Imperial College, Great Hall, London. Entrance was 50p.

23 February 1972
Chichester College.

25 February 1972
Avery College, Eltham, South London. Support, Armada (60p).

26 February 1972
Mayfair Suite, Belfry Hall, Sutton Coldfield.

28 February 1972
Glasgow City Hall.

29 February 1972
Sunderland Locarno. Six fans, who arrived at the venue in wheel chairs, amazingly sprang to their feet as David and group took the stage!

1 March 1972
Bristol University.

4 March 1972
Portsmouth Guildhall.

7 March 1972
Yeovil College.

11 March 1972
Guildhall, Southampton.

14 March 1972
Bournemouth, Chelsea Village.

17 March 1972
Birmingham Town Hall. Returns back to Beckenham with photographer/journalist Mick Rock for an interview for *Rolling Stone*.

14 April 1972
'Starman'/'Suffragette City' single released, his second single release for RCA. Television appearances on ITV's 'Lift Off' and also 'Top of the Pops'. (The latter recording featured Robin Lumley on piano.) Initial release in picture sleeve.

20 April 1972
The Playhouse, Harlow. (Tickets: 75p, 60p, 30p.)

April 1972
David's contract with Ken Pitt expires.

29 April 1972
High Wycombe Town Hall.

30 April 1972
The Guildhall, Plymouth.

6 May 1972
David and The Spiders play the Kingston College, where Angie once studied psychology. J.S.D. Band support.

7 May 1972
Hemel Hempstead Pavilion, supported by Lee Riders (75p).

11 May 1972
Worthing Assembly Hall (50p).

16 May 1972
BBC Radio I session for John Peel's 'Top Gear'.

14 May 1972
Oxford Polytechnic.

20 May 1972
Oxford Polytechnic.

May 1972
'Starman'/'Suffragette City' single released in the US (RCA).

May 1972
'Sound of the Seventies' Radio I series broadcast. David and The Spiders featured in session. 'Ziggy Stardust, 'Hang Onto Yourself', 'Suffragette City' and 'Moonage Daydream' were broadcast.

27 May 1972
Ebbisham Hall, Epsom, with Bob Harris (50p).

2 June 1972
Newcastle City Hall.

3 June 1972
Liverpool Stadium.

4 June 1972
Preston Public Hall.

6 June 1972
St George's Hall, Bradford.

'The Rise and Fall of Ziggy Stardust and The Spiders from Mars' LP released. After the huge success of the tour and many further bookings, David Bowie had really arrived in the eyes of the media and the public.

'Ziggy Stardust' was to be the real breakthrough record for David. Sales in the first week of release were 8,000, a high figure at that time. Less than a year later, 'Aladdin Sane' was released to advance orders of 100,000.

'The Rise and Fall of Ziggy Stardust and the Spiders from Mars' album released 6 June 1972 (RCA SF8287)

Side One
Five Years (Bowie)
Soul Love (Bowie)
Moonage Daydream (Bowie)
Starman (Bowie)
It Ain't Easy (R. Davies)

Side Two
Lady Stardust (Bowie)
Star (Bowie)
Hang Onto Yourself (Bowie)
Ziggy Stardust (Bowie)
Suffragette City (Bowie)
Rock 'N' Roll Suicide (Bowie)

Produced by David Bowie and Ken Scott

David Bowie (guitar, sax, vocals)
Mick Ronson (guitar, piano, vocals)
Trevor Bolder (bass)
Mick Woodmansey (drums)

'Ziggy Stardust' – 'I wasn't at all surprised 'Ziggy Stardust' made my career. I packaged a totally credible plastic rock star – much better than any sort of Monkees fabrication. My plastic rocker was much more plastic than anybody's.'

7 June 1972
Sheffield City Hall.

8 June 1972
Middlesborough Town Hall, J.S.D. Band support.

13 June 1972
Bristol Colston Hall. J.S.D. Band support.

16 June 1972
Torquay Town Hall.

17 June 1972
Oxford Town Hall.

19 June 1972
Southampton Civic Hall.

21 June 1972
Dunstable Civic Hall, billed as the 'Flame of the Home Counties', supported by The Flamin' Groovies from America (75p).

24 June 1972
Guildford Civic Hall.

25 June 1972
Croydon Greyhound, Park Lane. One thousand people turned away at the door.

30 June 1972
High Wycombe Grammar School concert cancelled because of over-booking. The show, in aid of the Wycombe Action Group, was filled in by Jonathan Kelly who was to have been the evening's support act.

July 1972

'Revelations – A Musical Anthology for Glastonbury Fayre' LP released by the concert promoters to try and recoup some of the £5,000 lost at the previous summer's concert (Revelation). All of the featured artists contributed their work in sympathy, David's offering being a Spiders update of 'The Supermen' recorded during the Ziggy Stardust sessions.

2 July 1972
Rainbow Pavilion, Torbay.

GAY NEWS ARTICLE JULY 1972 BY PETER HOLMES
'GAY ROCK–DAVID BOWIE IN CONCERT AT
THE ROYAL FESTIVAL HALL'

THE EVENT: Saturday 8 July Bowie played at London's Royal Festival Hall in benefit for the Friends of the Earth's Save the Whale campaign fund.

Two weeks before the concert you couldn't get a seat in RFH for deviant practices or money. Your reporter got in early with a couple of quid and there he was just a few yards out from the stage and enough amplification equipment to set up a small to medium sized radio station.

Kuddly Ken Everett is compere. Introduces Marmalade and the J.S.D. Band, who replace Mott. It seems podgy Scots boys with glasses are in this week. They get a reasonable reception. But we're waiting for the star. The crowd isn't noticeably campy, even though the aftershave lies slightly heavier on the air than at most concerts at the RFH. Then Ken Ev ('I even went a bit gay'! *Nova*) in a fetching jumpsuit of blue denim with massive white buttons showing how he got in and how he meant to get out says he fought his way through the feather boas to the star's dressing room.

'He insists on introducing himself in about four minutes' time, so here is the second greatest thing, next to God . . . David Bowie,' says Kuddly Ken. The speakers boom out the moog martial version of the 'Song of Joy' from 'A Clockwork Orange'.

The capacity plus crowd claps in time and in the dark as people sneak across the stage in the murk.

It ends. A single spot picks out a thin, almost drawn jester. Red hair, white make-up and a skintight, red and green, Persian carpet print, space suit. All this on top of red lace-up space boots.

'Hello, I'm Ziggy Stardust and these are The Spiders from Mars.' More lights and we have Mick Ronson, Trevor Bolder, Mick Woodmansey.

A few seconds and we have the mind blowing electric music of Bowie from the amps matched by the words that make Burroughs look like a slouch. And on stage, Bowie rampant.

Until now, Bowie's never been a star, but he's studied some of the best, like Garbo, Presley, and now he's on top and he knows what to do. Sometimes he plays guitar, sometimes just sings with his eerie thin voice, but sometimes that voice grows. Bowie is the understudy who's been waiting in the wings for years.

Finally his big day comes, and he's got every step, every note, every voice-warble right. A star is born.

He's a showman alright. Even the

David and The Spiders play the Royal Festival Hall in aid of Friends of the Earth, proceeds going to the 'Save the Whale' fund. The concert was also notable because it was the first UK appearance of Lou Reed who was the 'special guest'. The support for the evening was Marmalade and the J.S.D. Band, and the compere Kenny Everett. (Tickets: 50p – £2.)

Mott the Hoople, originally lined up as support, dropped out, unable to play their full set because of time restrictions and preferring, thus, not to play at all.

---

pubescent girls who'd spent their Saturday-mornings-at-Woolies wages on a seat, or crowded into the gangways, screamed.

He says, 'Tonight we have a surprise for you.' And everyone knows what it is. Lou Reed. The *NME* and other pop papers carried that secret during the week in inch-and-a-half caps.

'Tonight we're going to do a number by the Cream – "Free." ' Anticlimax swamps the hall.

But the Bowie voice is haunting in the few lines of the words at the beginning of the number. Then he leaves it to The Spiders to get on with it. They do, talented musicians that they are. Strobe lights on the gantry over them slow, then into a far from silent movie, one frame at a time.

Then our David's back. Now he's in a white satin space suit that leaves only how he got into it to the imagination.

Garbo on Mars.

And, offhand, he says: 'If you've seen us before, you'll know we do some numbers by the Velvet Underground. And tonight we have, for the first time on any stage in England, Lou Reed.'

And the Velvets's former leading light bounds on in black to match Bowie's white. We get a set of Velvet numbers.

David plays to Lou.

Lou plays to Mick. Mick plays to David. While they're having fun on stage there's enough electricity generated in the RFH to keep the national grid pulsing high voltage goodies all over the land.

They end, and the front several hundred of the 3,000-plus crowd mobs the stage. Time for the expected encore.

Ziggy and The Spiders reappear and do 'Suffragette City', orange handouts with their pictures on explode from the stage.

In this hour and a bit Bowie has passed from wild electric rock to simple ballads, such as 'Space Oddity' and a Jaques Brel poem 'The port of Amsterdam' and back to wild electric rock.

His words span concepts from science-fiction and the coming of a super race to sexual liberation.

And we all had a bloody good time.

David Bowie is probably the best rock musician in Britain now. One day he'll become as popular as he deserves to be. And that'll give Gay rock a potent spokesman.

14 July 1972

Kings Cross cinema, a warm-up show for the Aylesbury show of the following evening. This show also attended by various journalists and guests.

15 July 1972

Friars Aylesbury. US pressmen flown in especially for the show in a Mainman initiative to prepare ground for the US tour.

At one time, David was planning to relay a live concert from Aylesbury Friars to a huge video screen erected in the market square but this was never pursued further.

15 July 1972

Iggy and The Stooges play their first and only UK show at the Kings Cross cinema.

July/August 1972

Iggy and The Stooges record 'Raw Power' at the CBS studios, London. Iggy Pop and the Stooges now come under Mainman management. They are one of David's favourite groups of the time.

16 July 1972

Holds a day of interviews at the Dorchester Hotel, Lou Reed and Iggy Pop also being present. 'Any society that allows people like Lou Reed and I to become rampant is really pretty well lost.'

18 July 1972

Plays the Friars Aylesbury. J.S.D. Band Support.

28 July 1972

'All the Young Dudes'/'One of the Boys' single released by Mott the Hoople, A-side written by David who is also featured on the recording and production (CBS). Originally a demo of 'Suffragette City' was sent to Mott's bassist Overend Watts when David discovered that Mott had broken up. In the interim period David wrote a song he thought more appropriate for the group called 'All the Young Dudes', playing it on an acoustic guitar for the first time in his manager's office. A version cut by David and The Spiders and originally intended for the 'Aladdin Sane' LP has never been released.

August 1972

David, busy with concert preparations and recording with Lou Reed at Trident studios, moves temporarily in to the Grosvenor House Hotel to save time on runs to and from Beckenham.

'Hang Onto Yourself'/'Man in the Middle' single released by Arnold Corns though this group project had long been forgotten (B & C). This single was later reissued on the Mooncrest label.

19 August 1972

David and The Spiders play the Rainbow Theatre, London. The performance also featured Lindsay Kemp and mime company and backing singers The Astronettes. The afternoon rehearsal was filmed by Mick Rock, part of which was used for the promotional video of 'John I'm Only Dancing', shown on 'Top of the Pops' at the time. Loyd Watson and Roxy Music support, ex-Procol Harum pianist Matthew Fisher providing piano from backstage for David's set.

20 August 1972

Rainbow Theatre. Both shows a sell-out.

Bryan Ferry's comment on David's Rainbow performance, 'I don't think it worked.'

Lindsay Kemp only knew of the Rainbow show one week beforehand, when David telephoned him in Edinburgh. Angie travelled to Scotland to bring Kemp and company back to London for rehearsals.

August 1972

Lou Reed's 'Transformer' LP recorded at Trident studios, David and Mick Ronson producing.

28 August 1972

Locarno Electric Village, Bristol. Support Gnidrolog and Thin Lizzy (£1.25).

31 August 1972

Starkers, Bournemouth.

1 September 1972

'John, I'm Only Dancing'/'Hang Onto Yourself' single released by RCA (highest chart position No. 12). David and The Spiders play the Top Rank Suite, Doncaster. The show featured as part of the local St Leger Festival.

2 September 1972
Opening night of the Hard Rock, Manchester. David and The Spiders play. DJ Andy Peebles.

3 September 1972
The Hard Rock, Manchester. The show saw David and group perform without the glitter jumpsuits, playing just in denims.

4 September 1972
Top Rank Suite, Liverpool.

5 September 1972
Top Rank Suite, Sunderland.

6 September 1972
Top Rank Suite, Sheffield.

Above left: David Jones, aged 11, at Ravenswood School. *Kentish Times*

Above right: David Jones, aged 13, at Ravenswood School. *Kentish Times*

Left: 4 Plaistow Grove, Bromley

Below: Burnt Ash Junior School as it is today

The King Bee in 1964. *Decca*

David as Mod, 1966. *Decca*

David in 1966

At the Marquee Club,
London, in 1966.
Starzone Magazine

Above: The Lower Third's early publicity, 1966

Below: The only photos taken of David with The Buzz; they are pictured recording for 'Ready, Steady, Go'. *Pictorial Press*

Left: David writing 'Join the Gang' at Clapham Common's open-air café, 1966. *Pictorial Press*

Below: Davie Jones? Brian Jones? Spot the difference. Bowie in 1965. *Syndication International*

Above: David Jones and The Manish Boys outside the BBC in 1965. *Syndication International*

Right: Tony Hill, Hermione Farthingale and Bowie — the original Feathers line-up. *Stevenson*

Left: Feathers — Hermione Farthingale, Bowie, producer Tony Visconti and John Hutchinson wait for recording time at Trident studios, London, 1968. *Stevenson*

Below: David and Angie outside the Bromley Registry Office on their wedding day in 1970, with David's mother. *Beckenham Journal*

Angie Bowie with puppeteer Brian Moore in the Beckenham Arts Lab days

Bowie with Freddi Burretti in 1971

Above: David Bowie in 1969

Left: Rehearsing 'Space Oddity' for a charity concert in November 1969. *Stevenson*

Left: An out-take from the photographic session for the 'Ziggy Stardust' cover in 1972. *Ward*

Facing page

Above: From 'The Man Who Sold The World' (RCA) cover session

Below: On tour in 1972. *Mick Rock*

Halo. *Decca*

Left: Ziggy at the Palace Theatre, Watford in December 1973. *Watford Observer*

Right: Bowie in 1973. Note the shoes.
Pictorial Press

Below: Posing in 1971

Bottom: In concert, 1973

A star and stripes. *Pines/Elliot*

Bowie and Marc Bolan jam
together for a television
recording in 1977

Brian Eno, David Bowie and
Robert Fripp at Hansa by the Wall
studio, Berlin in 1978. *RCA*

From the 'Diamond Dogs' tour in 1974.
Pines/Elliott

Real spacemen pick up a pinta – early promotional picture for *The Man Who Fell To Earth*, 1975

Above: David Bowie in 1982. *EMI*

Left: The Thin White Duke, 1976

On and off the set of *The Hunger* with Catherine Deneuve. *MGM*

David Bowie in a scene from *The Hunger*. *MGM*

Above: In Japan, 1980

Right: Relaxing in Paris in 1977

Left: The honourable schoolboy
in 1980. *Recorded Picture Co.,
(NZ), photo by Ken George*

Below: On the set of *Merry
Christmas, Mr Lawrence* in 1982,
with Tom Conti and Jack
Thompson. *Recorded Picture
Co., (NZ), photo by Ken George*

7 September 1972
Top Rank Suite, Hanley, Stoke-On-Trent. Last night of David and
The Spiders's first UK tour.

8 September 1972
'All the Young Dudes' LP released by Mott the Hoople. Produced by
David (CBS).

Late September 1972
Arrives in New York on the *QE2* for his first tour of the United States.
David, group and personnel charter a Greyhound bus from New York
to Cleveland for their first concert.
　　Most of the LP 'Aladdin Sane' was written while travelling across
America from town to town.

September 1972
Mainman Organization established by Tony DeFries in New York.

22 September 1972
David and The Spiders play the Cleveland Music Hall. Support group
for the US tour, Fumble.
　　Interviewed for the November issue of *Rolling Stone* by Timothy
Ferris.

24 September 1972
Memphis Ellis Auditorium. Post-concert party held at the Memphis
Downtowner Motor Inn.

28 September 1972
Carnegie Hall, New York, David's New York debut, a complete sellout
and huge success, despite a bad attack of flu. Interviewed backstage
by Scott Osborne for the US television News Service.

s.o. *How would you describe youself?*
d.b. Partly enigmatic, partly fossil.

RCA announce that four hundred applications for one hundred press
passes were made for David's Carnegie Hall show.

29 September 1972
Kennedy Center, Washington DC.

1 October 1972
The Music Hall, Boston.

October 1972
RCA release 'The Jean Genie'/'Hang Onto Yourself' and rerelease 'Space Oddity' and 'The Man Who Sold the World' LPs in the US.

6 October 1972
'Do Anything You Say', 'I Dig Everything'/'Can't Help Thinking About Me', 'I'm Not Losing Sleep' EP released, a reissue of some of David's earlier Pye singles (Pye).
   Initial release in picture sleeve.

7 October 1972
Chicago Auditorium.

27–28 October 1972
San Francisco Winterland Auditorium. Support Sylvester.

8th October 1972
Fisher Theater, Detroit.

16 October 1972
Chicago.

20 October 1972
Santa Monica Civic Auditorium, Florida.

21 October 1972
Santa Monica Civic Auditorium. Second show added to meet demand.

November 1972
David is asked by CBS to mix the recently recorded LP by Iggy and The Stooges. Production had been disastrously left to Iggy Pop who had amazingly mixed most of the instruments onto one channel. David remixed the tapes in Hollywood, the finished LP still retaining the edge of Pop's wild recording technique.
   'Walk on the Wild Side'/'Perfect Day' single released by Lou Reed. David coproduced and mixed the single with Mick Ronson and Reed and also appears on it (RCA).

3 November 1972
'The Man Who Sold the World' LP rereleased (RCA LSP 4816). Track listing as first issued on the Mercury label. No remix.

9 November 1972
'David Bowie in America' article published in *Rolling Stone*.

11 November 1972
Majestic Theater, Dallas.

12 November 1972
The Music Hall, Houston.

14 November 1972
Lagola University, New Orleans.

17 November 1972
The Jai Alais Fronton at the Pirate's Cove, Miami, Florida. 'Space Oddity' LP rereleased, previously titled 'David Bowie' (RCA LSP 4813). Track listing as first issued (except for the removal of one unlisted track 'Don't Sit Down', a 20-second filler). No remix.

20 November 1972
The Municipal Auditorium, Nashville.

22 November 1972
The Warehouse, New Orleans.

24 November 1972
'The Jean Genie'/'Ziggy Stardust' single released by RCA, A-side recorded in New York, composed on the road by David and sung constantly by everyone on the tour bus while travelling from show to show (highest position no. 2).

28 November 1972
The Stanley Theater, Pittsburgh.

29 November 1972
Mott the Hoople play the Tower Theater, Philadelphia introduced by David who also joined them on stage for a memorable version of 'All the Young Dudes'.

30 November 1972
David and The Spiders play the Tower Theatre, Philadelphia.

November 1972
'Space Oddity', 'Moonage Daydream'/'Life on Mars', 'It Ain't Easy' promo EP issued (RCA).

1–2 December 1972
Tower Theater, Philadelphia.

10 December 1972
Back in New York, David stayed at the Warwick Hotel. Spends the evening chatting with Mott's Ian Hunter, playing tracks to him from his forthcoming album, 'Aladdin Sane', including an unfinished version of 'All the Young Dudes' which was eventually thought by David to be unsuitable for inclusion on the LP. Later the two talked all night at the delicatessen about the future Mott plans.

Mid-December 1972
Returns from New York on HMS *Ellinis*. During the journey home wrote 'Aladdin Sane'. The melody came first (like most of David's songs at the time) with the lyrics following.

8 December 1972
'Transformer' LP released by Lou Reed, produced and part arranged by David who also wrote the uncredited 'Wagon Wheel' track and lent backing vocals throughout. David contacted old sax tutor Ronnie Ross with the offer of session work on the LP.

December 1972
'Space Oddity'/'The Man Who Sold the World' single released in America only (RCA). With the issue of the single came a mimed video filmed in London's Trident studios, simply David with his guitar.
    '20 Fantastic Hits by Original Artists Volume 3' LP released including 'The Jean Genie' (Arcade).

23 December 1972
David and The Spiders play at the Rainbow, London.

24 December 1972
Christmas Eve show at the Rainbow, both shows supported by Quiver. The audience attending the Christmas Eve show were asked to bring

along a toy for the children in need. The following day a large delivery of presents was made to Dr Barnardo's homes in London.

December 1972
David, Angie and Zowie spend Christmas at home in Haddon Hall, their last Christmas there. David's fame well and truly established, fans camp in his garden, hoards of fan mail arrives and privacy vanishes. A decade of hard work and hope finally pays.

28 December 1972
Manchester, Hard Rock.

December 1972
Talking to *Rolling Stone* on his winter tour of the US: 'I very rarely have felt like a rock artist. I don't think that's much of a vocation, being a rock 'n' roller.'

Nothing matters except whatever it is I'm
doing at the moment. I can't keep track of
everything I say . . . I can't even remember
how much I believe and how much I don't
believe. The point is to grow into the person
you grow into. I haven't a clue where I'm
gonna be in a year. A raving nut, a flower
child or a dictator, some kind of reverend. I
don't know. That's what keeps me from
getting bored.

DAVID BOWIE 1973

After barely a week's break, it was up to Scotland to complete the last few UK shows before a second tour of America.

5 January 1973
Glasgow, Green's Playhouse (matinee and evening shows). Supported by Quiver.

6 January 1973
Edinburgh Empire Theatre. Support Quiver.

7 January 1973
Newcastle City Hall. Support Quiver.

9 January 1973
Preston Guildhall. Support Quiver.

17 January 1973
Appears on London Weekend Television's 'Russell Harty Plus' chat show, singing 'Drive In Saturday' and 'My Death'. The interview that followed had David with his tongue planted firmly in cheek.

R.H. *What kind of home did you come from?*
D.B. A small one. A home like an ordinary house. It was a lovely home with a dog and a budgie.
R.H. *Do you go back there at all? Is it still there?*
D.B. No, it isn't. My father died, my mother moved. But I still see my mother.
R.H. *They haven't put up a big notice outside it saying, you know, a blue . . .*
D.B Yes . . . 'For Sale'. No, they haven't.
R.H *Do you believe in God?*
D.B. What?
R.H. *Do you believe in God?*
D.B. I believe in an energy form, but I wouldn't like to put a name to it.
R.H. *Do you indulge in any form of worship?*
D.B. Um . . . life. I love life very much indeed.

The show was billed as a London Weekend 'pop' special and featured Elton John, Georgie Fame and Alan Price amongst others. Recorded at the LWT South Bank studios.

20 January 1973
Recording with The Spiders at Trident studios. A new (sax) version of 'John I'm Only Dancing' recorded and other preparatory work for 'Aladdin Sane', all part of a week's recording schedule there. 'Panic

in Detroit' and 'Lady Grinning Soul' were also recorded, but without David's vocals.

25 January 1973
Leaves Southampton on the *QE2* for America to begin a 100-day world tour.

13 February 1973
David and The Spiders spend all night rehearsing for the opening.

14 February 1973
New York, Radio City Music Hall, first night of the second US tour. The Valentine's Day performance was a triumph and New York once again took to David in a big way. The shows were a complete sellout, and even Andy Warhol found getting tickets a problem. One music paper called David 'The Darling of New York'. This was to be David's real breakthrough in the States.

   David, in need of a pianist, is introduced to an American piano teacher, Mike Garson, by Annette Peacock. Garson was to remain as David's pianist on and off for over three years.

15 February 1973
New York, Radio City Music Hall. Interviewed before the show by Michael Watts. Show attended by Johnny Winter and Todd Rundgren. Amongst those attending David's New York shows was Salvador Dali who has attended other performances by David in the States over the years. Support for the US tour were Fumble. David speaking later of their act said, 'I adore them. They're very unpretentious about revamping the whole era. It seems very natural with them, very James Dean.'

February 1973
'Images 1966–67' double LP released in the US (London). Re-packaged in 1977 as 'The Starting Point', a single LP minus eleven tracks featured on 'Images', also on the London label.

16–20 February 1973
Philadelphia, the Tower Theatre.

17 February 1973
First plans for a starring role announced. 'Stranger in a Strange Land', from the book by Robert Heinlein, was never made.

23 February 1973
Nashville, the War Memorial Theatre.

26–27 February 1973
Memphis, Ellis Auditorium.

1 March 1973
Detroit, the Masonic Auditorium. Interviews conducted at the Detroit Hilton. After the show David holds a small party for friends and is introduced to Michael Des Barres of US group Silverhead and to B. P. Fallon.

March 1973
The Image rerun at the Jacey cinema, Trafalgar Square, squeezed in between two other films *I Am Sexy* and *Erotic Blue*.

3 March 1973
Chicago, the Aragon Ballroom.
    David and crew check into the Beverly Hills Hotel, the same time as Andy Warhol and his entourage. Home from home for the Mainman crowd.
    During their stay in LA, while David and his travelling companion Freddi Burretti were dancing together at the Rainbow Grill, David was approached by a 'long-haired individual' and threatened. The interloper called David a 'punk' and threw a punch at him. He was hastily dragged away by the ever-present minder, Stuey George. The incident upset David enough to restrict trips outside of his hotel room for the rest of the US tour.

10 March 1973
Los Angeles, the Long Beach Auditorium.

11 March 1973
Los Angeles, the Long Beach Auditorium.
    Holds a dinner party for Ringo Starr and Klaus Voorman; later in the week he also attended the Bette Midler show at Long Beach Arena. Leaves the States in mid-March, travelling to Japan by boat for his first shows there.

6 April 1973
'Drive In Saturday'/'Round and Round' single released. B-side written by Chuck Berry. 'Drive in Saturday' was written on a train journey from Seattle to Phoenix and inspired by some unusual buildings David

caught sight of in the distance from his train window. No one could explain their purpose to him.

8 April 1973
Tokyo, Shinjuku Koseinenkin Kaikan. David and The Spiders's first performance in Japan. Receives a wild reception from a rock-starved audience and is an immediate success in Japan. The *Japan Times* commented on his Tokyo performance:

'Musically, he is the most exciting thing that has happened since the fragmentation of the Beatles, and theatrically he is possibly the most interesting performer ever in the pop music genre.'

Personnel for Japanese tour:
Mick Ronson (guitar, vocals)
Trevor Bolder (bass)
Aynsley Dunbar (drums)
Mike Garson (keyboards)
Ken Fordham (saxophone)
John Hutchinson (rhythm guitar)
David Bowie (vocals, guitar, saxophone)

10–11 April 1973
Tokyo, Shinjuku Koseinenkin Kaikan.

While in Japan, David attends a show by one of Japan's most popular Kabuki stars, Tomasa Boru. After the Tokyo show, David was introduced to Boru backstage at the venue.

12 April 1973
Nagoya, Kokaido.

13 April 1973
'Aladdin Sane' LP released to advance orders of 100,000, the first time such sales had been recorded since The Beatles. On the day of release, the LP qualified for a gold disc (RCA). The LP was originally to be titled 'Love Aladdin Vein' or 'Vein', but these titles were dropped because of the possible drug associations.

'Lady Grinning Soul', a track written for Claudia Lennear, replaced the originally listed track 'Zion'.

'Aladdin Sane' and single 'The Jean Genie' were banned before release in Rhodesia, authorities there considering the records to be 'undesirable'.

14 April 1973
Hiroshima, Yuubinchokin Kaikan.

16 April 1973
Kobe, Kobe Kokusai Kaikan.

17 April 1973
Osaka, Koseinenkin Kaikan.

20 April 1973
Tokyo, Shibuya Kokaido. Last show in Japan.

A triumphant show to end the Japanese tour. After fifteen minutes he returned for a third encore of 'Round and Round'. The show was slightly marred by hysteria spreading when the Japanese guards waded into the crowd to break up what they considered to be a riot. Angie helped trapped youngsters escape the crush, many of them caught under seats that had toppled in rows. No major injuries were reported.

'Aladdin Sane' album released 13 April 1973 (RCA RS 1001).

Side One
Watch That Man (New York)
  (Bowie)
Aladdin Sane (1913–1938–197?)
  (HMS *Ellinis*) (Bowie)
Drive In Saturday (Seattle–Phoenix)
  (Bowie)
Panic in Detroit (Detroit) (Bowie)
Cracked Actor (Los Angeles)
  (Bowie)

Side Two
Time (New Orleans) (Bowie)
The Prettiest Star (Gloucester Road)
  (Bowie)
Let's Spend the Night Together
  (Jagger, Richard)
The Jean Genie (Detroit and New
  York) (Bowie)
Lady Grinning Soul (London)
  (Bowie)

Produced by David Bowie and Ken Scott

Arranged by David Bowie and Mick Ronson

David Bowie (vocals, guitar, harmonica, saxophones)
Mick Ronson (guitar, piano, vocals)
Trevor Bolder (bass)
Woody Woodmansey (drums)
Mike Garson (piano)
Ken Fordham (Bux-saxophones, flutes)
Juanita 'Honey' Franklin/Linda Lewis/Mac Cormack (vocal backup)

'Aladdin Sane' – 'I ran into a very strange type of paranoid person when I was doing "Aladdin". Very mixed-up people, and I got very upset. It resulted in "Aladdin" . . . and I knew I didn't have much more to say about rock 'n' roll.

'I mean "Ziggy" really said as much as I meant to say all along. "Aladdin" was really "Ziggy" in America. Again, it was just looking around, seeing what's in my head.'

Before leaving Japan, Kansai Yamamoto, a fashion designer who had presented a spectacular costume gift to David in New York, gave David a further nine costumes based on the traditional Japanese Noh dramas. During his short stay David managed to see a few Noh performances and later commented, 'It was a great experience, I found them absolutely fascinating. There was an awful lot, particularly in the outlying villages and provinces, of very strange ritual dance performances that I hadn't seen before. A lot of them were from Shintoism.'

21 April 1973
Boards a boat from Yokohama to Nahodka, then a train to Vladivostok to catch the Trans-Siberian Express, travelling 'soft', the Russian equivalent of 'first class'.

The train journey was long. David passed the time occasionally writing and took a lot of film of Russia from the train. At one station, a particularly zealous guard tried to confiscate David's movie camera. Leee Childers, who was one of the few companions who braved the journey with him, managed to distract the guard long enough for David to get back on the train. Of Russia, David had surprisingly little to say. 'Russia is an impossible country to talk about. It's so vast. The people we found to be warm, generally. When we got to Moscow, they were colder.'

After the week-long journey across Russia, David and friends spent two days sightseeing in Moscow, catching the May Day parade before catching the Orient Express through East Germany, Poland and France. In Paris, David and Angie spent the night at the George V Hotel, (David's favourite Paris hotel) and overslept the following day. Arriving late at the Gare du Nord, missing their train and subsequently their ferry, they took the hovercraft from Boulogne back to England. Bowie was reluctant: this was too much like flying!

3 May 1973
Their last evening in Paris spent with Jacques Brel.

4 May 1973
Leaves Paris. Arrived at Charing Cross Station, London, having completed more than 8,000 miles over land. A few hundred fans mobbed him on the station platform as he ran to a waiting car. Interviewed on the journey home by Roy Hollingworth of the *Melody Maker*.

5 May 1973
David and Angie give a homecoming party in Haddon Hall, inviting all their friends. Tony Visconti and Mary Hopkin, Lindsay Kemp, Mick Ronson, George Underwood, Freddi Burretti, Sue Fussey (David's tour hairdresser) and Ken Scott.

May 1973
Just over a week later, barely recovered from the tour, it was back to UK touring with the first of two shows at Earls Court, London.

12 May 1973
David and The Spiders perform at Earls Court. It had been well publicized in the press that Japanese designer Kansai had prepared a startling new wardrobe for the new stage show. The Earls Court shows would premier these new costumes and also 'Aladdin Sane' – David's follow-up character to Ziggy Stardust.

The first show however, was less than a success: Earls Court was a new venue for rock concerts, David's being the first of this kind there. The 18,000 fans who attended the show proved too much to control and the show was halted twice to maintain order. Eventually David gave the audience an ultimatum and the show was completed. The second show, scheduled for 30 May, was cancelled. Both London shows had sold out in record time; the national press were writing of 'Bowie Mania'.

12 May 1973
Souvenir edition of the *Evening News* run to coincide with the first night show. David interviewed for the paper by John Blake.

15 May 1973
Leaves Kings Cross Station for Aberdeen to start what became known as the 'Aladdin Sane' retirement tour of Britain. UK tours often included matinee performances arranged by DeFries in Japan when he telephoned the already-booked support group Fumble to tell them that they would not be needed on the tour. The tour was a major sellout and complete success.

16 May 1973
Aberdeen Music Hall. Arriving the previous evening at Aberdeen Station, David was taken just fifty yards from the station to the Imperial Hotel in a grey Daimler. Tickets for the Aberdeen show had sold out in two hours. A second matinee was quickly added and also sold out. The opening night's success proved to be a precedent for the entire tour.

17 May 1973
Dundee, Caird Hall. After the show, David was nearly trapped by a mob of admirers outside the stage door. Bodyguard Stuey George managed to push David to safety.

18 May 1973
Glasgow Green's Playhouse (matinee show added). The evening performance went well again, except for slight crowd violence and the customary destruction of chairs, which is said to be the mark of a good show in Glasgow! David was safely whisked away under police escort after the show.

19 May 1973
Edinburgh, Empire Theatre. Matinee show added.

21 May 1973
Norwich, Theatre Royal. Matinee show added.

May 1973
'Images' double LP released in Germany, a collection of previously released and unreleased material from 1967 (London). Although this package was readily available in the UK and Europe generally, it wasn't released officially here until May 1975. 'Aladdin Sane' LP released in the US (RCA).

22 May 1973
Romford Odeon.

23 May 1973
Brighton Dome. Matinee show added.
   Damage caused by an excited audience at the venue lead the Brighton Dome management to ban David from ever appearing at the venue again.

24 May 1973
Lewisham Odeon. This date was added on from the original tour schedule.

25 May 1973
Bournemouth Winter Gardens.

27 May 1973
Guildford Civic Hall. Matinee show added.

28 May 1973
Wolverhampton, Civic Hall.

29 May 1973
Hanley, Victoria Hall.

30 May 1973
Oxford, New Theatre.

31 May 1973
Blackburn, King George's Hall.

1 June 1973
Bradford St George's Hall.
   'Raw Power' LP released by Iggy and The Stooges. The record was mixed by David and Iggy in Hollywood the previous summer. 'Time'/ 'The Prettiest Star' released in the US (RCA).

2 June 1973
Leeds University show cancelled six hours before it was scheduled to start because of bad stage and dressing room facilities. Said a Mainman representative, 'They were totally unsuitable. It would have meant David walking through the audience to get to the stage which is out of the question.'

3 June 1973
Coventry, New Theatre.

4 June 1973
Worcester Gaumont. Date added on from original tour schedule.

6 June 1973
Sheffield City Hall.

June 1973
Interviewed by German radio 'Rockspeak' programme.

7 June 1973
Manchester Free Trade Hall. Matinee show added.

8 June 1973
Newcastle, City Hall.

9 June 1973
Preston, Guildhall.

June 1973
Interviewed by BBC radio presenter Steve Dickson about the making of 'Aladdin Sane'.

10 June 1973
Liverpool, Empire Theatre. Matinee show added.

11 June 1973
Leicester, De Montfort Hall.

12 June 1973
Chatham Central Hall. Matinee show added.

13 June 1973
Kilburn Gaumont. Date added from original tour schedule.

14 June 1973
Salisbury, City Hall.

15 June 1973
Taunton Odeon. Matinee show added.

16 June 1973
Torquay Town Hall. Matinee show added.

18 June 1973
Bristol, Colston Hall. Matinee show added.

19 June 1973
Southampton Guildhall. The previously scheduled show on this day at
Portsmouth Guildhall cancelled before the start of the tour.

21 June 1973
Birmingham Town Hall. Matinee show added.

22 June 1973
Birmingham Town Hall. Matinee show added.
   'Life on Mars'/'The Man Who Sold the World' single released by
RCA due to the success of 'Life on Mars' in performance during the
tour. Highest chart position No. 3.
   'Life on Mars' was David's favourite track from the 'Hunky Dory'
LP and was inspired by 'My Way'. The single gained a silver disc,
selling over 250,000 copies, some copies issued in picture sleeves.

23 June 1973
Boston Gliderdrome.
   'The Prettiest Star'/'Love Around' single released by Simon Turner.
A-side written by David (UK 44) and featured on the LP 'Simon
Turner' (UKAL 1002).

24 June 1973
Croydon, Fairfield Hall. Matinee show added.

25 June 1973
Oxford, New Theatre. Matinee show added.

26 June 1973
Oxford, New Theatre. Matinee show added.

27 June 1973
Doncaster Top Rank.

28 June 1973
Bridlington Spa Ballroom.

29 June 1973
Leeds Rolarena. Concert added on through cancellation of the Leeds
University show earlier in the month. Matinee show added.

July 1973

'Let's Spend the Night Together'/'Lady Grinning Soul' single released in the US (RCA).

3 July 1973

Hammersmith Odeon, London. The famous final concert of the '73 tour. The film of the concert, shot by D.A. Pennebaker is at last available on video tape. The show was also recorded by RCA's mobile unit for an expected LP release of the event, recorded by Ken Scott. (The LP never officially materialized and is now just a remixed film soundtrack.) The show also featured a special guest, Jeff Beck, who appeared on 'The Jean Genie' and 'Love Me Do', which David augmented on harmonica.

After the show, David and some friends (including Mick and Bianca Jagger, who had attended the show) returned to the Inn on the Park for a small party.

4 July 1973

The Last Supper . . . David's retirement party held at the Cafe Royal in Regent Street. The guest list probably made the party the social rock event of the decade. Amongst the guests were Mick and Bianca Jagger, Ringo Starr, Paul McCartney, Keith Moon, Britt Ekland, Lulu, Tony Curtis, Cat Stevens (David's old Deram buddy), Richard Pennebaker, Lou Reed, Jeff Beck, Elliot Gould, Ryan O'Neil, Sonny Bono, Barbra Streisand, Peter Cook and Dudley Moore. The party trailed well on into the early hours. Live music was supplied by Dr John.

5 July 1973

Although every newspaper in the land was making mileage of the 'I quit' announcement from the Hammersmith show, *Disc* reporter Ray Fox Cumming, speaking to David in his last interview before leaving for France, asked David whether he would ever tour again. 'All I can say,' said David, 'is that at this time I do not want to do "live" concerts again for a long, long time – not for two or three years at least.'

7 July 1973

David visits Lou Reed while recording 'Berlin', his follow-up LP to 'Transformer'.

9 July 1973

Leaves Victoria Station for Paris to record an LP of his sixties' favourites at the Chateau d'Herouville in France. 'Pin-Ups' was to be the last record with The Spiders. In between tracks for 'Pin-Ups' David and assembled musicians also recorded Lulu's 'The Man Who Sold the World'/'Watch that Man' single.

14 July 1973

Interview on Radio Luxembourg with Kid Jenson at the Chateau broadcast.

July 1973

Another interview conducted at the Chateau in between recording was with Charles Shaar Murrey for the *NME*. During the interview he spoke vaguely of his plans for the future, but was more open about the past.

I knew such a lot when I was sixteen. I knew about hundreds of things which I have since forgotten. They seemed to have changed and got a lot bigger. The world and politics and things like that.

I knew that being a mod meant that I had to wear clothes that no one else was wearing. The reason there were mods is because there were rock 'n' roll stars.

In those days I was in the audience, but I never dressed like anybody else in the rock business.

The Who weren't really moddy until getting on for the end of the Hi Numbers. They were pretty much a Rolling Stonesy-type band and it was only when they realized that their audiences were London mods that they looked to see what the mods were wearing.

I'd got all past that. I was into flower power by that time. I was lucky because I got out of it before it built up to its climax. I got involved with a lot of very interesting people at the beginning, the intelligentsia of what was happening in London at the time, and I fast realized what a big anti-swing it was going to become.

I should have been a newsman, really. I should have been doing your job, observing and perceiving current affairs and seeing where they're really going.

23 July 1973

In the week beginning 23 July, all five of David's LPs were in the top 40, three in the top 15, unprecedented for a solo artist.

Late July 1973

David, Angie, Zowie and friends leave the Chateau for Rome for a holiday. During the break David wrote the backbone for the 'Diamond Dogs' LP, including '1984'.

115

August 1973
Returns to London. *Pork* director Tony Ingrassia travelled to London
from New York for discussions about David's hopes to stage an adaptation of '1984'.

8 September 1973
'The Laughing Gnome'/'The Gospel According to Tony Day' single
released by Deram (highest chart position No. 4). The single sold over
250,000 copies.

September 1973
Final 'Pin-Ups' mixing completed in London by David and Ken Scott.

12 October 1973
'Sorrow'/'Amsterdam' single released by RCA (highest chart position
No. 3). B-side written by Jaques Brel. Release slightly delayed from
the original scheduled date of 28 September.

18–20 October 1973
'The Midnight Special' American television show filmed by NBC at
the Marquee. The show, billed as David Bowie's '1980 Floor Show' also
featured The Troggs and three-piece vocal group, Carmen. Marianne
Faithfull sang 'I Got You Babe' in a duet with David.

Filming was conducted at the club over a three-day period, and was
the last time David and The Spiders played together. David made a
number of spectacular costume changes during the show, all designed
by himself and Freddi Burretti.

He sang eight songs: '1984', You Didn't Hear It from Me', 'Sorrow',
'Everything's Alright', 'Time', 'I Can't Explain', 'The Jean Genie' and
the duet with Marianne Faithfull (who was decked out herself in a
nun's habit – minus the cloth at the back.

The audience for the show were members of David's fan club, though
they were considered a nuisance by the NBC film crew who would
have preferred the place empty.

Each of the tracks used in the show had to be filmed over two or
three runs as there were only two camera positions available for each
run. The show has never been broadcast in the UK.

'The Midnight Special'

Produced and Directed by Stan Harris
Creative Consultant – Rocco Urbisci
Associate Producer – Jaques Andre

Concept and Design – David Bowie
Choreography – Matt Mattox
Backing Vocals – The Astronettes
Bowie's Costumes – David Bowie and Freddi Burretti
*Dooshenka's costume (featured in 'Sorrow') – Natasha Korniloff
Make-up – Barbara Daley
Hair by Billy the Kid
Graphics – George Underwood
Sound Mix – Ken Scott and Ground Control

A Bert Sugarman Inc. Production
*Dooshenka in reality being Amanda Lear

19 October 1973
'Pin-Ups' released with advance sales of 150,000. A kind of greatest
hits package of David's favourite songs from the sixties, all material
written by other artists (RCA).

The sleeve photo for 'Pin-Ups' was originally destined for the cover
of *Vogue* magazine (UK). Twiggy explains: 'The circulation manager
of English *Vogue* started to get nervous about putting a man on the
cover. I said he was crazy because they would sell more issues of that
Vogue because Bowie was on the cover than they'll ever sell in their
lives. So while he was thinking about it, David said, "Look this is
lovely, why don't we use it on the album cover". I know it doesn't
really look like me, in fact there are still a lot of people who don't
know that it's me, it's still one of my favourite pictures.'

'Pin-Ups' released 19 October 1973 (RCA RS 1003)

Side One
Rosalyn (Duncan, Farley)
Here Comes the Night (Berns)
I Wish You Would (Arnold)
See Emily Play (Barrett)
Everything's Alright (Crouch,
    Konrad, Stavely, James, Karlson)
I Can't Explain (Townshend)

Side Two
Friday On My Mind (Young, Vanda)
Sorrow (Feldman, Goldstein,
    Gottehrer)
Don't Bring Me Down (Dee)
Shapes of Things (Samwell-Smith,
    McCarty)
Anyway, Anyhow, Anywhere
    (Townshend, Daltrey)
Where Have All the Good Times
    Gone (Davies)

Produced by Ken Scott and David Bowie

David Bowie (vocals, alto and tenor saxes, harmonica, Moog synthesizer)
Mick Ronson (guitar, piano, backing vocals)
Trevor Bolder (bass)

Mike Garson (grand piano, electric piano, organ, harpsichord)
Aynsley Dunbar (drums)
Ken Fordham (baritone sax)
Mac Cormack (backing vocals)

'Pin-Ups' – 'These are all songs which really meant a lot to me then, they're all very dear to me.

'These are all bands which I used to go and hear down at the Marquee between 1964 and 1967. Each one meant something to me at the time. It's my London of the time.'

October 1973
David and new 'session' line-up start recording the next LP at the Olympic stuidos, Barnes. The schedule kept him busy for nearly five months. David was also working on the production of an album by The Astronettes (featured in 'The Midnight Special'). The LP was never completed.

November 1973
'Sorrow'/'Amsterdam' single released in the US (RCA). 'The Midnight Special' screened in the US to a mixed reception, though has since been regularly repeated on US television.

David invites Tony Visconti down to the Olympic studios to listen and advise him on the production of 'Diamond Dogs'.

4 December 1973
Attends *A Patriot for Me* by John Osborne at the Palace Theatre, Watford with a mystery blonde called Anna. David, arriving at the theatre in his white American limousine, stopped backstage after the production for a few minutes to chat with its star, Marianne Faithfull. The following day David was publicly barracked in the local press by Watford's Labour MP for leaving his car on double yellow lines throughout the three-hour play.

31 December 1973
Is awarded a plaque by RCA Records for having five different LPs in the charts for nineteen weeks that year.

December 1973
At this time, David, Angie, Zowie, Danielle (Angie's assistant) and Marion (Zowie's nanny) were living in Oakely Street, Chelsea, just

down from the Albert Bridge and the Embankment. David invited singer Ava Cherry to move in with them. She wasn't altogether welcomed by Angie. The Oakley Street home was rented to them by Diana Rigg. They lived there until the following March when arrangements for a new house purchase in Kensington were cleared. David had had his sights on this particular house since his school days, when he would travel into town at the weekends and wander around the area.

5 January 1974
Melody Maker poll for 1973 declares David as No. 1 best male singer (in the British section), best record producer, best composer, and best single release in 'The Jean Genie'. Freddi Burretti accepted the awards on David's behalf. *Sounds* poll declared David No. 2 male vocalist, No. 1 composer and producer.

11 January 1974
'The Man Who Sold the World'/'Watch that Man' single released by Lulu, featured David on backing vocals, saxophone and coproduction credits went to Mick Ronson (Polydor).
   Both tracks featured on the Lulu LP 'Heaven and Earth and the Stars' (US – Chelsea Records).

25 January 1974
'Love Me Tender'/'Slaughter on 10th Avenue' single released by Mick Ronson (RCA). This was the beginning of a DeFries masterplan to launch Ronson in the wake of David's retirement. Unfortunately for Ronson a spring tour that coincided with the release of the first LP was a dismal failure.

15 February 1974
'Rebel Rebel'/'Queen Bitch' single released by RCA, the A-side being a trailer for the forthcoming LP, the first since his retirement and the disbanding of The Spiders from Mars (highest chart position No. 5).

28 February 1974
William Burroughs interview with David published in *Rolling Stone*.

1 March 1974
'Slaughter on 10th Avenue' LP released by Mick Ronson, his first solo album. The record featured three of David's songs: 'Growing Up and

I'm Fine', 'Music is Lethal' and 'Hey Ma Get Papa' (the latter being David's lyrics only). David and Co. move into new home in Kensington. 'Slaugher on 10th Avenue', 'Growing Up and I'm Fine' (Mick Ronson) 'All Cut Up on You', 'Andy Warhol' (Dana Gillespie) promo only EP issued in the US. David wrote one track on the A- and B-side and was involved in the recording of Andy Warhol (RCA).

15 March 1974
'Now We are Six' LP released by Steeleye Span (Chrysalis). David featured on one track, 'To Know Him is to Love Him', playing saxophone.

22 March 1974
'Weren't Born a Man' LP released by Dana Gillespie (RCA). David wrote two songs for the record, 'Andy Warhol' and 'Backed a Loser'. He also coproduced the LP.

11 April 1974
Arrives in New York on the SS *France* to live in America for nearly two years. Checks in to the Sherry Netherlands Hotel on 5th Avenue. 'Rock 'N' Roll Suicide'/'Quicksand' single released by RCA (highest chart position No. 22).

April 1974
Mick Ronson prepares for his first solo UK tour in an appearance at the Rainbow attended by David before he left for the States. Ronson's tour officially opening in Preston Guildhall on 10 April, then on to Manchester Free Trade Hall (11 April), Edinburgh Odeon (12 April), Newcastle City Hall (13 April), Dundee Caird Hall (16 April), Birmingham Town Hall (23 April), Bournemouth Winter Gardens (24 April), Hemel Hempstead Pavilion (27 April), Leicester De Montfort Hall (28 April), Sheffield City Hall (29 April).

Backing group for the tour included Trevor Bolder and Mike Garson.

April 1974
David spends the first part of his stay in New York piecing together a new tour band, persuaded by DeFries.

Around this time, David would frequent gigs in Harlem at normally strictly black venues like the Apollo seeing The Temptations, The Spinners and Marvin Gaye. Other shows attended were to see Roxy Music and Todd Rundgren's set at the Carnegie Hall (which, incidentally, was David's first public appearance since arriving in New York the week before). He attended the post-concert party.

'Television' and 'Leather Secrets' were two of the smaller acts David caught in between plans and rehearsals for the 'Diamond Dogs' tour.

23 April 1974
Performance artist Chris Burden is nailed to the top of a Volkswagen car in Venice, California. The modern-day-performance crucifixion became the cut-up inspiration four years later for David's 'Joe the Lion' from the 'Heroes' album.

24 April 1974
'Diamond Dogs' LP released and greeted by disapproval by most rock critics. The LP was a testament to David's biggest change to date and was the first LP for almost five years that he was to work on with an almost entirely new line-up. In a 1976 interview for BBC Radio One he admitted the whole experience as being very daunting, finding himself virtually alone in the studio once again (RCA).

The notorious cover artwork was by Belgian artist, Guy Peellaert, who was also, at that time preparing cover artwork for Jagger and The Rolling Stones ('It's Only Rock 'n' Roll').

David commissioned Peellaert after visiting his London exhibition of 'Rock Dreams' work.

'Diamond Dogs' released 24 April 1974 (RCA APL I. 0576)

Side One
Future Legend (Bowie)
Bewitched, Bothered and
  Bewildered (Rodgers)
Diamond Dogs (Bowie)
Sweet Thing (Bowie)
Candidate (Bowie)
Sweet Thing (Reprise) (Bowie)
Rebel Rebel (Bowie)

Side Two
Rock 'N' Roll With Me (Bowie,
  Peace)
We Are the Dead (Bowie)
1984 (Bowie)
Big Brother (Bowie)
Chant of the Ever Circling Skeletal
  Family (Bowie)

Produced by David Bowie

Arranged by David Bowie
String Arrangement by Tony Visconti
David Bowie (vocals, guitar, saxophones, Moog, mellotron)
Mike Garson (keyboards)
Tony Newman/Aynsley Dunbar (drums)
Alan Parker (guitar on '1984')

121

'Diamond Dogs' – 'It was frightening trying to make an album with no support behind me. I was very much on my own. It was my most difficult album. It was a relief that it did so well.'

Corinne Schwab became David's personal assistant in the early part of 1974, and has been David's closest friend and aide ever since. She has proved indispensable to David's hectic schedule, running their 'suitcase' office while travelling. (The only office base for Bewlay Brothers/Isolar, is New York.)

David later spoke of her appointment, 'I found her in a want ad, I rang her up and asked her, "Do you want to work for me?" ' Corinne's reaction to the offer, as told to an American reporter a couple of years later, 'I'd never heard of him and I hate rock 'n' roll!' She took the job and has been travelling with him ever since.

May 1974
'Diamond Dogs' LP released in the US (RCA).

'Rebel Rebel'/'Lady Grinning Soul' single also released in the US. Initial pressings of the A-side were substantially different to the LP and UK single versions, similar in style to the live version featured later on the 'David Live' release (RCA).

The Diamond Dogs US Tour, 1974
The 1974 tour of the United States was a fast return to the stage. The stage show idea initially came about as a plan for a West End revue of *The 1980 Floor Show*, this idea never getting further in the UK than the Marquee show production for 'The Midnight Special'.

The power of the image took precedence as David Bowie opened in Toronto on 16 June 1974 on the first leg of his North American tour with a string of Canadian dates.

In a show characterized by elaborate staging, special effects and a crucial attention to detail, Bowie returned to the concert trail in a feat of theatrical sensual delight for the eyes and ears.

And if at times he seemed about to be dwarfed by the props surrounding him, it's also true that he proved himself the hub of this extravaganza and a forceful figure whose presence overshadowed all.

Personnel for the 'Diamond Dogs' tour were
Tony Newman (drums)
Pablo Rosario (percussion)
David Sanborn (alto sax, flute)
Richard Grando (baritone sax, flute)

122

Mike Garson (piano, mellotron)
Earl Slick (guitar)
Herbie Flowers (bass)
Gui Andrisano (vocal backings)
Warren Peace (vocal backings)
Michael Kamen (electric piano, Moog, oboe)

June 1974
'Diamond Dogs'/'Holy Holy' single released in the US (RCA).

Early June 1974
Final dress rehearsal completed in New York before the 600-mile journey to Montreal.

14 June 1974
Montreal Forum, Canada. The extravagant 'Diamond Dogs' tour opens heralding David's return to the stage. The show itself was David's most spectacular and theatrical yet, completely choreographed. The set itself, 'Hunger City', was David's concept with Jules Fischer. Phallic shapes, moving catwalks and many other special effects were employed to make the show a complete aural and visual experience. 'Diamond Dogs'/'Holy Holy' single released in the UK by RCA to coincide with the start of the tour in the US, the tour that Britain was never to see (highest chart position No. 21).

15 June 1974
Ottawa Civic Centre.

16 June 1974
Toronto O'Keefe Auditorium. David had laryngitis.

17 June 1974
Rochester Memorial Auditorium, New York.

18 June 1974
Cleveland Public Auditorium. 'Diamond Dogs' tops the album charts.

19 June 1974
Cleveland Public Auditorium. These two shows a great success, most of the opening night problems with failing props and general problems now put right. It was a frequent occurrence, however, for certain props not to work on occasions.

20 June 1974
Toledo Sports Arena.

21 June 1974
Detroit Cobo Hall. Show transferred at the last minute from the Ford Hall because the stage was too big!

22 June 1974
Detroit Cobo Hall.

23 June 1974
Columbus Mershon Auditorium.

24 June 1974
Dayton Harra Arena.

25 June 1974
Akron Civic Theater.

26–27 June 1974
Pittsburgh Auditorium.

28 June 1974
Charleston, WV Civic Center.

29 June 1974
Nashville, Municipal Auditorium. Show attended by Linda and Paul McCartney.

30 June 1974
Memphis, Mid-South Coliseum.

July 1974
'1984'/'Queen Bitch' single released in the US (RCA).

1 July 1974
Atlanta, Fox Theater.

2 July 1974
Tampa, Curtis Hixon Hall, Florida.
 During the journey from Atlanta to Tampa, a driver was stung by a bee and the truck containing most of the set thus ended up in a ditch

with a nest of rattle snakes. The show at Tampa went on, however, without props. After receiving a twenty-minute ovation, David returned for an encore.

3 July 1974
West Palm Beach Auditorium.

4 July 1974
Jacksonville Exhibition Hall.

5 July 1974
Charleston, SC Municipal Auditorium.

6 July 1974
Charlotte Park Center.

7 July 1974
Norfolk Scope.

8–15 July 1974
Philadelphia Tower Theater.
   The Tower Theater shows on 14 and 15 July were nearly cancelled at the last moment when David's backing band, after hearing the news that the shows were to be recorded for an LP, refused to play without an increased fee in line with the normal recording rates. The normal show fee of $150 for a member of the group was increased to $5,000 after David negotiated with DeFries.

July 1974
UK promoters turn down the chance to stage the 'Diamond Dogs' tour at the Empire Pool, Wembley, because of the amount of money asked for by Mainman. Tickets would have had to have been about £7.00, unacceptable then as a reasonable price.
The recordings at the Tower Theater on 14 and 15 July became David's first live LP release, 'David Live'. It was recorded without Tony Visconti who was held up when his car broke down travelling from New York. This resulted in various instruments used not being recorded exactly as Visconti had really wanted and thus making the mixing much more difficult. A few days after the Philly shows, David and Tony Visconti travelled to Manhattan's 'Electric Lady' recording studios to mix the LP together. All of this was due to a Mainman –DeFries intiative to secure the record's release for the Christmas market.

16 July 1974
Boston Music Hall.

17 July 1974
Hartford, Bushnell Auditorium.

19 July 1974
New York, Madison Square Garden.

20 July 1974
New York, Madison Square Garden. New York shows videotaped. After the last Madison show, a small party was held at the Plaza Hotel. Amongst the regular friends and Mainman crew were Rudolf Nureyev, Mick Jagger and Bette Midler, who disappeared with David into a closet for half an hour.

The end-of-tour party for the road crew was held at the 'Ice Palace Discotheque'.

The sets for the shows at Madison Square Garden had to be unloaded in the street outside the venue because the trucks were too big to clear the back entrance.

August 1974
'Andy Warhol'/'Dizzy Heights' single released by Dana Gillespie, coproduced by David and Mick Ronson (RCA). A-side written by David who originally wrote the song for her.

David books studio time at Philadelphia's Sygma Sound studios, the studio famed for it's 'Gamble & Huff' recording connections. David was particularly excited by the sound he heard there after sitting in on an Ava Cherry session.

Drummer Tony Newman and bass guitarist Herbie Flowers leave the tour group (which David retained for the second leg of the tour in September). Replacements were Willie Weeks and Andy Newmark.

David goes to an early Bruce Springsteen concert at Max's Kansas City, New York. David is later introduced to Springsteen and David decides then to cut three of Springsteen's songs for the new LP, 'Spirits in the Night', 'It's Hard to be a Saint in the City' and 'Growing Up'. These songs were later replaced by other material on the LP and have never been released. David has since used Springsteen's keyboard player, Roy Bittan, on several recordings.

Other shows attended around this time included the Jacksons's Madison Square Garden show. The recording of the soul LP 'Young Americans' over August went well and as usual, David ended up with a lot more material than one LP could use. During their time in the

126

studio, Philadelphian Bowie fans would camp outside in the hope of meeting him. For their patience, at the end of recording, David invited them into the studio and played them the finished master tape for the record, miming and dancing to the music and sharing wine.

Some of the recording for 'Young Americans' was filmed by the BBC for 'Cracked Actor'.

'Rock 'N' Roll With Me'/'The Divine Daze of Deathless Delight' single released by Donovan, produced by Andrew Loog-Oldham (Epic). A-side written by David/Peace.

2 September 1974
Los Angeles Universal Ampitheater. One show filmed by the BBC for 'Cracked Actor'.

3 September 1974
Los Angeles Universal Ampitheater. Interviewed by Robert Hilburn for *Melody Maker*.

4–8 September 1974
Los Angeles Universal Ampitheater.

11 September 1974
San Diego Sports Arena.

13 September 1974
Tuscon Convention Centre.

'Knock On Wood'/'Panic in Detroit' single released, David's first live single release by RCA (highest UK chart position No. 10). A-side written by Floyd and Cropper.

'Rock 'N' Roll With Me'/'Panic in Detroit' live single released in the US (RCA).

14 September 1974
Phoenix Coliseum. Robert Hilburn interview published (*MM*).

16 September 1974
Phoenix Coliseum.

September 1974
Drummer Willie Weeks and bassist Andy Newmark (who joined the tour to help David out) leave to fulfil recording commitments with George Harrison.

24 September 1974
'Knock On Wood' enters the top 20, in the UK.

The September part of the 1974 US tour was still technically the 'Diamond Dogs' tour, but now mixed with the new soul feel David picked up in Philadelphia. Six singers now backed David and included along with Warren Peace and Ava Cherry, four black singers: Luther Vandross, Anthony Hinton, Dianne Summler and Robin Clark.

October 1974
D. A. Pennebaker's Hammersmith Odeon show from July 1973 broadcast for the first time on US television (ABC). Angie did some solo interviews on Philadelphia WMMR radio and the Mike Douglas TV show in Hollywood

5 October 1974
After a short break, the 'Diamond Dogs' show becomes the 'Soul tour'. David, fed up with the hassles of a complicated tour and happy that he had fulfilled all that he could from a performance within it, replaces the massive set with a simple white screen backdrop for his shadow to be thrown against. The move, once again, left his young American audience baffled, having only just accustomed themselves to the idea of 'Halloween Jack', the character David portrayed during the 'Dogs' tour.

The backing group now adopted the name of The Garson Band, named after keyboardsman, Mike Garson.

Along with the six backing singers came replacement drummer and bassist, Dennis Davis and Emir Ksasan.

10–11 October 1974
Wisconsin, Madison Auditorium.

16 October 1974
Michigan Palace, Detroit.

22–23 October 1974
Chicago, Arie Crown.

28 October 1974
New York, Radio City Music Hall.

29 October 1974
New York, Radio City Music Hall.
'David Live' double LP released of David's US 'Diamond Dogs' tour (RCA).

30 October 1974
New York, Radio City Music Hall.

'David Live' released 29 October 1974 (RCA APL2.0771)

Side One
1984 (Bowie)
Rebel Rebel (Bowie)
Moonage Daydream (Bowie)
Sweet Thing (Bowie)

Side Two
Changes (Bowie)
Suffragette City (Bowie)
Aladdin Sane (Bowie)
All the Young Dudes (Bowie)
Cracked Actor (Bowie)

Side Three
When You Rock 'N' Roll With Me
  (Bowie, Peace)
Watch that Man (Bowie)
Knock on Wood (Floyd, Cropper)
Diamond Dogs (Bowie)

Side Four
Big Brother (Bowie)
Width of a Circle (Bowie)
Jean Genie (Bowie)
Rock 'N' Roll Suicide (Bowie)

Produced by Tony Visconti

David Bowie (vocals, guitar)
Earl Slick (guitar)
Michael Kamen (electric piano, synthesizer, oboe)
Mike Garson (grand piano, mellotron)
David Sanborn (alto sax, flute)
Richard Grando (baritone sax, flute)
Herbie Flowers (bass)
Tony Newman (drums)
Pablo Rosario /Gui Andrisano/Warren Peace (backing vocals)

'David Live' – 'God, that album. I've never played it. The tension it must contain must be like a vampire's teeth coming down on you. And that photo on the cover. My God, it looks as if I've just stepped out of the grave.

'That's actually how I felt. That record should have been called, "David Bowie is alive and well and living only in theory".'

November 1974
David Bowie and Elizabeth Taylor announce that they are to appear together in a film, *The Bluebird of Happiness*, which was eventually

made without David. When he viewed the script, he considered it to be, 'Too dry and boring'. He liked her though, because, he said, she had likened him to James Dean.

2 November 1974
New York, Radio City Music Hall.

3 November 1974
New York, Radio City Music Hall. Last night in New York.

6 November 1974
Cleveland Public Auditorium. The show was marred by sound problems. After the show, David stayed up all night in the hotel bar, dancing and miming.

8 November 1974
Buffalo Memorial Auditorium.

11 November 1974
Washington DC, Capital Center.

14–16 November 1974
Boston Music Hall.

18–24 November 1974
Philadelphia Spectrum Theater.

While in Philadelphia, David and friends, Mike Garson, Warren Peace, Ava Cherry and two bodyguards were held for identity paper checks while drinking at the Artemis Club. The police, checking for underage drinkers, asked David for proof of his age. A startled Bowie replied 'You don't believe I'm twenty-one years of age? Incredible! That's quite flattering actually. Why, everyone knows that I'm at least fifty-two.'

25 November 1974
Uniondale, New York.

28 November 1974
Memphis, Mid-South Auditorium.

30 November 1974
Nashville Municipal Auditorium

November 1974
Interview with Bruno Stein *Creem* magazine during the 'Soul tour':

He looked relaxed in a loose fitting, uncolourful overall outfit, though
somewhat tired from the energetic performance he gave to a packed
audience less than an hour before. His eyes seemed weary and his voice was
a bit hoarse, as the conversation twisted and turned among the subjects,
extra-terrestrials and political conspiracies, he gradually grew animated and
energetic, jumping to make a point, stalking around the hotel suite while
listening to someone else, dancing while seated in a chair and singing along
as he played tapes of his forthcoming soul album.
   'I used to work for two guys who put out a UFO magazine in England
about six years ago. And I made sightings six, seven times a night for about
a year, when I was in the observatory.' After listening to four numbers, Ava
and her girlfriends persuaded David to leave with them. Ava knew a
millionaire who lived not far away in a modernistic mansion full of strange
delights. David gulped down another cup of coffee, with cream and sugar,
put on a striking green coat, it looked like mohair, and followed them out
of the suite.
   It was 2.30 a.m. and the sluggish night crew of the small but elegant hotel
barely looked up as the red-haired rock star and four giggling black girls
made their way through the lobby to the waiting limousine.

1 December 1974
Atlanta Omni.

2 December 1974
Tuscaloosa, University of Alabama. Last show of the 1974 US tour.

4 December 1974
Appears on the Dick Cavett 'Wide World of Entertainment' show,
sharing the billing with British actor Roy Dotrice. After an introduction
from Cavett, David sang '1984' and the then new song, 'Young Americans', many critics picking up the reference to Nixon.
   The conversation that ensued between David and Dick Cavett was
covered with some wonder by the press, David being more evasive
than ever, poking the carpet with a cane and continually sniffing.
   Cavett, *sans* tie for an interview with a difference, didn't help proceedings by continuing the interview on a simplistic level and not
pursuing areas that may have drawn David out:

D.C. *What kind of person would you describe yourself as?*
D.B. I'm a person of diverse interest, I'm not very academic.
D.C. *David, what kind of student were you in school?*
D.B. As I've said, not very academic, I suppose I was considered arty. I went to a technical college near London and did an art course for people from twelve up who couldn't do anything else much like maths or physics or chemistry, so I took art.
D.C. *What does your mother think of you?*
D.B. She pretends I'm not hers. We've never been that close but we have an understanding.

For the main part the conversation mostly flowed around Cavett and the commercial breaks but David finished up the show with a cover version of 'Footstompin', the blueprint sound for 'Fame'.

The show was made in New York (NBC).

December 1974
'Young Americans' video filmed in New York, David dressed in his 'Soul tour' gear and looking his thinnest ever.

25 December 1974
Christmas spent with Angie and Zowie and close friends at their rented New York house.

A Brazilian concert tour cancelled because of poor road conditions.

All costumes for every concert tour David has made since the early seventies are kept in storage in New York.

January 1975
David, resting in New York, sends Tony DeFries a telegram informing him that his and Mainman's services would no longer be required and legal action had begun to free him (David) of all existing contracts.

'Young Americans'/'Knock on Wood' single released in the US (RCA).

Final touches are completed to the 'Young Americans' LP by producer Tony Visconti. David had lost interest in the record and was spending most of his time working on a 'Diamond Dogs' video project in his house in New York. Most evenings were spent with Mick Jagger and the whole experience for Visconti, who was trying to finish the LP on time, was reminiscent of the recording of 'The Man Who Sold the World'. 'He made just two sessions, just like "The Man Who Sold the World" when he was preoccupied with Angie.'

On the town excursions with Mick and Bianca and Ava Cherry included a night at Madison Square Gardens to see Led Zeppelin. David showed particular interest in their laser show system. Later in the week, David and Ava Cherry visited Zeppelin at the Plaza Hotel, Jimmy Page and John Paul Jones being old friends of David's. (Page had played guitar on David's second single in 1965.)

Other excursions included a visit to Trude Heller's club with Cherry Vanilla to see Lance Loud's band, a night at CBG's to see Patti Smith and her support for the evening, Television. With Jagger he saw Manhattan Transfer at the Café Carlyle, then haggled with the management over the bill for the meal according to the British rock press at the time.

26 January 1975
Angie makes her first UK television interview appearance on 'Russell Harty Plus' and spoke of her proposed film and modelling career and life on and off the road with David (London Weekend).

26 January, 1975
'Cracked Actor', an omnibus documentary about David, is broadcast. The film, by Alan Yentob, traced David's career up to and including the 1974 US tour. A valuable piece of television that gave the UK the only indications of the 'Diamond Dogs' show and the Soul tour that followed. The interview material with Yentob was gleaned from a number of conversations in hotel rooms and in cars. It gave Nicolas Roeg the idea of using David in his forthcoming film, *The Man Who Fell to Earth*. Roeg used almost identically the 'Cracked Actor' in-car footage situation for his own film (BBC 1).

February 1975
David is visited by English film director Nicolas Roeg, who made *Performance* and *Walkabout*.

Roeg had arrived in New York only to discover that David had forgotten their appointment. David arrived home eight hours later to find a determined Roeg patiently sitting in the kitchen. The rest of the night was then spent discussing the project, David almost sold on the project from the start. Up to that point Peter O'Toole had been Roeg's leading choice for the alien role.

21 February 1975
'Young Americans'/'Suffragette City' single released by RCA (highest chart position No. 18), the A-side being a preview of the forthcoming LP of the same name.

A film of David singing 'Young Americans' at the height of his Soul tour in late 1974, was broadcast on 'Top of the Pops', David looking thinner than ever, and strumming a guitar with the Soul tour backing group.

March 1975

Officially announced that David and Tony DeFries had started legal proceedings against each other. A lawsuit initially filed through David's UK solicitors terminating all connections with DeFries and Mainman was made. The result of heavy legal action between David and Mainman has never been fully announced, though a connection with Mainman is still maintained. David leaves New York for California to avoid the upsetting legal complications.

The lawsuit, announced by David's solicitors, declared a motion to end all agreements between David and Mainman, including publishing, management and recording controls.

1 March 1975

David is featured on the Grammy Awards ceremony, broadcast from the Uris Theater in New York. (The Grammy award is the US musical equivalent to the Oscar.) David presented the 'Best female soul singer' award to Aretha Franklin, giving a three-minute speech which was broadcast live on US television.

Also present at the awards ceremony were John and Yoko, Simon and Garfunkel, Roberta Flack, Bette Midler, Stevie Wonder, Sarah Vaughan, Tony Orlando and Dawn, The Hudson Brothers, Ann-Margret and David Essex.

March 1975

David attends Rod Stewart's Madison Square Garden show with Ava Cherry and Warren Peace, later dropping backstage for the post-concert party.

7 March 1975

'Young Americans' LP released, David's major excursion into the world of 'white plastic soul' and his personal reaction to the radio of the United States of that time. The LP was recorded at the Sygma Sound studios in Philadelphia and later with John Lennon, at the Electric Lady studios in New York. The latter recorded work made after the completion of the original and unreleased version of 'Young Americans'. David inserted the two new tracks with Lennon and

134

removed 'Who Can I Be Now' and 'Come Back My Baby' to make way for them, which upset Visconti who was unaware of this change until the record was released. In the US, the LP was temporarily held up from release after Tony DeFries served an injunction on the record as major litigation between David and DeFries over contracts was underway. This was soon removed by RCA and the UK release was unaffected.

Earlier working titles for the LP were, 'Somebody Up There Likes Me', 'One Damned Song' and 'Fascination'. Other unused Philadelphian material included another reworked 'John, I'm Only Dancing' and the three Bruce Springsteen tracks.

'Young Americans' released 7 March 1975 (RCA RS. 1006)

Side One
Young Americans (Bowie)
Win (Bowie)**
Fascination (Bowie, Vandross)**
Right (Bowie)**

Side Two
Somebody Up There Likes Me
(Bowie)**
Across the Universe (Lennon,
McCartney)***
Can You Hear Me (Bowie)***
Fame (Bowie, Lennon, Alomar)***

Produced by *Tony Visconti/**Tony Visconti, Harry Maslin/***David Bowie, Harry Maslin
Vocal arrangements by David Bowie, Luther Vandross
String arrangements by Tony Visconti

David Bowie (vocals, guitar, keyboards)
Carlos Alomar/Earl Slick (guitars)
Mike Garson (piano)
David Sanborn (alto sax)
Willie Weeks/Emir Ksasan (bass)
Andy Newmark/Dennis Davis (drums)
Larry Washington/Pablo Rosario/Ralph McDonald (percussion)
Ava Cherry/Robin Clark/Luther Vandross/Jean Fineberg/Jean Millington
   (backing vocals)
John Lennon (vocals, guitar)

'Young Americans' – 'My own recent music has been good, plastic soul, I think. It's not very complex, but it's enjoyable to write. I did most of it in the studio. It doesn't take very long to write . . . about ten, fifteen minutes a song. I mean, with "Young Americans" I thought I'd better make a hit album to cement myself over here, so I went in and did it. It wasn't too hard, really.'

135

April 1975
'The Special of the Week' American radio interview broadcast. David sounded very despondent. 'I've rocked my last roll,' he said (KULA).

May 1975
'London Boys'/'Love You Till Tuesday' released as a single for the first time, a track recorded in 1966 and featured on the B-side of 'Rubber Band' when it was originally released (Decca).

'Images' double LP released in the UK, although all material (David's complete Deram catalogue of released material) had already been previously available on import in the cartoon cover sleeve. That sleeve was substituted for an up-to-date 'Soul tour' shot from 1974 (Decca).

David and Iggy Pop attempt some recording in Hollywood. After the aborted session with Iggy, David spends the rest of the night writing a new song, calling it 'Movin' On'.

During the early part of his stay in LA, David moved into the home of Deep Purple bassist, Glen Hughes, an old friend of David's and, at that time, touring with Purple.

David was driving around LA in a borrowed VW. Later he moved into his new manager's home in central Hollywood. Michael Lippman had now become David's manager, but the arrangement lasted little over six months because of Lippman's alleged bad management of Bowie's affairs.

Interviewed by Cameron Crowe for *Rolling Stone* (published 12 February 1976).

'Images' released May 1975 (Deram DPA 3017/3018)

Side One
Rubber Band (Bowie)
Maids of Bond Street (Bowie)
Sell Me a Coat (Bowie)
Love You Till Tuesday (Bowie)
There is a Happy Land (Bowie)

Side Two
The Laughing Gnome (Bowie)
The Gospel According to Tony Day (Bowie)
Did You Ever Have a Dream (Bowie)
Uncle Arthur (Bowie)
We Are Hungry Men (Bowie)
When I Live My Dream (Bowie)

Side Three
Join the Gang (Bowie)
Little Bombardier (Bowie)
Come and Buy My Toys (Bowie)
Silly Boy Blue (Bowie)
She's Got Medals (Bowie)

Side Four
Please Mr Gravedigger (Bowie)
London Boys (Bowie)
Karma Man (Bowie)
Let Me Sleep Beside You (Bowie)
In the Heat of the Morning (Bowie)

Produced by Mike Vernon and *Tony Visconti
Arranged by Dek Fearnley, David Bowie and *Tony Visconti

David Bowie (vocals, guitar, saxophone)
Dek Fearnley (bass)
Derek Boyes (organ)
John Eager (drums)
Session musicians

June 1975
Iggy Pop, who had failed to show up at further booked studio sessions, is discovered by David to have checked in the UCLA Neuropsychiatric Institute near LA, as a voluntary patient. David visited Pop who later revealed that David was the only person to do so.

David tried to encourage Iggy out of the institute to return to recording. That idea had to be aborted when Pop again disappeared.

This same month it was announced that David was to star in *The Man Who Fell to Earth*, an adaptation of the novel by Walter Tevis.

David travelled to New Mexico to begin production on the film, taking the famous Santa Fe Super Chef railway.

Production on the film had been scheduled to last eleven weeks. David and friends stayed at the Hilton Inn in Albuquerque for the main part of the filming, only making rare excursions to the bar and rarely out of the hotel except for filming. Other projects were simultaneously firing his imagination, the main one being his autobiography, tentatively titled *The Return of the Thin White Duke*, a section of which was featured in *Rolling Stone* magazine (12 February 76):

Vince was American and came to England, then went to France.

Then he came back to England and we spoke of our findings. He wore a white robe and sandals and we sat in the busy London street with a map of the world and tried to find the people who were passing by and scowling at us. They were nowhere on the map. Vince went back to France, then I heard about the famous show where he had told his band to go home and appeared in front of the curtains in that old white robe and sandals telling the French people about the comings and goings due upon us. He was banned from performing.

My records were selling and I was being a man in demand. I thought of Vince and wrote 'Ziggy Stardust'. I thought of my brother and wrote 'Five Years'. Then my friend came to mind, standing the way we stood in Bewlay Bros and I wrote 'Moonage Daydream'.

During this period, David reached his well-publicized 'low-point', his general interview copy becoming increasingly bizarre. Suffering at times from severe depression, this was worsened by his increased interest in cocaine. Filming helped, though he never fully recovered until he made the break from the States to Europe in 1976.

July 1975
'Life on Mars'/'Down by the Stream' single released by The King's Singers, A-side written by David (EMI).

As filming begins on *The Man Who Fell to Earth* romantic links are reported in the press as David is joined on the set by Sabrina Guinness. David would also read furiously, practise filming on his own 16mm newsreel camera and write anything from new songs to short stories. Some of those songs were intended for the soundtrack of the film, others going on 'Station to Station'. Bowie has never discussed the short stories except to say they will never be published. Of a visit to Carlsbad Caves in Artesia, New Mexico David later spoke to an American journalist, Rex Reed. 'It was completely dark except for one hole in the top. Suddenly there was a whistling sound like rats screaming. Thousands of bats flew out of the rocks and up through the hole. They return every morning at 4 a.m. I'd love to do my next concert there, with thousands of vampire bats descending on the audience's heads.'

Filming also had its problems; one scene had to be shot at an old Aztec burial ground. Near to the site a group of rowdy local Hell's Angels had camped, and if that wasn't enough to worry about, whilst drinking a glass of milk on set David noticed, 'Some gold liquid swimming around in shiny swirls inside the glass'. David was ill for two days afterwards and is still to this day unsure of what actually happened. No trace of any foreign element was detected in tests though there were six witnesses who said they had seen the strange matter in the bottom of the glass. That, together with cameras jamming for no reason, was enough for David to feel jinxed. David described the whole location as 'Very bad Karma'.

20 July 1975
Sunday Times magazine interview feature published titled 'The Bowie Odyssey' by Tina Brown. Interview made while David was in Los Angeles working on the 'Station to Station' album.

138

'Actually, I want to say a few things on the album.

'Like "Right" is putting a positive drone over. People forget what the sound of man's instinct is – it's a drone, a mantra. And people say: "Why are so many things popular that just drone on and on". But that's the point really. It reaches a particular vibration, not necessarily a musical level. And that's what "Right" is . . .

'Oh, all right . . . let's talk about the rest of the album. Very decadent this is (laughs). "Somebody Up There Likes Me" is a "Watch out mate, Hitler's on his way back" . . . it's your Rock and Roll sociological bit.

'And "Across the Universe", which was a flower power sort of thing John Lennon wrote. I always thought it was fabulous, but very watery in the original, and I hammered the hell out of it. I like it a lot and I think I sing very well at the end of it.

'People say I used John Lennon on the track . . . but let me tell you . . . no one *uses* John Lennon. John just came and played on it. He was lovely.

' "Can You Hear Me" was written for somebody but I'm not going to tell you who it is. That is a real love song. I kid you not. And the end of the thing is "Fame" which was more or less sung about what we're doing now.

' "Win" was a "get up off your backside" sort of song really – a mild precautionary sort of morality song. It was written about an impression left on me by people who don't work very hard, or do anything much, or think very hard – like don't blame me 'cause I'm in the habit of working hard.

'You know, it's easy – all you got to do is win.'

This statement-filled interview ('Rock and Roll is dead – a toothless old woman. It's embarrassing.') was filled with political preoccupations David felt at that time, which were to get even wider coverage in May 1976 when it was picked up by the nationals. In between politics and occasional references to the filming, David spoke of the 'Young Americans' LP.

'I'll still make albums with love and with fun, but my effect is finished. I'm very pleased. I think I've caused enough rumpus for someone who's not even convinced he's a good musician.'

In another interview published the same day with David Lewin in a piece titled 'Will the real David Bowie stand up?' David was unusually reminiscent:

My sister married an Egyptian sixteen years ago. I haven't seen her since. I was not lonely as a child – but a loner. I still am. I have one friend only – and I've known him since we were eight and at school together.

My father worked for Dr Barnardo's homes. We had a four-roomed house in Brixton, South London and one room was let out to a girl who I found out later was a prostitute.

A figure in a green jumpsuit walks down the dim corridor. As he passes the glass doors leading outside, a flood of evening light illuminates him. The shock of red hair alone is enough to identify him as David Bowie. His shoulders rock from side to side and he has a springy step of one endowed with an overabundance of energy, even though he has just completed a full day's shooting in 90-degree heat. Stopping in front of a room, he knocks but gets no response. As he turns to leave, he meets the reporters who have tracked him here and are ready to pounce like Diamond Dogs.

'We're from Creem magazine and we've been trying to talk to you for a couple of days,' says John. 'C'mon, let's go sit outside,' he says without a moment's hesitation.

Sitting on the porch overlooking the parking lot he shakes hands as introductions are made and seems genuinely friendly.

Can this be the David Bowie who is called cold and aloof, even by his friends?

There is an introduction as a burly, goateed man wearing Bermuda shorts and tank top enters the scene to hover over David like a protective mother. He appears to be a bodyguard.

'Do you want me to stay and wait with you?' he asks, sliding a glance at the two strangers questioning Bowie. 'No, that's OK, go on, I'll be all right', he replied to the guard.

Cut to: clapperboard snapping shut. 'Scene 105 A, take thirteen.' The servant knocks, but instead of calling, 'Come in.' Bowie pauses then signals. 'Cut, let's go onto the next one.' Apparently he'd rather skip that take thirteen and move on to a more auspicious number. But four-year-old Zowie Bowie, who'd been entertaining himself elsewhere, chooses this as a time to pay a visit. 'I want to get in bed with daddy,' says little Z clambering over a tangle of cables just off camera. A crewie takes him gently by the hand and guides him to safe territory. 'You can't get in bed with dad right now, he's busy.'

Zowie settles for a mock shoot out with daddy from the sidelines, then scurries away to another part of the set.

JOHN: What kind of films do you like?

DAVID: I don't see too many, actually. I think the last film I saw at a theatre was Clockwork Orange, and before that was The Hustler with Paul Newman. But the ones I like mostly are pre-1930 German films. They're very stylized, that's the kind of film I like, but no one makes them like that now.

STEVE: Do you mean expressionism?

DAVID: Right.

STEVE: Like The Cabinet of Dr Caligari?

DAVID: Yeah, that's a good one. I have copies of my favourite and that's usually what I look at when I want to view a film. I think this (The Man Who Fell to Earth) will have some of those qualities.

1 August 1975

'Fame'/'Right' single released, the second single taken from the 'Young Americans' LP (RCA).

The single, issued in the States at the same time, became David's first and only US No. 1 to date and stayed in the top slot for four weeks (highest chart position in the UK No. 17).

August 1975
'A Mother's Anguish – David Never Comes To See Me' interview with Mrs Margaret Jones, David's mother, by Charles Shaar Murray (NME).

'My husband and I lived for David. We approved of his work. My husband said to me, "Love, if we don't let David go into this business he'll be frustrated for the rest of his life." '

8 September 1975
Attends Peter Sellers's forty-seventh birthday party in Los Angeles. Bill Wyman and Ron Wood, also there, team up with David and run through a few blues numbers, David taking time out from work on the film.

26 September 1975
'Space Oddity'/'Changes', 'Velvet Goldmine' single released. A re-release of David's '69 epic and released as part of RCA's Maximillion series. This became David's first UK No. 1, 'Velvet Goldmine' being an unissued 'Hunky Dory' out-take. Initial release in picture sleeve.

A special film clip of 'Space Oddity' was shown on 'Top of the Pops', with a completely different soundtrack. The clip was taken in its original form from the 1968 film, *Love You Till Tuesday* – the film that the BBC once rejected.

Late 1975
Playboy interview published. Interviewed by Cameron Crowe:

c.c *How much have drugs affected your music?*
D.B. The music is just an extension of me, so the question really is, what have drugs done to me? They've fucked me up, I think. Fucked me up nicely and I've quite enjoyed seeing what it was like being fucked up.
c.c. *Then you agree with your reviewer who called your 'Young Americans' album 'a fucked-up LP from a fucked-up rock star'?*
D.B. Well 'The Man Who Sold the World' is actually the most drug-oriented album I've made. That was when I was the most fucked up. 'Young Americans' is probably a close second, but that is from my current drug period. 'The Man Who Sold the World' was when I was holding onto some kind of flag for hashish. As soon as I stopped using that drug, I realized it dampened my imagination. End of slow drugs!
c.c. *Let's start with one question you've always seemed to hedge: How much of your bisexuality is fact and how much is gimmick?*
D.B. It's true, I am bisexual. But I can't deny that I've used the fact very well. I suppose it's the best thing that has ever happened to me. Fun, too.
c.c. *Why do you say it's the best thing that ever happened to you?*
D.B. Well, for one thing, girls are always presuming that I've kept my heterosexual virginity for some reason. So I've had all these girls to try to

get me over to the other side again: 'C'mon, David, it isn't all that bad. I'll show you.' Or, better yet, 'We'll show you.' I always play dumb.

On the other hand, I'm sure you want to know about the other hand as well. When I was fourteen sex suddenly became all-important to me. It didn't really matter who or what it was with, as long as it was a sexual experience. So it was some very pretty boy in class in some school or other that I took home and neatly fucked on my bed upstairs, and that was it. My first thought was, well, if I ever get sent to prison, I'll know how to keep happy!

I've always been chauvinistic, even in my boy-obsessed days. But I was always a gentleman. I always treated my boys like real ladies. Always escorted them properly and, in fact, I suppose if I were a lot older, like forty or fifty, I'd be a wonderful sugar daddy to some little queen down in Kensington. I'd have a houseboy named Richard to order around.

c.c. *Some psychiatrists would call your behaviour compulsive. Does the fact that there is insanity in your family frighten you?*

D.B. My brother Terry's in an asylum right now. I'd like to believe that the insanity is all genius, but I'm afraid that's not true. Some of them, a good many, are just nobodies. I'm quite fond of the insanity, actually. It's a nice thing to throw out at parties, don't you think? Everybody finds empathy in a nutty family, everybody says, 'Oh, yes, my family is quite mad.' Mine really is. No fucking about, boy. Most of them are nutty in, just out of, or going into an institution. Or dead.

c.c. *What did you think of Barbra Streisand's recording 'Life on Mars'?*

D.B. Bloody awful. Sorry Barb, but it was atrocious!

September 1975
Filming for *The Man Who Fell to Earth* completed. The final cut for the film was made by Nicolas Roeg at Shepperton later in the year.

David and the group travel to Los Angeles to start work on a new LP, 'Station to Station', at the Cherokee studios in Los Angeles.

4 November 1975
'Soul Train' appearance recorded for Dick Clark's 'American Bandstand', US TV's main pop/rock show. David mimed to 'Fame' and 'Golden Years', and before his performance answered questions from the audience. David later said that he made himself 'A little drunk. Something I never normally do,' he added.

7 November 1975
'Space Oddity' released. Reaches No. 1 for the first time.

17 November 1975
'Golden Years'/'Can You Hear Me' single released (RCA) (highest chart position No. 8).

23 November 1975
David records appearance on the 'Cher Show' in the US. He sang 'Fame', 'Can You Hear Me' and 'Young Americans' with Cher, then a medley of songs with Cher including, 'Song Sung Blue', 'Wedding Bells', 'Da Doo Ron Ron', 'Daytripper', 'Blue Moon', 'Only You', 'Young Blood' and finished off with 'Young Americans' (CBS TV).

27 November 1975
Russell Harty satellite interview recorded.

28 November 1975
'Russell Harty Plus' show broadcast featuring an exclusive satellite interview with David direct from 'Downtown Burbank', California (London Weekend). The big exclusive revelation for Harty being, 'I'm coming home in May to play shows, look at you and be English again.' He refused to give up booked satellite space when it was announced that Spain's General Franco had died.

December 1975
'The Spiders from Mars' (minus Mick Ronson and, of course, David) undertake a small tour of the UK to promote their new single 'White Man, Black Man' and LP 'Spiders from Mars' (Pye).

2 December 1975
European tour details released for David's 1976 tour.

25 December 1975
Christmas spent at Keith Richard's Jamaican home, rehearsing the new band for his return to world touring. Guitarist Earl Slick decided not to join David on this tour. An immediate replacement was found in Stacey Heydon, a previously unknown Canadian bar-room guitarist. On David's arrival in Jamaica, finding that no arrangements had been made for him there, David telephoned manager Michael Lippman to tell him that he was fired.

December 1975
Rumours developed in the press suggesting that David was intending to star in a bio-pic of Frank Sinatra. David later furiously denied these when interviewed on tour in 1976.

143

3 January 1976

Appears on the 'Dinah Shore Show' and sang 'Stay' and 'Five Years', the latter being a reminiscent performance similar to his 1972 appearance on 'The Old Grey Whistle Test'. Also on the show, actress Nancy Walker and actor Henry 'Fonzie' Winkler. The show, made in Hollywood, also showed David practising karate.

10 January 1976

Interview published with Nicolas Roeg in *Street Life*, conducted by Mike Flood Page:

'He has before him a miniature Sony cassette machine and offers an exclusive preview of the Bowie soundtrack just in from LA. It's a simple melodic instrumental based around organ, bass and drums, with atmosphere courtesy of studio wizardry all put together and performed by Bowie himself.'

Roeg went on to explain to Page the character of Newton in the film, and the comparisons between Newton and Howard Hughes. 'There is this line that he speaks in the film which is quite indicative of his attitude: "My life is not secret, but it is private," which is typical of Hughes. It seems to me that irritates a lot of people.'

23 January 1976

'Station to Station' – LP released by RCA to herald, 'The Return of the Thin White Duke . . .' – David's emotional return to Europe after an absence of three years.

Initial release of this record was delayed when David, unhappy with the colour of the sleeve and wanting a simpler black-and-white cover to complement the tour idea he was developing, ordered a change.

'Station to Station' released 23 January 1976 (RCA APLI–1327)

Side One	*Side Two*
Station to Station (Bowie)	TVC 15 (Bowie)
Golden Years (Bowie)	Stay (Bowie)
Word on a Wing (Bowie)	Wild is the Wind (Tiomkin, Washington)

Produced by David Bowie, Harry Maslin

Arranged by David Bowie

David Bowie (vocals, guitar, alto sax)
Carlos Alomar/Earl Slick (guitar)
Roy Bittan (piano)
George Murray (bass)
Dennis Davis (drums)

'Station to Station' – ' "Station to Station" was really my preface for "Low" and my return to Europe.'

The 1976 World Tour
David's first world tour for five years opened in Vancouver, Canada to wide press coverage.

The show was far removed from anything previous, starting hauntingly with the Salvador Dali/Luis Bunuel 1922 film, *Un Chien Andalou*. The film, strongly surrealist and black and white, suited perfectly the monochromatic of the whole show.

The startling effect of white light on black setting was a hugely successful innovation and a shrewd assessment of stage lighting. The image was followed through completely with black trousers and waistcoat, crisp white shirt and a packet of Gitanes tucked neatly in a pocket.

David's group for the tour were: Carlos Alomar, Dennis Davis, Tony Kaye (ex 'Yes' keyboards man), George Murray and last-minute replacement, Stacey Heydon. Backing singers Ava Cherry and Claudia Lennear were dropped at the last moment by David when he decided that such singers had no place in the new show.

The large traditional entourage that David and Mainman had developed had been dispensed with, David reducing every aspect of the presentation down to a minimum.

Patrick Gibbons was now acting manager (David, since Lippman's departure, has maintained overall control over his affairs). Corinne Schwab was David's personal assistant and to this day is the only survivor from the Mainman period. Barbara de Witt handled worldwide press and publicity. Tony Mascia had become David's bodyguard. David's closest travelling companion for the tour was Iggy Pop (or Jimmy as he is known to his friends) who attended almost every show.

The white light effect employed on the tour was said to have been inspired from some old photographic effects pioneered by Man Ray.

2 February 1976
Vancouver, Canada. The opening night of David's 1976 world tour.

3 February 1976
Seattle Coliseum.

4 February 1976
Portland.

6 February 1976
San Francisco, Cow Palace. After the show, David was presented with a silver cape and guitar and a gold disc for 'Fame' by promoter Bill Graham. 'It was a lovely night,' said David 'and should be even better in Los Angeles.' Interviewed before the show by Robert Hillburn for London's *Melody Maker*.

8 February 1976
Los Angeles, Englewood Forum. The post-concert party held by David and Angie as usual drew glittering guests, including Rod Stewart and Britt Ekland, Alice Cooper, Ringo Starr, Ray Bradbury, Linda Ronstadt, Carly Simon, Henry Winkler, Valerine Perrine and Steven Ford, son of the then US president. David and Ford chatted, David wanting to talk about politics, Ford more interested in Peter Frampton. Little Zowie was allowed to stay up to see the concert.

9 February 1976
Los Angeles, Englewood Forum. After the show, Patti Smith stopped by and spilt beer all over Angie's mink.

11 February 1976
Los Angeles Englewood Forum. After the show, David introduced to David Hockney by Christopher Isherwood.
   During the LA shows Iggy turned up backstage to see his old friend. David invited Iggy to join him as a travelling companion for the rest of the tour.

12 February 1976
Cameron Crowe interview published in *Rolling Stone*.

13 February 1976
San Diego Sports Arena.

For the tour, David was reported to be practising karate regularly to keep in shape. He would often employ karate movements on stage.

15 February 1976
Phoenix Coliseum.

16 February 1976
Albuquerque.

17 February 1976
Denver, Colorado.

20 February 1976
Milwaukee.

21 February 1976
Kalamazoo.

22 February 1976
Evansville.

23 February 1976
Cincinnati.

25 February 1976
Montreal.
Filming of *The Eagle Has Landed* started without David, who had originally agreed to appear in the film. The problem was David's tour commitments, as director Jack Wiener explained: 'It's unfortunate, because we would have liked very much to have had him, but when you are working on a movie with a 5½-million-dollar budget you can't afford to have one of the cast involved with something else at the same time.'

26 February 1976
Toronto, Maple Leaf Gardens.

27 February 1976
Cleveland Auditorium.

28 February 1976
Cleveland Auditorium.
'Play Don't Worry' LP released by RCA, the second solo release for Mick Ronson. David's only involvement was the backing track for 'White Light/White Heat' recorded during the 'Pin-Up' sessions in France. David mentioned in 1980, that he was hoping to release his own version of the song some time.

29 February 1976
Detroit, Cobo Arena.

February 1976
Two-million-dollar lawsuit filed by David against former manager, Michael Lippman. David contended that Lippman had been taking fifteen per cent of his earnings instead of the agreed ten per cent, and that he also froze $475,000-worth of David's assets after he was fired. David had to ask RCA to underwrite expenses at the start of the tour.

1 March 1976
Detroit, Cobo Arena. David interviewed pre-concert by Christ Charlesworth at the Pontchertrain Hotel. 'I couldn't do anything but survive now. Once you've made the initial bloom, what else do you have to do?'

3 March 1976
Chicago Ampitheater.

5 March 1976
St Louis.

6 March 1976
Memphis, Mid-South Coliseum.

7 March 1976
Nashville Municipal Auditorium.

8 March 1976
Atlanta.

11 March 1976
Pittsburgh Auditorium.

12 March 1976
Norfolk Scope. Stays at the local Holiday Inn, after the show giving an early rendition of 'Sister Midnight' (which was written on the '76 tour and occasionally sung live) in the hotel bar.

13–14 March 1976
Washington DC, Capital Center.

15–16 March 1976
Philadelphia, Tower Theater.

17 March 1976
Boston, The Gardens.

18 March 1976
The Man Who Fell to Earth premiered at the Leicester Square Theatre, London, attended by Angie, James Coburn, Lee Remick, Rick Wakeman, John Peel, Amanda Lear, Stomu Yamashta, and stars from the film, Candy Clarke, Rip Torn, Alf Martin and John Walters.

19 March 1976
Buffalo, New York. David struggles through the show with severe flu. The following day he is kept in bed until the afternoon before the drive to the Rochester show.

20 March 1976
Rochester, New York. Interviewed before the show by Al Rudis, David was still suffering. 'I had 800,000 units of penicillin the other day, and then I've been taking doses of 400,000 a day, and that and brandy really puts you out. The doctor said it was cool to drink with penicillin, because I had to have something to take the pain away.'

A.R. *After your European tour, are you going to concentrate on acting for a while?*
D.B. No, no, no, the first thing I'm doing is I'm gonna finish off some silk screens and lithographs that I've worked on. I did some earlier this year, which I thought were very successful.
A.R. *Will they be exhibited?*
D.B. No.

As the '76 tour progressed, David's backing group picked up the title Raw Moon as a monicker, regressing, it would seem, from Mars!

21 March 1976
Springfield, Massachusetts. Before the show, in the early hours of the morning, David, Iggy Pop, Dwain A. Vaughn, a friend, and a girl, Chivah Soo are arrested at the Flagship Americana hotel in Rochester on suspicion of possession of 8 oz of marijuana. David later given bail of $2,000. He also put up the bail of $2,000 each for the other three.

22 March 1976
New Haven.

23 March 1976
Uniondale New York, Nassau Coliseum.

25 March 1976

Appears in court in Rochester, New York, charged along with the three other suspects, of possession of marijuana. The case was adjourned and dropped one year later. David later appeared on Channel 5 news leaving court.

26 March 1976

New York, Madison Square Garden, final show of the US segment of the 1976 world tour. After the show, a small party was held at the Penn Plaza Club for David and the crew. At the party David described that evening's show as getting the best reaction he had ever received, 'I was so nervous, I nearly threw up!' David spent most of the evening in a corner chatting with Iggy.

27 March 1976

A private screening of *The Man Who Fell to Earth* David had arranged for friends had to be cancelled when David couldn't get a print of his own film.

Late March 1976

Sails from New York for Cannes to continue the tour.

'David Bowie Special' released March 1976 (Japan Only) (SRA–9503–04)

Side One
Starman (Bowie)
Moonage Daydream (Bowie)
Five Years (Bowie)
Hang on to Yourself (Bowie)
Suffragette City (Bowie)
Rock 'N' Roll Suicide (Bowie)

Side Two
The Jean Genie (Bowie)
Time (Bowie)
Let's Spend the Night Together
   (Jagger, Richard)
The Prettiest Star (Bowie)
Watch that Man (Bowie)
Aladdin Sane (1913–1938–197?)
   (Bowie)

Side Three
Space Oddity (Bowie)
The Man Who Sold the World
   (Bowie)
The Wild Eyed Boy from Freecloud
   (Bowie)
Cygnet Committee (Bowie)

Side Four
Changes (Bowie)
Life on Mars? (Bowie)
Fill Your Heart (Rose, Williams)
Andy Warhol (Bowie)
Black Country Rock (Bowie)
The Width of a Circle (Bowie)

Produced by David Bowie, Gus Dudgeon, Ken Scott
   and Tony Visconti

150

April 1976
'TVC 15'/'We are the Dead' single released in the US (RCA).

Early April 1976
David, while returning from a stopover trip to Moscow, is held at the Russian/Poland border while customs men confiscated some Nazi books. The books were for research.

'I'm working on a film on Goebbels and they found all my reference material,' David later said. David elaborated more on his Nazi fascination in an interview with Angus Mackinnon for *NME* 1980.

That whole 'Station to Station' tour was done under duress. I was out of my mind totally, completely crazed. Really. But the main thing I was functioning on was – as far as that whole thing about Hitler and the Rightism was concerned – was mythology . . . I had found King Arthur. It was not as you probably know . . . I mean, this whole racist thing that came up, quite inevitably and rightly. But – and I know this sounds terribly naive – but none of that had actually occurred to me, inasmuch as I'd been working and still do work with black musicians for the last six or seven years. And we'd all talk about it together – about the Arthurian period, about the magical side of the whole Nazi campaign, and about the mythology involved.

7 April 1976
Munich, Olympia Hall, Germany.

8 April 1976
Dusseldorf, Philips Halle, Germany.

10 April 1976
Berlin, Deutchlandhalle, Germany. Interviewed earlier in the day by Stuart Grundy for the 'David Bowie Story', broadcast in May on Radio One.

11 April 1976
Hamburg, Congress Centrum Halle, Germany. Further interviews conducted with Stuart Grundy for the 'David Bowie Story' on BBC Radio One.

13 April 1976
Frankfurt Festhalle, Germany.

14 April 1976
Zurich, Switzerland. David saw the new house he and Angie had rented for the first time. Originally, the tour schedule included another

German show in Ludwigshafen Franz-Eberthalle, but was cancelled in favour of a Swiss date.

15 April 1976
Frankfurt Festhalle.

16 April 1976
David stopped off for the evening in a Frankfurt club and made a rare off-the-cuff guest appearance with a local group, Linus Band.

17 April 1975
Bern Festhalle, Switzerland.
 Spends some time resting at his new home in Switzerland.

24 April 1976
Helsinki, Masshallen, Finland. Earlier in the day a press conference is held.

26 April 1976
Stockholm, Kungliga Tennishallen, Sweden. After the show, pursued by a persistent Swedish reporter, David made his infamous and ill-fated remark about fascism, a remark that David has since repudiated on many occasions.
 'As I see it I am the only alternative for the premier in England. I believe Britain could benefit from a fascist leader. After all, fascism is really nationalism.'

27 April 1976
Stockholm, Kungliga Tennishallen, Sweden.

28 April 1976
Gothenburg, Falkoner Teatret, Denmark.

29 April 1976
Copenhagen, Falkoner Teatret, Denmark.

30 April 1976
Copenhagen, Falkoner Teatret, Denmark.
 Swedish radio interview broadcast, made a few days earlier (Skivspegelen Radio).
 'TVC 15'/'We are the Dead' single released by RCA, the second single taken from 'Station to Station' (highest chart position No. 33).

2 May 1976
David arrives at Victoria Station to a well-publicized return to the UK, after an absence of over two years, the national press showing particular interest in him after the political declaration made a few days earlier in Stockholm.

A photographer catches David in mid-wave to fans. He seems to be making a Nazi salute. David furious at the claim that he was.

David had been interviewed during the journey from Dover to Victoria on the specially chartered train by Maggie Norden for Capital Radio. The interview was broadcast thirty minutes later on Capital's 'Hullaballo' show.

M.N. *Did you like Russia?*
D.B. Yes, it's er . . . no Penge but it's quite good, quite fun. I didn't stay there for long, eight hours.
M.N. *What did you miss about London?*
D.B. That's it really, London. I couldn't, having grown up here, take a bit out. I missed the toilet paper!'
M.N. *How many people have you been travelling with?*
D.B. Me personally? . . . three. With the road crew there's about twenty-five people in all.

For David's arrival at the station RCA supplied a PA system on the platform for him to make a speech on arrival. This never actually took place, David leaving the station after only thirty seconds waving to excited fans. The PA system had evidently broken down.

'The David Bowie Story', Radio One, four-part weekly special broadcast, part one, all written and produced by Stuart Grundy.

3 May 1976
Wembley, Empire Pool, London. David's first live show in the UK for practically three years. David apparently cried from emotion at the end of the show.

4 May 1976
Wembley, Empire Pool. Interviewed earlier that day by Jean Rook for the *Daily Express* in his only press interview while on tour. 'I tell my son that the make-up is how daddy makes his money.'

5 May 1976
Wembley, Empire Pool.

6 May 1976
Wembley, Empire Pool. David introduces himself on stage as David 'Winston' Bowie.

'Cracked Actor' documentary repeated 'Omnibus' (BBC 2).

7 May 1976
Wembley, Empire Pool. David and Brian Eno discuss plans for recording together.

8 May 1976
Wembley, Empire Pool. David's last show in the UK. All six shows a complete sell-out. Mick Jagger, Keith Richard and Billy Preston watch the final show from backstage.

9 May 1976
The Man Who Fell to Earth put on general release in the UK. David remains in London for a few days before continuing the European tour in Holland.
    'The David Bowie Story', part two broadcast (BBC Radio One).

13 May 1976
Rotterdam, Ahoy Sports Stadium, Holland.

16 May 1976
'The David Bowie Story', part three broadcast (BBC Radio One).

17–18 May 1976
Paris, Pavillon de Paris, Porte de Patin.

19 May 1976
Last Paris show cancelled because of poor ticket sales. After the show on 18 May, David and famous transvestite Rommy Haag visit the Alcazar club in Paris to celebrate the end of a successful world tour, Haag suggesting to David that he should visit Berlin.

20 May 1976
'ChangesOneBowie' LP released by RCA, David's first compilation LP, an odd but sensible cross section of recorded work to date, all tracks selected by David. Cover portrait again in black and white and taken by Tom Kelly (famed for taking the Marilyn Monroe nude calendar photograph).

23 May 1976
Fourth and final part of 'The David Bowie Story' broadcast.

June 1976
Bowie family move into the rented cuckoo-clock house near Montreux in Corsier-sur-Vevey, to relax after the tour. After a short stay there,

154

David and Iggy Pop leave for the Chateau d'Herouville in France to continue their holiday. After a relaxing couple of days, the lure of the recording studio became too much, and David and Iggy booked recording time to work on a new LP for Iggy – the LP that later became 'The Idiot'.

'ChangesOneBowie' album released 20 May 1976 (RCA RS.1055)

Side One
Space Oddity (Bowie)*
John, I'm Only Dancing (Bowie)
Changes (Bowie)
Ziggy Stardust (Bowie)
Suffragette City (Bowie)
The Jean Genie (Bowie)

Side Two
Diamond Dogs (Bowie)
Rebel Rebel (Bowie)
Young Americans (Bowie)
Fame (Bowie, Lennon, Alomar)
Golden Years (Bowie)

Produced by David Bowie, Ken Scott, Gus Dudgeon, Tony Visconti and Harry Maslin
Arranged by David Bowie and *Paul Buckmaster

28 May 1976
Zowie Bowie's fifth birthday.

July 1976
Work on 'The Idiot' continues throughout July at the chateau near Paris, though still not complete at the end of the month (the studio having been previously booked by other artists for August).

9 July 1976
'Suffragette City'/'Stay' single released by RCA, issued as a promotional track from the 'ChangesOneBowie' LP and cashing in on the recent London concert successes. Initial release in picture sleeve.

August 1976
'Stay'/'Word on a Wing' single released in the US (RCA). David, Iggy and the chateau's studio engineer travel to Munich to complete recording on 'The Idiot' at the Musicland studios there. After recording completed, David and Iggy then travelled on to Berlin, for the final mix at Hansa by the Wall studios. First use of these studios.

September 1976
Ex-Spider Trevor Bolder is announced as replacement for John Wetton in the heavy rock group Uriah Heap.

1 September 1976
David, Brian Eno, Tony Visconti, Carlos Alomar, Dennis Davis, Ricky Gardiner, George Murrey and Roy Young arrive at the Chateau d'Herouville to start work on David's next LP, 'Low'. Production on the LP was not easy for David, as he had to take a few days out for court proceedings in Paris against Michael Lippman. (David maintained that one of the reasons for the dissolution with Lippman was in part due to the fact that Lippman had pledged to David that he would get the rights for David to score *The Man Who Fell to Earth*. These actually went to John Phillips.) 'Subterraneans', the last track on side two of 'Low', was actually composed for the soundtrack, which David had worked on with Paul Buckmaster. David spent four days in Paris dealing with the deposition. Eno used David's absence to prepare the groundwork for 'Warszawa'.

October 1976
David moves to the Schoeneberg district of West Berlin. In an interview with the *Berliner Morgen Post* he said, 'Berlin gives me something I don't get from London or Los Angeles.' This was to be David's last press interview in Berlin. His well-publicized reclusiveness prompted German photographers to stalk him with telephoto lenses. After David's two-and-half-week stint at the chateau in France, where eight tracks were laid down, David and Eno continue the recording at Hansa studios, Berlin.

Ricky Gardiner, interviewed later about the recording, said, 'As for the style of music, I think you'll find that David doesn't reject any kind of music. He's not a musical pseudo-intellectual. He likes Mantovani, for example, which may make some people go into double-think.

'In actual fact it makes complete sense. Mantovani is brilliant, there's no getting away from that, and David knows it. I think he was very disappointed by the music for *The Man Who Fell to Earth*. He spent quite some time writing a score for it, and he wasn't pleased it wasn't used in the film. He let us hear it and it was excellent, quite unlike anything else he's done.'

November 1976
David interviewed on Australian television show, 'Countdown'.

News breaks that David had suffered a coronary in Berlin. Later reports revealed a less serious incident. A hospital spokesman at the Berlin British Military hospital where David was taken said:

In the early hours one morning, the hospital received a call from a lady in some distress saying her British husband had had a heart attack.

Though we don't usually admit non-military personnel, as an act of mercy we sent out an ambulance to get him. He'd just overdone things, and was suffering from too much drink. We ran various tests and proved he hadn't had a coronary.

According to Angie, it wasn't the effects of hard work and drink that made David ill, but, 'Music people winding him up'.

Angie appears at the Little Theatre, St Martin's Lane, in a lunchtime show entitled *Krisis Kabaret* with Roy Martin and friends. The troupe later became known as the 'Soul House Company' and released one single, 'Soul House'/'What's Going On' (Track Records 2094 132).

December 1976
David awarded the US Academy of Science, 'Fiction, Fantasy and Horrors' best actor of the year award for *The Man Who Fell to Earth*.

25 December 1976
Christmas at the rented chalet near Montreux with Angie and Zowie.

January 1977
'Pop Shop' German radio programme broadcast featuring the first part of three one-hour specials on David's music.

8 January 1977
David celebrates his thirtieth birthday with Iggy and Rommy Haag and friends in a Berlin nightclub.

'Fascination'/'We Just Want to Play for You' single released by Fat Larry's Band, A-side written by David (WMOT), and also appears on the 'Feel It' LP.

Most leisure time in Berlin for David was spent exploring art galleries. According to Tony Visconti David's knowledge of art was now approaching that of the connoisseur. 'Every time I go there he's into something new. Also, he's the only guy, who, when he's on tour, never stays in his hotel room. He always puts on a disguise and goes out into the streets.'

14 January 1977
'Low' LP released. A new departure for David into cybernetics, synthesizer sound construction. This LP also heralded the joining of forces with ex-Roxy Music keyboards man, Brian Eno. The LP was recorded at Hansa studios, Potsdamer Platz, Berlin.

Home for David in Berlin at this time was a modest flat above a car spares shop, at Haupstrasse 152, Schoeneburg. The flat, which was only walking distance from the studios, was in a very poor area of the city, mostly populated by a Turkish community.

Brian Eno later commented to Michael Watts about the record's production:

I know he liked 'Another Green World' a lot, and he must've realized that there were these two parallel streams of working going on in what I was doing, and when you find someone with the same problems you tend to become friendly with them.

He said when he first heard 'Discreet Music' he could imagine in the future that you would go into the supermarket and there would be a rack of 'Ambience' records, all in very similar covers.

And – this is my addition – they would just have titles like 'Sparkling', or 'Nostalgic' or 'Melancholy' or 'Sombre'. They would all be mood titles, and so very cheap to buy you could chuck them away when you didn't want them anymore.

Eno also made further comments on the recording of 'Low' later in 1970.

The way he worked impressed me a lot. Because it reminds me of me. He'd go out into the studio to do something, and he'd just come back hopping up and down with joy. And whenever I see someone doing that I just trust that reaction. It means that they really are surprising themselves.

Brian Eno first came to the public's attention in 1972 as part of the original celebrated Roxy Music line-up.

Roxy Music and Eno's first meeting with David came in the summer of '72 when they supported David at the famed 'Ziggy Stardust', Rainbow concerts, adding their own brand of futuristic elegance. It was there that David and Eno formed a friendship that was to prove fruitful five years later. Eno by this time was attracting as much interest as anyone in the group. His own brand of camp futuristic fashion and simple-but-effective synthesized sound made him an obvious focus of attention, even more so than Bryan Ferry, at one point.

Eno left Roxy Music at their height in late 1972, and began work from that point on as a solo artist, his first album release as such being 'Here Comes the Warm Jets', an LP dismissed by many journalists.

Undeterred Eno, with Robert Fripp, moved even further into the obscure, releasing two LPs of pure electronic drones, 'No Pussyfooting' and 'Evening Star'. The LPs underlined Eno's interest in pure progression.

David and Eno logically linked up in late 1976 to record and expand ideas they had both been working towards for some years. The LP recorded at the Chateau d'Herouville in France became 'Low', the first in triptych ('triptych, because I like the word "triptych" and wanted the chance to use it', David later said).

With the release of 'Lodger' in May 1979, the trilogy was completed; Eno now was spending more time travelling than in the studio.

In 1983 Eno is as busy as ever, mainly producing people like Talking Heads, Devo and John Cale. All such albums bear his own trademark.

'Low' album released 14 January 1977 (RCA PL. 12030)

Side One
Speed of Life (Bowie)
Breaking Glass (Bowie, Davis, Murray)
What in the World (Bowie)
Sound and Vision (Bowie)
Always Crashing in the Same Car (Bowie)
Be My Wife (Bowie)
A New Career in a New Town (Bowie)

Side Two
Warszawa (Bowie, Eno)
Art Decade (Bowie)
Weeping Wall (Bowie)
Subterraneans (Bowie)

Produced by David Bowie and Tony Visconti.

Arranged by David Bowie

David Bowie (vocals, Arp, tape horn, brass, synthetic strings, saxophones, tape cellos, guitar, pump bass, harmonica, piano, prearranged percussion, Chamberlain)
Brian Eno (vocals, splinter mini-Moog, Report Arp, Rimmer EMI, guitar treatments, piano, Chamberlain)
Carlos Alomar (rhythm guitars, guitar.)
Dennis Davis (percussion)
Ricky Gardener (guitars)
George Murray (bass)
Roy Young (pianos, Farfisa organ)
Peter and Paul (cellos)
Eduard Meyer (cellos)
Mary Visconti/Iggy Pop (backing vocals)

'Low' – 'It does sound very mathematic and icy, but that doesn't defeat its ultimate musical impact. The impact is definitely an arrangement and presentation of some emotive force, and it does touch one.'

February 1977
Cherry Vanilla, David's ex-publicist, begins her first concert tour of the UK.

11 February 1977
'Sound and Vision'/'A New Career in a New Town' single released, the first single taken from 'Low'. The single was a substantial hit from an album considered by some at RCA to be almost commercial suicide. The record gained extensive radio and TV airing.

Late February 1977
Letter received by *Melody Maker* from David in Berlin published: 'I would like to correct the misconception that Iggy Pop is managed by myself. Iggy looks after his own business affairs. I would appreciate a printed correction. David Bowie, Berlin.'

1 March 1977
Iggy Pop, beginning his first UK tour, appears at the Friars Hall, Aylesbury – with David on keyboards. Rumours of David's appearance with Iggy before the shows, but no one was sure until the show actually started. After the afternoon soundcheck at the hall, David, Iggy and friends were seen drinking in the Gun bar of the Bell hotel for half an hour before departing for the dressing room at the hall where they stayed for three hours before the show.

   Although the Friars Hall was only ninety-five per cent full for Iggy's first show, he was well received. Most of the audience were unaware that it was David Bowie at the keyboards, as he was not lit.

2 March 1977
Iggy Pop at the Newcastle City Hall.

3 March 1977
Iggy Pop at the Manchester Apollo.

4 March 1977
David and Iggy check into the Montcalm Hotel, London. Rainbow Theatre, London, Iggy's first London show.

While in London, David is taken for lunch to Toscanini's in the Kings Road by Marc Bolan. After the meal, David and Bolan, both slightly drunk, wandered down the Kings Road singing. At one point, when in view of a packed open-topped double-decker bus full of school children, the two jumped up and down trying to attract the children's attention shouting alternately, 'I'm David Bowie', and 'I'm Marc Bolan'. Although the school children were none too interested in their

David is a great singer . . . he can sing anything, almost. I remember him when he was in The Lower Third and he used to go to gigs in an ambulance. I used to think he was very professional. He was playing saxophone then and singing. I suppose it was a blues band then and he was produced by Shel Talmy.

He did a record which I'm sure everybody has forgotten. It was 'Pop Art' – yer actual feedback. I can't remember what it was called.

After that he went to Decca around the time I was doing 'The Wizard'. He was into . . . bombardiers then. Don't you remember 'The Little Bombardier'?

He was very Cockney then. I used to go round to his place in Bromley and he always played Anthony Newley records. I haven't spoken to him about it, but I guess that was how he got into mime.

Newley did mime in *Stop the World I Wanna Get Off*. The funny thing is that 'The Laughing Gnome', which was one of David's biggest singles here, came from that early period.

It came at the height of his supercool image. And that's very 'Strawberry Fair' . . . 'the donkey's eaten all the strawberries!' That was his biggest single, so it just shows you it doesn't pay to be cool, man!

Rock 'n' Roll suicide hit the dust and the laughing gnomes took over. We were all looking for something to get into then. I wanted to be Bob Dylan, but I think David was looking into that music-hall humour.

It was the wrong time to do it, but all his songs were story songs, like 'London Boys'. They had a flavour, a very theatrical flavour, with very square kinda backings.

But in those days there weren't any groovy backings being laid down. I think if he played back those records now he'd smile at them, because he was an unformed talent then. He was putting together the nucleus of what he was eventually going to be.

When he had 'Space Oddity' he was on tour with me in Tyrannosaurus Rex. He had a mime act and used to open up the show. He didn't sing at all but had a tape going and he'd act out a story about a Tibetan boy. It was quite good actually, and we did the Festival Hall with Roy Harper as well.

I remember David playing me 'Space Oddity' in his room and I loved it and said he needed a sound like the Bee Gees, who were very big then. The stylophones he used on that, I gave him. Tony Visconti turned me onto stylophones.

The record was a sleeper for months before it became a hit, and I played on 'Prettiest Star', you know which I thought was a great song, and it flopped completely.

But I never got the feeling from David that he was ambitious. I remember he'd buy antiques if he had a hit, when he should have saved the money. David got his drive to be successful once I'd done it with the T. Rex thing. At the beginning of the seventies it was the only way to go.

antics, they did manage to attract some Bowie fans who couldn't believe their luck when David obliged with an autograph and a chat.

March 1977

Angie tells the *Daily Express* that she and David are broke. 'David's been robbed blind.'

5 March 1977

Rainbow Theatre. Iggy's second London show continued through slight crowd troubles after David and group had taken the stage and some of the crowd raced to the front. Fans were ejected as the show started when scuffles with security men broke out and seats were damaged.

7 March 1977

A third London show at the Rainbow added to meet demand on tickets. Iggy's last UK show.

Support for all of Iggy's UK dates – The Vibrators.

March 1977

'China Girl'/'Baby' single released by Iggy Pop, cowritten and produced by David who is also featured on the single (RCA).

David spent four days at Marc Bolan's flat working together on a film with the Mainman. Apart from writing the script, they planned the soundtrack and to appear in glorious Technicolor themselves.

'I hope it's going to be out in the year,' says Marc. 'All I can tell you is that it's about a future society and reflects our own feelings. We're also bringing out an album, doing a side each.

'What a combination it's going to be, the two greatest musical influences of the seventies joined together.'

10 March 1977

David and Iggy leave Heathrow for the US to continue Iggy's concert tour there. This was the first time David had flown in six years, and he has now conquered his fear of flight. On his arrival in New York David said to reporter Lisa Robinson. 'I flew for the first time in five or six years. I think the airplane is really a wonderful invention.'

That evening David and Iggy went nightclubbing at the Lower Manhattan Ocean Club with friends David Johansen and wife Cyrinda Foxe. Music supplied for the evening by the Patti Smith group, Iggy joining the group on stage for a wild version of '96 Tears'. David spent the evening quietly chatting, sipping Möet et Chandon and smoking French cigarettes.

13 March 1977

Montreal, Le Plateau Theater, Iggy's concert tour continued.

14 March 1977

Toronto Convocation Hall.

16 March 1977
Boston, Harvard Square Theater.

18 March 1977
New York Palladium, the show was attended by Mick Jagger and Keith Richard amongst others.
'The Idiot' LP released by Iggy Pop with David on keyboards and backing vocals, David also writing all the music, Iggy supplying all the lyrics (RCA). The cover photo was taken by David in Berlin (RCA).

19 March 1977
Philadelphia, Tower Theater.

21 March 1977
Cleveland, Agora Ballroom. The show was attended by unknown group Devo from Akron, Ohio. The group managed to slip a demo tape of their music to David, though it was Iggy who then drew David's attention to it.

22 March 1977
Cleveland, Agora Ballroom.

27 March 1977
Chicago, Riviera Theater.

28 March 1977
Chicago, Illinois.

29 March 1977
Pittsburgh, Leona Theater.

30 March 1977
Columbus.

31 March 1977
Angie in London to model a £700 wedding dress for the autumn collection of designer Yuki. Angie agreed to do the assignment because Yuki 'is a close friend'.

1 April 1977
Milwaukee, Oriental Theater.

4 April 1977
Portland, Paramount Theater.

5 April 1977
Seattle, Paramount Theater.

7 April 1977
Vancouver Gardens.

13 April 1977
San Francisco, Berkely Theater.

15 April 1977
Los Angeles, Santa Monica Civic Auditorium.
   While in LA, David and Iggy are interviewed together on 'The Dinah Shore Show' preceding the interview with 'Sister Midnight' and 'Funtime' with David on keyboards and backing vocals.

DINAH: *Jimmy, you've known each other for years I suppose.*
IGGY: Six years.
DINAH: *How did you meet?*
IGGY: In a bar in New York. We scored. We were both unrecognized. We had a lot in common.
DINAH: *David, what about recording?*
DAVID: In the studio, Jimmy would make up lyrics on the spot and keep everything he did, and occasionally change a line after he recorded it. I'd never seen anyone able to make up lyrics just out of the head, to a track. He'll hate me for this, but, it's more like the beatnik era.

Late April 1977
David and Iggy return to Berlin to begin preparations on Iggy's new LP 'Lust for Life'.

May 1977
'Be My Wife'/'Speed of Life' single released in the US (RCA).

6 May 1977
'Raw Power' LP by Iggy and The Stooges rereleased (Embassy). 'I Got a Right'/'Gimme Some Skin' single released by Iggy and The Stooges, mixed by David (Holland–Siamese Records).

June 1977
Freddy Mercury of Queen interview published in *Sounds*.

Why do you think people like David Bowie and Elvis Presley have been so successful?
F.M. Because they give their audiences champagne for breakfast, they're what the people want. They want to see you rush off in limousines. They get a buzz.

17 June 1977
'Be My Wife'/'Speed of Life' single released, the second release from 'Low' and a less successful choice than 'Sound and Vision' (RCA).

27 June 1977
David apears on French TV on 'TFI Actualities', interviewed by Yves Marousi.

Appears the same day on another French channel on 'Midi Premiére' for an interview with Danielle Gilbert.

July 1977
David attends the French premiere of *The Man Who Fell to Earth* at the Gaumont Theatre in the Champs Elysées, Paris.

After the screening, David, with actress Sydne Rome, got caught in a throng of admirers avoiding strangulation by donating his scarf to the person pulling the end of it. In the evening bustle a pickpocket tried to steal his wallet, and David, out of character, swung out and punched, breaking his own thumb in the action but retaining his wallet.

While in Paris, a video for the single 'Be My Wife' was made but never broadcast in the UK.

Sydne Rome had travelled to Paris for discussions with David on the possibilities of work on *Wally*, the film David was hoping to make about expressionist artist Egon Schiele. The film was never made because of problems finding a suitable script. David and Sydne Rome worked together later on *Just A Gigolo*.

'An Evening with Johnny Rotten' radio interview broadcast – 'Bowie was good for a while but you couldn't really get into it 'cos you didn't believe that he was doing what he believed in. I dunno what he was up to.

'He was like a real bad drag queen. Some drag queens are very good, he wasn't. Bad stuff. "Rebel Rebel" was a good single. It's about the New York Dolls, I think.'

'Rock et Folk' interview conducted by Phillip Manoeuvre and Jonathen Farren in Paris:

P.M. *You seem to be fascinated by cities like Berlin. . .*

D.B. Berlin, because of the friction. I've written songs in all the Western capitals, and I've always got to the stage where there isn't any friction between a city and me. That became nostalgic, vaguely decadent, and I left for another city.

At the moment I'm incapable of composing in Los Angeles, New York or in London or Paris. There's something missing. Berlin has the strange ability to make you write only the important things – anything else you don't mention, you remain *silent*, and write nothing . . . and in the end you produce 'Low'.

P.M. *The only person The Sex Pistols seem to admire in their heart of hearts, is David Bowie . . .*

D.B. Oh, if Ziggy Stardust had had a son . . . yes! When Ziggy fell from favour and lost all his money, he had a son before he died . . . Johnny Rotten!

Late July 1977

David and Bianca Jagger seen dining and dating in Paris, Bianca in Paris for work on a film called *Flesh Coloured*. The two later travelled to Spain for a short holiday.

3 August 1977

Iggy Pop and David interviewed over the telephone for Japanese radio.

September 1977

'Heroes' (long version)/'Heroes' (short version) promo-only 12-inch single issued (RCA).

9 September 1977

David records appearances on 'Marc' – Bolan's television show, singing a live version of his forthcoming single 'Heroes'. The recording ended with a jam between David and Bolan, a song they created on the spot called 'Standing Next to You'. It ended in chaos when Bolan accidentally slipped off the stage and fell about laughing. As the recording was already running over time, it could not be rerecorded and the unfinished version was the one broadcast. This was to be Bolan's last TV show before his death. Later, after a meal in the Manchester Post House, the two retired to Bolan's room there to demo a few tracks on cassette, the main one being 'Madman', a track that was later properly pieced together and issued by Cuddly Toys.

After killing a few hours with Bolan, David caught the train from Manchester to Euston, sharing a carriage with Eddie and The Hot

Rods, who also recorded for the Bolan show. Also with The Rods at the time was reporter Tim Lott, hardly able to believe his luck at an exclusive interview which was later published in *Record Mirror*.

T.L. *I note the crucifix hanging around his neck, resting between the few long hairs on his chest. Not another God-squad casualty?*
D.B. It has some religious significance, but not necessarily as a Christian symbol. Before Christianity the crucifix had quite a different significance; the vertical line represented heaven, the horizontal, earth. The crucifix was the meeting of the two. Cabalism is based on numerology, astrology's predecessor, and the missing scrolls of the Old Testament. I have a spirit and I believe that comes from God.

The conversation between David, Tim Lott and Eddie and The Hot Rods was wide and varied and included David's thoughts on 'Low'.

T.L. *The section of 'Low' that most critics found confusing was side two.*
D.B. You want me to explain that to you? It's my reaction to certain places. 'Warszawa' is about Warsaw and the very bleak atmosphere I got from the city. 'Art Decade' is West Berlin – a city cut off from its world, art and culture, dying with no hope of retribution. 'Weeping Wall' is about the Berlin Wall – the misery of it. And 'Subterraneans' is about the people who got caught in East Berlin after the separation – hence the faint jazz saxophones representing the memory of what it was.

9 September 1977
'Lust for Life' LP released by Iggy Pop. David again collaborating with Pop to supply most of the musical content, and Iggy, the lyrics. David also coproduced the LP with Iggy and supplied backing vocals (RCA).

11 September 1977
David records an appearance on 'Bing Crosby's Merrie Olde Christmas' TV show, filmed for ATV at Elstree in the setting of a grand country mansion. David again sang 'Heroes', this time adding some mime. The highlight of the show was a duet with Crosby, 'The Little Drummer Boy'. This was Bing Crosby's last TV appearance before his death in October. 'Peace On Earth'/'The Little Drummer Boy' became a top ten hit when released in November 1982 for the Christmas market.

16 September 1977
Marc Bolan killed in Barnes, southwest London when his car, driven by girlfriend Gloria Jones, ran off the road into a tree. Gloria Jones was seriously injured in the accident. They had one child, Rolan.

17 September 1977
An *NME* interview with Iggy Pop published:

Bowie gave me a chance to apply myself because he thinks I have some talent . . . originally we were just going to do 'Sister Midnight' but I think he respected me for putting myself in a looney bin. He was the only guy who came to visit me . . . nobody else came . . . nobody. Not even my so-called friends in LA . . . but David came. Bowie and I have a very abrasive relationship; it's a clash. How can two friends make an album sound like that?

20 September 1977
Marc Bolan buried at The Chapel, Golders Green, London. David flew in from Switzerland to attend.

23 September 1977
'Heroes'/'V–2 Schneider' single released by RCA as a preview to the LP of the same name. The single was aided by a number of television appearances, including his first appearance on 'Top of the Pops' for five years (highest chart position No. 24).

25 September 1977
Iggy Pop starts a new tour of the UK to promote LP 'Lust for Life'. David did not feature this time on the tour. Support – The Adverts.
   'Helden'/'V–2 Schneider' single released in Germany. 'Heroes' sung in German (RCA).
   'Heroes'/'V–2 Schneider' single released in France. 'Heroes' sung in French (RCA).

28 September 1977
'Marc' TV show broadcast, the last show featuring David (Granada).

29 September 1977
A trust fund was set up for Rolan Bolan by David.

30 September 1977
'Success'/'The Passenger' single released by Iggy Pop, featuring David on keyboards, production and writing credits (RCA).

1 October 1977
David visits Rome to promote 'Heroes'. Makes two television appearances, one on 'L'altra Domenica' (a different Sunday), recording a short interview. The other was on 'Odeon', a longer feature including general conversation, a performance of 'Heroes' and David playing

piano for a version of 'Sense of Doubt'. One radio recording was also made for 'Radio 21, 25' a half-hour show dedicated to analysis of 'Heroes'.

13 October 1977
David telephones Capital Radio from Amsterdam to inform them of an interview later in the month.

14 October 1977
'Heroes' LP released, David's second collection of European/Berlin images and the second in the Bowie/Eno trilogy. The LP was again recorded at Hansa studios, Berlin, in the summer (RCA).

The LPs issued in Germany and France varied from the English release, both LPs containing split versions of 'Heroes' in English and either German or French (RCA).

16 October 1977
French interview with Michel Drucker broadcast on 'Le Rendez-Vous Du Dimanche' (TFI).

French radio interview broadcast with Jean-Bernard, including a phone-in for David's French fans (RTC).

While in Paris, David stayed at the Plaza Athénée Hotel in the Avenue Montaigne, avoiding the George V where the fans now waited whenever David was in Paris.

19 October 1977
Arrives at Heathrow airport for a short promotional visit. Records an appearance on 'Top of the Pops' the same evening, bass on the television recording supplied by Tony Visconti. After the show, David and Tony Visconti went on to Soho for a drink, David pleasantly surprised at not being recognized. It was the first London pub David had visited for five years.

During his short London stay David was seen in the company of nineteen-year-old actress, Suzy Bickford, who later told a reporter, 'He wants to go back to painting'.

'Heroes' album released 14 October 1977 (RCA PL. 12522)

Side One	*Side Two*
Beauty and the Beast (Bowie)	V–2 Schneider (Bowie)
Joe the Lion (Bowie)	Sense of Doubt (Bowie)
'Heroes' (Bowie, Eno)	Moss Garden (Bowie, Eno)
Sons of the Silent Age (Bowie)	Neuköln (Bowie, Eno)
Blackout (Bowie)	The Secret Life of Arabia (Bowie, Eno, Alomar)

Produced by David Bowie and Tony Visconti

David Bowie (vocals, keyboards, guitar, saxophone, koto)
Carlos Alomar (rhythm guitar)
Robert Fripp (lead guitar)
Brian Eno (synthesizers, keyboards, guitar treatments)
George Murray (bass)
Dennis Davis (drums, percussion)
Tony Visconti/Antonia Maass (backing vocals)

'Heroes' – 'I believe in the last two albums, more than anything I've done before. I mean, I look back on a lot of my earlier work and, although there's much that I appreciate about it, there's not a great deal that I actually like. I don't think they're very likeable albums at all.'

20 October 1977
A heavy press schedule at the Dorchester Hotel. The early evening spent at a private viewing of an unknown film which David had been asked to score.

Evening spent at Capital Radio for an interview with Nicky Horne for 'You're Mother Wouldn't Like It', including a phone-in.

N.H. *Your association with Brian Eno and also Robert Fripp is slightly reminiscent of the Arts Lab in Beckenham which is like the days of your youth. Have you ever thought about that, in a way you're sort of going back to that now?*
D.B. It's sort of reminiscent in as much as we have this, well on my part, naive ideal that we should keep re-evaluating a musical position. And I know Brian wants to put music to work, he wants music to go out and get a job. He wants it to do something apart from entertain. And so it has something of the lets-try-and-do-something-with-the-music-that-is-stimulating-on-any-other-level-than-just-pure-enjoyment. As well as enjoyment, I mean.
N.H. *Yes, it's still got to be fun hasn't it?*
D.B. I don't know if it's got to be *fun*, I wouldn't get that flippy about it. I think it has to be enjoyable, I think there are various degrees of enjoyment. I mean it depends if you're S or M you know!
N.H. *Good evening to Alan, who's on the blower at the moment.*
Q. *Hello. Good evening David. The question I'd like to ask is, could you tell me, who are, or were 'The Bewlay Brothers'? And I don't mean the music company.*
D.B. Yes. The Bewlay Brothers were, I suppose, very much based on myself and my brother. My brother was one of the bigger influences in my life. In as much as he told me I didn't have to read the choice of books that I was recommended at school, and that I could go out to the library and go and choose my own, and sort of introduced me to authors that I wouldn't

170

have read probably. You know, the usual kind of things like, the Jack Kerouac's, the Ginsberg's and e. e. cumming's and stuff.

Q. *I understand you're very interested in Burroughs as well?*

D.B. Yes, Burroughs, was very instrumental, as soon as I met him. I mean he convinced me about the marvellous things you can do with the cut-up technique and I incorporated that in some of the stuff like 'Diamond Dogs' and I've never dropped it. In fact it reveals itself to it's fullest extent I guess, on 'Heroes', more than anything else.

21 October 1977

Leaves Heathrow for a safari visit to Kenya staying overnight at Tree-tops, the treehouse visited by the Queen and Prince Philip in 1952. Most of the time in Kenya spent with the Masai, whom David had received official permission to visit. He was accompanied by an appointed local who translated for him.

29 October 1977

'Rock On' radio interview with Stuart Grundy broadcast. Recorded earlier in the month. The conversation centred on 'Heroes' (Radio 1).

6 November 1977

'Pop Shop' television interview with Vic Dennis made in early October in Amsterdam broadcast on Dutch TV.

V.D. *Is the fact that you have moved to Berlin connected with politics?*

D.B. Some newspapers asserted that it could have been in relation to politics but it's absolutely wrong. I am apolitical and I think a real artist is apolitical, because an artist is a dreamer . . .

V.D. *What about your private life?*

D.B. I don't like talking about that. It's not easy to live with me. I'm not blaming Angie. I've got many things to do and I have not got much time for others. I know that, but what can I do? I'm selfish by nature though I know it's a shame. The only person I really love is my son. He's six years old and he's quite often with me. I don't want reporters to see him because I think he's too young for that kind of thing. He's not very interested in music. He prefers mathematics. I think he could become an engineer or something like that.

Three videos were made for the release of 'Heroes'. The tracks were 'Blackout', 'Sense of Doubt' and 'Heroes'. David's clothes for all three videos were exactly the same as the LP sleeve.

December 1977

'Before and After Science' LP released by Brian Eno (Polydor).

'Beauty and the Beast'/'Sense of Doubt' single released in the US. A 12-inch radio promo-only copy of this single was also issued in the States and backed with 'Fame' (RCA).

David travels from Kenya to New York to continue LP promotion there. He also recorded the narration of Prokofiev's 'Peter and the Wolf', the traditional children's story. The music was supplied by the Philadelphia Symphony Orchestra and conducted by Eugene Ormandy.

While in New York David was best man for bodyguard Tony Mascia (who played Arthur, David's driver in *The Man Who Fell to Earth*). Mascia later said of David: 'David's a cool kid to work for, I got offered twice the money to work for Rod Stewart, but I turned it down. David's a brilliant guy, the painting, the writing. He's a very generous kid, very shy, but with me he can be himself. I'm like his father.'

The wedding, which was held on Hudson Street, was also attended by Iggy Pop.

David records an appearance for the 'Superstars' Radio Network', interviewed by Sony Fox. Later in the week he introduced Devo on stage at Max's Kansas City and saw a performance of *Dracula*, then a Broadway hit. David was not impressed.

Melody Maker readers' poll declares David's 'Heroes' the album of the year. *NME* declares David No. 1 singer and songwriter and 'Heroes' the second best LP behind The Sex Pistols.

'Over the Wall We Go'/'Beauty Queen' single released by Ivor Bird (Paul Nicholas). A-side written by David (RSO).

1 December 1977
Interview with David broadcast by John Tobler (Manchester–Piccadilly Radio).

3 December 1977
*NME*s Eno interview published. Eno asked about the general recording work with David.

ENO: That time was really confused. It was much harder working on 'Heroes' than 'Low'. The whole thing, except 'Sons of the Silent Age', which was written beforehand, was evolved on the spot in the studio. Not only that, everything on the album is a first take! I mean, we did the second takes but they weren't nearly as good. It was all done in a very casual kind of way.'

Q. *How did the rest of the finished album strike you?*
ENO: I never really listen to lyrics. I just hear bits and pieces. Like in 'Joe the Lion' where he says 'It's Monday'. That's a real stunner.'
Q. *What about Bowie?*
ENO: He gets into a very peculiar state when he's working. He doesn't eat. It used to strike me as very paradoxical that two comparatively well-known people would be staggering home at six in the morning, and he'd break a raw egg into his mouth and that was his food for the day, virtually.

It was really slummy. We'd sit around the kitchen table at dawn feeling a bit tired and a bit fed up – me with a bowl of crummy German cereal and him with albumen from the egg running down his shirt.'
Q. *Do you have much in common in terms of approach?*
ENO: We used oblique strategies a lot. 'Sense of Doubt' was done almost entirely using the cards, and we did talk about work methods. But no, I don't think we have that much in common. But that's fine, so long as there's give and take.'

24 December 1977
'Bing Crosby Christmas Show' broadcast on ITV. Bing's reaction to their work together? 'He sings a lovely counterpoint.'

25 December 1977
Christmas for David spent with Zowie in Switzerland.

January 1978
'Bowie Now' promo LP issued in the US, featuring tracks from 'Low' and 'Heroes' (RCA DJLI–2697).

6 January 1978
'Beauty and the Beast'/'Sense of Doubt' single released by RCA, the second from the 'Heroes' album (highest chart position No. 39). Initial release with picture sleeve.

7 January 1978
Amanda Lear interviewed for the *Melody Maker* by Chris Brazier.

'With David it was great because it was a kind of symbiosis, an exchange, it wasn't just take, take, take. I introduced him to Germany, to expressionism and to Fritz Laing. I told him about Dali (one of Amanda's old friends) and he used 'Un Chien Andalou' on his tour. Before I met him I was reading Tolkien and Herman Hesse, now I read Machiavelli.'

January 1978
David and Zowie leave Switzerland for Berlin with Zowie's Scottish nanny, Marion. Angie had stayed in New York over Christmas, fuelling a row which had been growing between herself and David for some years. David, furious that she hadn't even telephoned Zowie at Christmas, was accused of 'kidnapping' by Angie, who arrived back at their Swiss home on 2 January to find the place empty. In a rage she took an overdose of sleeping pills and fell down the stairs, breaking her nose. She was admitted to the Samaritans' hospital in Vevey and discharged herself the following day.

9 January 1978
Statement issued by David in Berlin, in answer to Angie's accusations:

My wife was not aware that my son was with me. A few days before Christmas she decided she would leave Switzerland and spend the holidays with friends elsewhere. From that day to her arrival back in 2 January, she didn't phone me or the boy to say where she was.

13 January 1978
Zowie is returned to Switzerland with David's permission by Marion. David quashes rumours that he had filed for divorce. But Angie and David *had* made an agreement together and actually celebrated the split. Divorce proceedings started later, instigated by Angie.

January 1978
David, back in Berlin, begins filming his second starring film role in *Just a Gigolo*, directed by David Hemmings, who had visited David in late 1977 in Switzerland. David later admitted the real draw to the picture. 'Marlene Dietrich was dangled in front of me.'

22 January 1978
An interview made with David in 1977 broadcast in New York, an eighty-minute special featuring mainly 'Heroes' material.

February 1978
Filming of *Just a Gigolo* continues at the Cafe Wien on the Kurfurstendamm in Berlin. Press interviews are conducted in between shooting, including one for the *Melody Maker* by Michael Watts.

M.W. *You once told me, 'I'm an actor, not an intellectual,' and yet critics see you in your records rather than your emotions.*
D.B. I've decided I'm a Generalist now! I thought that just about covers all grounds. It encompasses anything I wish to do, really. I find, for instance,

I really want to paint seriously now, and not toy with it, and I am painting very seriously now, every available moment.

And I'd like to be known as a painter one day when I get up enough nerve to show them. But I want at the moment to be known as a Generalist rather than as a singer or a composer or an actor . . .

M.W. *And how about your professed knowledge of politics?*

D.B. I have absolutely no interest whatsoever. Never have had, probably never will.

M.W. *You were needling us all again?*

D.B. Very definitely, yes.

M.W. *You have no interest in the political situation in Germany for instance?*

D.B. The kind of interest one has if one lives in a foreign country. But may I live and die an artist! Through the ages, though, a lot of artists have used those very spikey little things just to get people at it.

8 February 1978
Film synopsis for *Just a Gigolo* issued by David Hemmings; at that point the film was titled simply, 'Gigolo'.

After filming, David, fired with inspiration, would spend the rest of the evening painting and working on various woodcuts. He would then take Polaroids of the paintings and mount them in a photo album, showing these only to a selected few.

18 February 1978
'Confessions of an Elitist' interview by Michael Watts, published in the *Melody Maker*.

20 February 1978
1978 world tour plans announced and included in the itinerary is the first UK tour for five years, starting in Newcastle and finishing in London.

Late February 1978
Filming of *Just a Gigolo* completed. David leaves Berlin for Kenya for a holiday before joining rehearsals in the States for his world tour.

March 1978
'David Bowie with Eugene Ormandy and The Philadelphia Orchestra/ Peter and the Wolf' LP released in the US. Initial pressings of the LP were featured in translucent green (RCA Red Seal RI–12743).

Side One: David Bowie Narrates Prokofiev's 'Peter and the Wolf' (Op. 67)
Side Two: Benjamin Britten's 'Young Person's Guide to the Orchestra'
Produced by Jay David Saks

The 1978 World Tour

The 1978 world tour was the most thorough trek around the globe David had made to date. It included dates in the US, Europe, the UK, Australia and Japan. These shows were the first since the '76 'Station to Station' tour and included mostly the new material from 'Low' and 'Heroes'. David had to increase the size of the band to maintain the sound built on those two records.

Visually, David had developed the white neon tube effect originally used in 1976, suspending the lights at the back of the stage and overhead to box in the effect more. He also brought in coloured spots again to soften the effect.

David's wardrobe was designed for him by old friend, Natasha Kornilof, who has done much work with the Ballet Rambert. David called her from America requesting some ideas. Natasha came up with the opposite of what was then happening on the London fashion scene supplying David with, amongst other things, a white sailor's outfit, very baggy trousers and shirt, covered by a snakeskin jacket and a sailor's hat.

Musically, as well as including sections of the two most recent LPs, David made the whole show more palatable by including a major slice of the '72 album, 'Ziggy Stardust'. The inclusion of this material surprised everyone but was enthusiastically greeted by the fans, many of whom had never had the chance to hear or see 'Ziggy' perform live.

A record of the tour was made, reflecting the structure of the show.

15 March 1978

Stops off from Kenya at Heathrow Airport for a day in London, prior to flying on to the States for rehearsals.

16 March 1978

Flies on to Dallas to join rehearsals.

25 March 1978

David with tour band and crew travel on to San Diego to prepare for the first show. They all spend the evening at a huge bowling alley complex, David having a bash at pool for the first time.

1978 tour band as on 'Stage' LP rundown (8 September 78).

29 March 1978

San Diego Sports Arena, the first show in the 1978 world tour.

30 March 1978
Phoenix Coliseum.
Interviewed for *Hit Parade* US magazine by Liza Robinson.

I'm incredibly happy now, because I'm not ambitious anymore. I do have a strong paternal streak. I'm a born father. I want more children, but not ego children, I'd like to adopt when my house is a little more in order. I get such enjoyment out of being with children, now they are enjoyable things. You can stuff all your punk bands, give me three children instead.

April 1978
Interviewed by Flo and Eddie for *Phonograph Record* magazine.

Radio interview broadcast on KULA.
'Midnight Special' interview with Flo and Eddie broadcast on US TV. David, dressed in a kimono, talked about 'Aladdin Sane' and the re-creation of 'Ziggy Stardust' for the '78 tour.

F.E. *Tell us about Kenya.*
D.B. I didn't know what to expect before I got there. I went there to show my son how animals really live, that they're not always behind bars, because he's seen the Berlin Zoo and things like that and that's about it. I mean, he's only six and he's only seen them in zoos. So we got there and he started looking at all the animals and found it was a real country, with real people, it wasn't just one big safari. And there were all kinds of people I've never come across before, tribes that have led an existence unchanged for seven to eight hundred years, a humbling experience.

2 April 1978
Fresco Convention Center.

3–4 April 1978
Los Angeles Forum.

5 April 1978
San Francisco, Oakland Coliseum Arena.

6 April 1978
Los Angeles Forum. Part of Flo and Eddie interview broadcast on the radio in LA.

7 April 1978
'I Got a Right'/'Sixteen' single released by Iggy Pop, coproduced by David and Iggy Pop (RCA).

9 April 1978
Houston Summit.

10 April 1978
Dallas Convention Center. The show was filmed as an early document of the tour.

11 April 1978
Baton Rouge, Louisiana State University.

13 April 1978
Nashville Municipal Auditorium.

14 April 1978
Memphis, Mid-South Coliseum.

15 April 1978
Kansas City Municipal Auditorium.

17–18 April 1978
Chicago, Arie Crown Theater.

20–21 April 1978
Detroit, Cobo Hall.

22 April 1978
Cleveland, Richfield Coliseum. After the show David and group rested in the hotel bar and listened to a local group who rather nervously acknowledged David's presence. David nodded.

24 April 1978
Milwaukee Exposition Center.

26 April 1978
Pittsburgh Civic Arena.

27 April 1978
Washington DC, Capital Center.

28–29 April 1978
Philadelphia, Spectrum Arena. Both shows recorded for the 'Stage' double live LP released later in the year. Tony Visconti then went to New York to mix the tapes (within two weeks) for quick release to thwart bootleggers who cashed in on David's 1976 tour when they put out 'The Thin White Duke' double live bootleg recorded in New York State.

1 May 1978
Toronto, Maple Leaf Gardens.

2 May 1978
Ottowa Civic Center.

3 May 1978
Montreal Forum.

5 May 1978
Providence Civic Center.

6 May 1978
Boston Gardens.

7–8 May 1978
New York, Madison Square Garden.

9 May 1978
New York, Madison Square Garden. Last show of the '78 US tour. David leaves the Regency Hotel in New York after the last show with Brian Eno to celebrate, picking up Bianca Jagger en route to attend a party at Studio 54, then onto CGB's to catch a live group. When leaving the latter on returning to the limousine they discovered the tyres slashed.

Brian Eno was asked by David if he would come on the tour, even to play on only a few numbers if necessary. Eno, establishing a policy of no live work, turned the offer down.

May 1978
Dana Gillespie, actress and musician friend of David and Angie's, interviewed for *Sounds*.

I first went to the Marquee when I was fourteen, Clapton had just emerged, The Yardbirds had just formed. About the fourth time I went, it was very romantic actually, there was this blond guy there. He was called David Jones then, and was with his band called Manish Boys. I was brushing my hair in the mirror, and he walked up to me, took the brush from my hand and started to brush my hair for me. He was the first guy I'd met who didn't meet my parents' approval. When I introduced him to my parents they visibly paled. It was their first encounter with the music business. It was definitely jailbait . . .

12 May 1978
'David Bowie and Eugene Ormandy and The Philadelphia Orchestra/ Peter and the Wolf' LP released in the UK. David's first venture into classical music was for son Joe. This story and piece of music being a favourite. David narrates on side one only, the other side featuring Benjamin Britten's 'Young Person's Guide to the Orchestra' (RCA – Red Seal).

'TV Eye' live LP released by Iggy Pop, David playing on four tracks (RCA). Early May 1978 David flies from the US to continue the '78 tour in Europe.

14 May 1978
Hamburg, Congress Centre.

16 May 1978
Berlin, Deutschland. Earlier that day David is interviewed by Alan Yentob for BBC 2's 'Arena Rock' programme.

The Berlin show was halted during 'Station to Station' when David noticed a steward manhandling a fan in the audience. David called to the steward in German to stop. When he did so the show was resumed and the whole of 'Station to Station' was played.

17 May 1978
Zurich, Switzerland.

18 May 1978
Essen, Gruga Halle, Germany.

19 May 1978
Cologne, Koln Sports Palast.

20 May 1978
Munich, Olympia Halle.

21 May 1978
Bremen. David and group record appearance on 'Musikladen Extra' at the television studios in Bremen, treating their appearance as a regular '78 concert. Last show in Germany.

22 May 1978
Vienna. After the show, David was greeted by RCA's local record company officials and attended a small party held for him.

23 May 1978
David travels to Cannes for the Film Festival. Stays up all night with film people after watching a private French-dubbed screening of *Just a Gigolo*.

24–25 May 1978
Paris, Pavillon de Paris, Porte de Pantin.

26 May 1978
Lyon, Palais des Sports.

27 May 1978
Marseilles, Parc Chaneau. Last show in France.

31 May 1978
Copenhagen, Falkoner Teatret, Denmark.

1 June 1978
Copenhagen, Falkoner Teatret.

2 June 1978
Stockholm, Kungliga Tennishallen.

4 June 1978
Gothenberg, Scandanavium.

5 June 1978
Oslo, Ekeberg Hall.

7–9 June 1978
Rotterdam, Ahoy Sports Palace.

11–12 June 1978
Brussels.

14–15 June 1978
Newcastle City Hall. David's first UK tour for five years underway.

16 June 1978
Newcastle City Hall. Interviewed for Tyne Tees 'Northern Lights' programme.

19 June 1978
Glasgow, Apollo. Interviewed for 'Reporting Scotland' TV show.

20 June 1978
Glasgow, Apollo. Interviewed earlier by Jonathan Mantle for *Vogue* (September edition).

21–22 June 1978
Glasgow, Apollo.

24–26 June 1978
Stafford, Bingley Hall.

29 June–1 July 1978
Earls Court, London.

Backstage was as crowded as ever with celebrities, including Dustin Hoffman, Bianca Jagger, Bob Geldof and Iggy, for David's London shows. Amongst the paying audience was David's mother in the royal box, Brian May and Roger Taylor from Queen, Ian Drury, David Hemmings and his clipboard – he was directing the film David was making of the Earls Court shows. Janet Street-Porter interviewed for a film on the second night. Film director Clive Donner, Melvyn Bragg and others attended.

While in London, David saw the second of Iggy's 'Music Machine' gigs in Camden Town. While backstage with Iggy ex-Pistol Johnny Rotten arrived. David and Rotten had nothing to say to each other. David later said, 'I just sat back and listened.'

During the UK tour David decided to stay in rented or borrowed flats rather than hotels. The flats were not even known to the promoter or band. The film made at Earls Court and one of the Stafford shows were to be part of David's documentary record of the tour, and one of the first Bewlay Brothers productions. The film has never been released except for two clips shown on 'The London Weekend Show'. At the end of the tour Bromley Council presented David with a bill of £38.31 for unpaid rates; a sum that had earlier been written off by the council but remembered by someone working for the borough!

The last Earls Court show marked the end of the first leg of the 1978 world tour, which was continued later in the year in Japan and Australia.

8 July 1978
'London Weekend Show' broadcast featuring concert extracts from the second Earls Court show, interview with fans, and a pre-concert interview with David by Janet Street-Porter.

4 August 1978
'Musikladen Extra' television show broadcast in Germany, recorded earlier in the summer in Bremen. The 45-minute special included: 'Sense of Doubt', 'Beauty and the Beast', 'Heroes', 'Stay', 'The Jean Genie', 'TVC 15', 'Alabama Song' and 'Rebel Rebel' as an encore.

12 August 1978
David, Iggy and friends attend the opening night of new Berlin disco, '50 36', arriving at about 5 a.m. to see the Berlin group, PVC.

September 1978
'Liza Jane'/'Louie Louie Go Home' single rereleased (Decca). This was David's first single recorded in 1964. It was unattractively packaged in a white sleeve. It created little interest.

8 September 1978
'Stage' double live LP released featuring a strangely edited account of David's 1978 tour, recorded again in Philadelphia, at the Spectrum Theater on 28 and 29 April 1978 (RCA). David seen browsing in Jubilee market in Covent Garden, looking through old photographs.

The release date for 'Stage' was delayed until 25 September. This was explained as being part of a growing argument between David and RCA over contracts. David apparently expected 'Stage' to be counted as two LPs but RCA claimed it was worth one because it was taken from a live performance.

'Stage' released 8 September 1978 (RCA PLO2913/(2)

Side One
Hang Onto Yourself (Bowie)
Ziggy Stardust (Bowie)
Five Years (Bowie)
Soul Love (Bowie)
Star (Bowie)

Side Two
Station to station (Bowie)
Fame (Bowie, Lennon, Alomar)
TVC 15 (Bowie)

Side Three
Warszawa (Bowie, Eno)
Speed of Life (Bowie)
Art Decade (Bowie)
Sense of Doubt (Bowie)
Breaking Glass (Bowie, Davis, Murray)

Side Four
Heroes (Bowie, Eno)
What in the World (Bowie)
Blackout (Bowie)
Beauty and the Beast (Bowie)

Produced by David Bowie and Tony Visconti

David Bowie (vocal)
Adrian Belew (lead guitar, backing vocals)
Carlos Alomar (rhythm guitar, backing vocals)
Simon House (electric violin)
Sean Mayes (piano, string ensemble, backing vocals)
Roger Powell (keyboards, synthesizer, backing vocals)
George Murray (bass, backing vocals)
Dennis Davis (drums, percussion)

September 1978
Vogue (UK) issue including feature and interview with David by Jonathan Mantle and photographs by Snowdon, taken in Berlin just after *Just a Gigolo* filming in February.

25 September 1978
David arrives in Paris to work on a third *Vogue* photo session, this time for Italian *Vogue* (December edition). He sported a beard especially grown for this session. While in Paris, David was interviewed on the telephone from Sydney, Australia for a radio series, 'The Golden Years of David Bowie'. This interview was broadcast on the last night of David's Sydney concerts later that year.

Q. *Is there something that you have not achieved that you wanted to?*
D.B. Swimming (laughs). You've gotta believe this, I only learnt to swim last week. I'm very proud of myself. I can do the crawl. I can only do one length. I've got very good . . . sort of lung power and can hold my breath

184

'cos I can't breathe yet. So I can't . . . I can't come back (laughs). When I get to the other end I'm stuck 'cos I'm out of breath.

But I like snorkeling a lot, so I really want to learn to swim. So I learnt to crawl and as long as I've got a snorkle in my mouth, I'll go round anywhere, any distance. I'm pretty foolhardy about water, that's why I love ships and I love sailing.'

October 1978
The world premiere of *Just a Gigolo* cancelled in Germany for one month because of difficulties in the translation from English to German. The main cut of the film was drastically different to the version later seen in England.

8 October 1978
Jaques Brel, Belgian singer/songwriter/actor died in hospital aged forty-nine. David much admired Brel, covering two of his songs and meeting him once in Paris in 1973.

A press release was issued from David's office to answer rumours that he was preparing to leave RCA for another label:

In answer to the numerous rumours concerning my recording activities, I wish to clear the air and set the record straight. At present and for the foreseeable future I am under contract to RCA Records and at no time have I engaged in any negotiations to alter that status. My relationship with RCA has been a long and rewarding one and any rumours that I am signing with another label are completely false and erroneous.

With that rumour cleared, another opened, this time David to star in a Buster Keaton bio-pic. This hasn't come off but David is known to be keen about it still.

November 1978
The 'Oz Tour' – David's first tour of Australia. He arrived quietly in Australia in early November. No arrival date was given to the press. On the flight the captain announced that he was closing down one of the engines because it was spilling oil. 'Awfully decent of him to tell us,' David told a small gathering of Australian press. Large press conferences were ruled out by David who preferred to call a number of smaller meetings over the next two days. The interviews were arranged through the tour promoter. David described how he felt about the Australian tour. 'I'm looking forward to it. It's a long way to go and there have been times in the past when I considered it. But now we're about to start, I'm very happy.'

11 November 1978
Adelaide. The first of six Australian shows.

14 November 1978
Perth. Interviewed for 'Countdown', an Australian TV programme. The interviewer seemed more interested in David's sex life than anything else.

David's regular keyboardman for the '78 tour, Roger Powell, was not available for the latter part of the tour, so his place was taken by Australian, Denis Garcia. The rest of the tour band was the same as for the US and European shows.

16 November 1978
The world premiere of *Just a Gigolo* (*Schoner Gigolo – Armer Gigolo*) at the Gloria Palast, Kurfürstendamm, Berlin. The show was attended by most of the cast of the film (except David). It was badly received in the press and David Hemmings immediately started work on a new edit. It was taken off the German circuit before being seen by the public. Film recut by Hemmings in London.

17 November 1978
'Breaking Glass'/'Art Decade', 'Ziggy Stardust' single released by RCA, David's second live single. Some initial pressings were on coloured vinyl and came in a picture sleeve (highest chart position No. 54).

18 November 1978
Melbourne Cricket Ground. The show was billed, 'Come Rain Or Shine' – it poured! But a capacity audience of twenty thousand made the most of the visit. The *National Times* said, 'The light show, like the artist when illuminated, was an example of true excellence.'

21 November 1978
Brisbane. David, as usual while on tour, caused controversy. A Brisbane newspaper reported:

David Bowie today (22 November 78) received some noisy feedback from Queensland's minister in charge of noise, Mr Russ Hinze, following the pop star's open-air concert last night. 'These pop singers come out here to make a quick quid by disturbing our peace and tranquillity,' Mr Hinze said. 'The fact that he's a pommie as well wouldn't help.' Mr Hinze, who is the minister for local government, said the newly-formed noise abatement authority will investigate complaints that last night's Bowie concert at Lang Park, Brisbane, disturbed the peace.

It was reported that the noise was loud enough to be heard 6 km away. Residents of the suburbs of Paddington, Bardon and Milton described it as 'intolerable'.

It is estimated that 40,000 kg of equipment will accompany the thirty-one-year-old cult hero, including an intricate system of fluorescent lights. A fleet of seven semi-trailers will be used to transport the equipment around Australia.

To capitalize on the excitement *The Man Who Fell to Earth* was rereleased on the Australian circuit.

24 November 1978
Sydney Show Ground.

25 November 1978
Sydney Show Ground. The last of David's sell-out Australian shows. Support group for all Australian concerts was The Angels. This was the first time for over five years David had had a support act.

The piano used on tour, a Bechstein, was originally wood grain coloured. It was painted black for studio work, blue for a TV special, black for private use, white for Rod Stewart's 1977 tour of Australia, and black again for David!

Tickets for the Sydney concerts cost $12.50 (approximately £8.00). While in Sydney, David was awarded a plaque for 'Outstanding sales' by the Australian office of RCA. It was later given to a charity.

28 November 1978
Last appearance in Australia on TV. Interviewed on a current affairs programme by Mike Willisee.

Early December 1978
Australian rock magazine *Juke* article published:

Rumours . . . that bizarre rocker David Bowie was paid for his Australian tour in gold to avoid customs and taxation, and made it into jewellery . . . Rumours have been established as false, a spokesman for the tour said . . . 'If he'd been paid in gold he would have lugged around a nugget as big as a bumper bar.'

David left Australia as quietly as he had arrived, travelling on to Japan to finish his tour.

Early December 1978
David arrives in Japan.

6 December 1978
Osaka, Koseinenkin Kaikan. David's first Japanese show of the '78 tour.

7 December 1978
Osaka, Koseinenkin Kaikan.

During the tour, David appeared on a number of radio and TV shows. Interviews on either TV or radio in Japan tend to be slow and very uninformative because of translation problems.

Q. *You have a son and his name is Zowie?*
D.B. One of his names.
Q. *Is there a meaning to Zowie?*
D.B. No.
Q. *And how old is he?*
D.B. Seven-and-a-half.
Q. *Does he look like you?*
D.B. Yes.
Q. *Which bit?*
D.B. Um, not the eyes (laughs). He's blond and very lively. He's not interested in music at all.
Q. *He's not going to take after you?*
D.B. No, he likes mathematics (laughs).
Q. *Weren't you very smart when you were a boy?*
D.B. No, I used to fall over a lot!

9 December 1978
Osaka, Banpaku Hall.

11 December 1978
Tokyo, NHK Hall. The 'Young Music Show' recorded for television. When broadcast the show was condensed to one hour.

12 December 1978
Tokyo, NHK Hall. David's last show in Japan, and the end of his world tour.

December 1978
Just a Gigolo premiered in Japan. The official party took place at the Roppongi disco. David attended dressed in a recently-tailored silk suit with lady friend, Dewi Sukarno.

David spoke of his work at that time: 'I think, without being pompous, that my way of working is as important as method. Style is only a superficial juxtaposition of things as they are, arranged against each other to offset their individual qualities and meanings.'

25 December 1978
David spends Christmas in Tokyo.

January 1979
Takes a short break with Zowie, mostly in Kyoto.

Early February 1979
Returns to London to promote *Just a Gigolo*, making various radio and TV interviews.

2 February 1979
'Musikladen Extra' repeated in Germany. The same broadcast as August 1978 (DR).

9 February 1979
Attends an early Human League concert at Nashville, Tennessee. After the show goes backstage to meet the group. David was particularly interested in the simultaneous slide show provided by Adrian Wright. He later said of the show, 'They were great. It was like watching 1980!'

12 February 1979
'Afternoon Plus', ITV interview made by Mavis Nicholson, mainly to promote *Just a Gigolo* and to generally talk about his career.

M.V. *You played the role of an alien in the film* The Man Who Fell to Earth, *and that was a man who was in his own void in a way . . .*
D.B. Yes, yes, very much.
M.V. *Do you feel that yourself?*
D.B. Thematically I've always dealt with isolation in everything I've written, I think. So it's something that triggers me off if it always interests me in a new project.
M.V. *Do you feel isolated though?*
D.B. Not really, but I can quite imagine how it must feel to be isolated so I have often put myself in circumstances and positions where I am isolated just so that I can write about them.

Later David appeared on 'Thames at Six' for another short interview, this time with Rita Carter.

A third television interview was conducted by Valerie Singleton for 'Tonight' (BBC I):

v.s. *There is this tremendous tendency to think of rock stars or pop stars as being a bit thick and obviously there's a lot more to you than that. Did it worry you that people had that kind of image?*

D.B. No, I'm very thick.

v.s. *Are you?*

D.B. Yes, I became a rock star . . . I could have been a painter.

v.s. *Why? As a need to get something out of your system?*

D.B. No, no, I wanted to be some kind of artist. I wanted to prove myself in some field as an artist and I didn't think I was a very good painter, so I went to music.

13 February 1979

The afternoon was spent with Jean Rook in a specially hired suite at the Dorchester. The *Daily Express* journalist once again captured the exclusive.

J.R. *How will David Bowie face up to his unmasked, lined face at fifty?*

D.B. I shall welcome it, yes. An ageing rock star doesn't have to opt out of life. When I'm fifty, I'll prove it.

J.R. *How did you drag yourself free from the deeper, more dangerous hooks which finally tore apart Moon and Vicious?*

D.B. I don't really know what happened to them, their deaths were terrible. If I knew that, I'd be one of them. I nearly was, I realized just in time that I was destroying myself. I loathed the pop scene, I never wanted to be a pop star. I was David Jones from Brixton who wanted to do something artistically worthwhile. But I hadn't the courage to face the audience as myself. It takes tremendous courage to face up to the adulation, the pressure, without cracking. That's why some of us crack.

Later that day he was interviewed for Capital Radio's 'Your Mother Wouldn't Like It' by Nicky Horne. The programme included a phone-in and David's favourite records. David arrived at Capital's Euston Tower through the front door, having to run the gauntlet of about seventy fans. The five assigned policemen and three bodyguards were lost in the tussle of trying to get David safely inside. Nicky Horne's opening remark to David: 'Welcome David, glad to see you've got in without losing too much hair!'

The interview was scattered with songs chosen by David and included 'Baby's on Fire' by Brian Eno, 'Shapes of Things' by The Yardbirds, 'The Batman Theme' by Link Wray, 'China Girl' by Iggy and 'White Light–White Heat' by The Velvet Underground.

N.H. *Now with the benefit of hindsight, do you think actually being with Lindsay Kemp and around him at that time, that you actually gained a lot of what you are today?*

D.B. Oh God, an extraordinary amount. As you probably have gathered over the past few years, I'm pretty eclectic, and I borrow and steal everything that fascinates me. I'm sort of a jackdaw, or is it a magpie? I can never remember. And Lindsay introduced me to things like Cocteau and the Theatre of the Absurd and Antonin Ateau and the whole idea of restructuring and going against what people generally expect. Sometimes for the shock value, sometimes as an educational force. He just gave me the idea that you could experiment with the arts and do things and take risks that you wouldn't do in real life. And so you can use it as a kind of experimental area for trying out new life styles without having to take the consequences.

N.H. *But you've always taken those chances in real life . . .*

D.B. Yes, when I started with the character, I would put myself through terrible experiences and terrible positions to write about what I thought they would feel. Until I really cottoned on to the idea, mainly through Brian Eno, who put it more into focus for me, that you could do all the experimentation in the creating of the music and not actually have to put your body through the same kind of risks.

14 February 1979

Fifteen-minute press conference held at the Cafe Royal, Regent Street. David's arrival at the midday meeting was preceded in the foyer by a short photo session with Sydne Rome, the two supplying the national press with a Valentine's Day kiss.

The conference was dull; too many questions and not enough time.

Q. *You've started a book of short stories.*

D.B. But the stories won't be published or sold. They're strictly for me to see if I'm any good at it.

Q. *Has Isherwood had as much influence on your writing as he did on your going to Berlin?*

D.B. Initially yes, but then I suppose I moved back to Burroughs.

In the evening, *Just a Gigolo* was premiered at the Prince Charles cinema, Leicester Square. For the guests attending both the reception and the premiere, twenties-style dress (or black tie) was compulsory. David and his date for the evening, actress Viv Lynn, however, wore kimonos. David's was blue, worn with black baggy trousers and wooden clogs.

21 February 1979

'Just a Gigolo' LP released, the soundtrack from the film. David's only contribution to the record was 'David Bowie's Revolutionary Song', performed by The Rebels with David humming at the beginning (Jambo).

'David Bowie's Revolutionary Song'/'Charmaine' single released in Japan, A-side written by David who also sang on it (Overseas Records).

'Just a Gigolo' released 21 February 1979 JAMBO (JAM I)

Side One
Just a Gigolo – Marlene Dietrich
  (Casucci, Caesar)
Salome – The Pasadena Roof
  Orchestra (Stolz)
Johnny – The Manhattan Transfer
  (Hollander, Fishman)
The Streets of Berlin – The Gunther
  Fischer Orchestra (Fischer)
Charmaine – The Pasadena Roof
  Orchestra (Pollock, Rapee)
Don't Let It Be Too Long – Sydne
  Rome (Fischer, Hemmings)
Ragtime Dance – The Ragtimers
  (Joplin, Masters)
Jealous Eyes – The Manhattan
  Transfer (Erdelyi, Fishman)

Side Two
David Bowie's Revolutionary Song –
  The Rebels (Bowie, Fishman)*
Easy Winners – The Ragtimers
  (Joplin, Masters)
I Kiss Your Hand, Madame – The
  Manhattan Transfer (Erwin,
  Rotter, Lewis, Young)
Kissing Time – The Gunther Fischer
  Quintet (Herbert, Gunther,
  Absalom)
Black Bottom – The Pasadena Roof
  Orchestra – (DeSylva, Brown,
  Henderson)
Jealous Eyes – The Barnabas
  Orchestra (Erdelyi, Fishman)
Just a Gigolo – Village People
  (Casucci, Caesar)
I Ain't Got Nobody – Village People
  (Williams, Graham)

Produced by Tim Hauser and Jaques Morali

Arranged by John Altman and Frank Barber

Original Soundtrack recording supervision by Jack Fishman

*Features David Bowie (vocal refrain, guitar)

March 1979

David meets Tony Visconti to complete the mix on the next LP 'Lodger' at Record Plant studios in New York. David made the most of his visit to the city, stopping off with David Byrne of Talking Heads for a night at Hurrahs.

Later in the week, David attended the Steve Reich/Phillip Glass show billed as 'The First Concert of the Eighties' with John Cale. During the performance David and Cale joined in for one number, Cale's 'Sabotage'. David (dressed in a black kimono) scratched away on a viola, the first time he had played one.

David later said, 'My mum would have been proud of me!' He also attended the Roxy Music show in New York, talking backstage with Bryan Ferry.

2 March 1979

'I Pity the Fool', 'Take My Tip'/'You've Got a Habit of Leaving', 'Baby

Loves That Way' EP released, made up of two old Parlophone singles. The A-side being old Manish Boys recordings, the B-side recorded by Davy Jones and The Lower Third in 1965 (EMI NUT EP). Initial release in picture sleeve.

3 March 1979
David, Debbie Harry and Chris Stein spend the evening at Hurrahs and go on to Mudds for a Ramones post-concert party.

7 April 1979
Attends the Siouxsie and The Banshees concert at the Rainbow, mainly to see the support group, The Human League.

10 April 1979
David, back in London for some early promotion for 'Lodger', attends a Lou Reed show, spending the end of the evening with Reed at the Chelsea Rendezvous. A friendly evening ends in uproar when Reed turned on David and started hitting him about the head. The shouting soon died down, but when it seemed that the quarrel was over, it was sparked off again, Reed again shouting at and hitting David. The event was witnessed and reported in the *Melody Maker* (21 April) by Alan Jones, who pushed his luck a little when he asked David what had upset Reed. David, upset and shaken, gave Jones short shrift. David finally left the restaurant alone, leaving a trail of broken potted plants and shrubs on the way (he later paid for all the damage). The affair has never been fully explained. Both parties have remained friends despite it.

17 April 1979
Evening spent at an Indian restaurant with Bette Midler.

18 April 1979
'Conversations with Bowie' Capital Radio special recorded at Tony Visconti's Good Earth studios in Soho.

Twelve Capital listeners (six boys and six girls) chosen by David after a special competition to find the best descriptive written piece about 'Bowie the Traveller'. The twelve were picked from thousands who bombarded the foyer in the hope of meeting the main man.

For the recording the twelve fans were met by David at the studio, who, on their arrival, said, 'Hello, how lovely to meet you. Do please grab some food and something to drink.' They had smoked salmon, prawns, spareribs and champagne laid on by David.

193

The show was broadcast on 14 May 1979. After the show David saw old manager and friend, Ken Pitt.

Bowie the Traveller. A winning entry by Alison.

Who am I?
Am I a light source without a switch? What are the cracked
images reflected in the bathroom mirror . . .
I was a De Kneig stylized facade, and then, like a space
permutating Pompidou centre I landed amongst the homogenous
coloured jungle of an old city.
I was the plastic edifice in a set of a movie I never wanted
to see. Now the bleak austerity of a weeping wall.
Why do the soulless duple clones cling to me? And the
colour supplement contributing pseudo wait on my command?
What is my life?
My portrait is of an empty room, a broken lipstick, a nomad
in a journey of time, the last cigarette.
The artist haunted with time.

19 April 1979
Evening spent with friends at the Café Un Deux Trois in London.

A little recording David made while in London was used on a friend's telephone answering machine: 'Hi, I'm David Bowie and I'm here with three Beatles and Eric Clapton, why not pop around . . .?

23 April 1979
David featured on 'The Kenny Everett Video Show' singing 'Boys Keep Swinging'. At the end of the song Kenny Everett as one of his characters, 'Angry of Mayfair', chased David around the rooftop set shouting, 'I fought for men like you in the war . . . and I never got one!'

27 April 1979
'Boys Keep Swinging'/'Fantastic Voyage' single released by RCA, a taster from the forthcoming LP – (highest chart position No. 7). Initial release in picture sleeve.

April 1979
A contemporary of David's, ex-Genesis vocalist Peter Gabriel interviewed for the *NME*.

There are various areas which Bowie and Devo have been into which I've consciously tried not to tread in because I don't want to.
  I think Bowie does things with a lot more style and fashion consciousness

194

than I do. I get the feeling that he's much more calculating. There's not too much coincidence that emanted from things labelled Bowie. With me there is still quite a large functioning of randomness, accident and mistakes.

Outside 'Exposure' (a 'Lowesque' track on the second Gabriel album), I can't really see we've got too much in common musically.

I like Bowie a lot. Any artiste who's prepared to sacrifice what he is, for what he might be . . .

Q. *Which is what you've done . . .*

That's what I intend to do, and I think that's a prerequisite for doing anything else. You must let go of what you've got 'cause if you try and clutch on to something which you think is yours it withers and dies.

May 1979

David travels to Rockfield recording studios in Wales to add some backing vocals to an Iggy Pop track (written by David) called 'Play It Safe', later featured on the LP Iggy was preparing then called 'Soldier'.

12 May 1979

David records a two-hour spot on Radio I's 'Star Special' (broadcast on 20 May).

After the taping, David interviewed by Stuart Grundy for Radio I's Saturday afternoon 'Rock On' show, discussion in the interview being mainly about 'Lodger' and three tracks from it, 'Fantastic Voyage', 'Boys Keep Swinging' and 'Yassassin'.

14 May 1979

'Bowie the Traveller/Conversation with Bowie' Capital Radio broadcast. David played each track from 'Lodger', talking about that track and the production. The first hour of the programme was used for a question session.

David opened the show. 'What I really wanted to do, I thought was, I'm going to do this a lot more in the future because when I talk to press people I don't get the same kind of questions that I get from people who come and see the shows and buy the albums and things. So I thought that publicly it might be better if I get a reaction from people who are actually involved in what I'm doing more than earning their money from being reviewers or critics . . . and I'll probably get more evil questions!'

Q. *When are you going to start directing films?*

D.B. Oh, I do every night, I've directed so many films, but in reality I think I'll give it . . . I've had two pieces of advice, one from a very good friend who said that I should plunge into it immediately, and go for a full-scale

195

thing. Another person who I also admire very much said it would just be a waste of time and I shouldn't bother. So I've got two attitudes there. Every time I finish an album I think 'Oh God I can't stand this anymore, I've got absolutely nothing to contribute, it's no good, all hell has broken loose in my mind, you know completely . . . illogical about the whole thing, I just curl up and die for a couple of weeks after making it. I don't know, it's always been like that with me, not one album that I've made that I've walked happily away from and gone about my business. None of it's pleasure anymore, it started off not as pleasure and it's now still not pleasure.

Q. *Why do you do it then?*

D.B. I've got to do it.

17 May 1979

Rolling Stone feature: 'The place: a Burger King on Eighth Avenue, New York. Elvis Costello occupies one corner of the small restaurant with Bebe Buell while David Bowie and his date occupy another. The two English stars leave each other alone . . .'

18 May 1979

'Lodger' LP released, the completion of the trilogy devised with Brian Eno over a two-year period (RCA). Early working titles were 'Despite Straight Lines' and 'Planned Accidents'.

Three videos were prepared in London to promote 'Lodger' and were of 'Boys Keep Swinging', 'Look Back in Anger' and 'D.J.'. David made some outside shots in Earls Court, wandering down a street. A trail of interested fans gathered. Most just wanted to kiss him.

'Lodger' album released 18 May 1979 (RCA BOW LP.I)

Side One	*Side Two*
Fantastic Voyage (Bowie, Eno)	D.J. (Bowie, Eno, Alomar)
African Night Flight (Bowie, Eno)	Look Back in Anger (Bowie, Eno)
Move On (Bowie)	Boys Keep Swinging (Bowie, Eno)
Yassassin (Bowie)	Repetition (Bowie)
Red Sails (Bowie, Eno)	Red Money (Bowie, Alomar)

Produced by David Bowie and Tony Visconti

David Bowie (vocals, piano, synthesizer, Chamberlain, guitar)
Adrian Belew (guitar, mandolin, rhythm guitar)
Carlos Alomar (guitar, rhythm guitar, drums, vocals)
Brian Eno (ambient drone, prepared piano, cricket manace, synthesizers, guitar treatments, horse trumpets, eroica horns, piano)
George Murray (bass, vocals)
Dennis Davis (drums, percussion, bass, vocals)

Sean Mayes (piano)
Roger Powell (synthesizers)
Simon House (violin, mandolins)
Tony Visconti (bass, mandolins, rhythm guitar, vocals)
Stan (saxophone)

'Lodger' – 'I'm so pleased that the conclusion of these three albums has been so up. You never know until you come out of the studio exactly what you've done, and I think it would have been terribly depressing if the third one had been down. At least this one has a kind of optimism.'

20 May 1979

'Star Special' broadcast on BBC Radio I featuring David playing a selection of his favourite records. He managed to squeeze in twenty-seven songs, explaining his choice between tracks.

'Love Street' by The Doors.
  'Lovely, I remembered seeing him [Jim Morrison], at the Roundhouse, one of their early shows there.'
'TV Eye' by Iggy Pop.
  'That brings back fond memories of the tour playing piano with him.'
'Remember' by John Lennon.
  'Rivetingly depressing, lovely piano, I think it's Billy Preston.'
'96 Tears' by Question Mark and The Mysterions.
  'Growing up and being angry, that's what this one is all about.'
'A Wagon–The Nursery Suite' by Edward Elgar.
  'This is a punk thing that I was incredibly impressed with when I first heard it. It's classical music but it's very good.'
'Inchworm' by Danny Kaye.
  'I thought that this was an extraordinary thing to use numbers as backing vocals.'
'Trial Prison' by Phillip Glass.
  'Now a modern use of number – Phillip Glass from an opera that he wrote which was about fifteen-and-a-half years long, from the LP 'Einstein on the Beach' .'
'Sweet Jane' by The Velvet Underground.
  'The first single that I heard when I first went to America, on the first day that I got there and in New York. I was taken over to a writer's apartment somewhere, probably on 8th Avenue, and he played me a new album that had just come out and he was very excited about this track and so was I . . .
'Helen Forsdite'
  'From the sublime to the ridiculous, from a compilation LP by Brian Eno of New York bands. The voice reminds me of 'Min' from the Goon Show!
'He's a Star' by Little Richard.

'This is quite absurd as well. I couldn't believe this when I first heard it, how he changed his voice so much I'll never know.'
'21st-Century Schizoid Man' by King Crimson.
'One from young Robert Fripp. If you sort of fancy yourself as a schizophrenic, this becomes your theme song, I used to love this.'
'Warning Sign' by Talking Heads.
'Here's a band that I admire very much. This song took me back to the old days of The Yardbirds, I don't know why.'
'Beck's Bollero' by Jeff Beck.
'I think they must have done this in about four-and-a-half minutes, it really sounds as if it's been thrown together but like all classics, it still shoots out of the speakers.'
'Try Some, Buy Some' by Ronnie Spector.
'Here's a song that made me fall in love with the singer. Absolutely incredible. My heart went straight out to her.'
'20th-Century Boy' by Marc Bolan.
'Here's a guy that probably did as much for the early seventies sound in England as Spector did to the sound in America. He single-handedly changed a lot, sound-wise, of what was happening in England, it's my old buddy, Marc Bolan.'
'Where Were You' by The Mekons.
'Here are some guys who are following, I suppose, in some of the tradition laid down by Marc Bolan . . .'
'Big City Cat' by Steve Forbert.
'Here's a singer, well he's new to me anyway, his name's Steve Forbert. I like it particularly because one of my old band is on it, Dave Sanborn playing saxophone.'
'We Love You' by The Rolling Stones.
'I'm running out of things to play you. This is called 'We Love You', and I'm sure they mean it!'
'2 HB' by Roxy Music.
'This is a very deserving band. This song is very good if you like Humphrey Bogart, it's called '2 HB', a very good pun.'
'Saint in the City' by Bruce Springsteen.
'Here's a great writer, I don't like very much what he is doing now. After I heard this track, I never rode the subway again.'
'Fingertips' by Stevie Wonder.
'Here's one that also scared me because it was so incredibly adventurous when it was released.'
'Rip Her to Shreds' by Blondie.
'Let's bring back the good weather again. Let's leave it to Blondie . . .'
'Beautiful Loser' by Bob Seger.
'Now, I'm not sure about this one, I think it's quite nice. I only played it because it's got the word lodger in it and that's the name of my new album.
'Talking about my new album, this is a track from it called 'Boys'.'
'Boys Keep Swinging'.

198

'Now that song really does have a problem!'
'Yassassin'.
'Here's a song that I started to write in Berlin and ended up in New York. It's got a sort of Turkish quality to it, it's one of my favourite tracks on the album. "Yassassin" means "long life" in Turkish, I didn't know that, I read it on a wall . . .'
'The Books I Read' by Talking Heads.
'They're different from me, they actually go and read books, they don't read walls . . .'
'For Your Pleasure' by Roxy Music.
'I think the Ta Ra at the end is a wonderful gesture . . .. I saw them in concert the other week in New York, very good . . .'
'Something on Your Mind' by King Curtis.
'This is um . . . this is a mess, not really!'
'Lies' by The Staple Singers.
'Here are three girls that have a very musical dad and one of the girls is very sexy and I keep playing her records over and over again when I'm on my own.'

'I'm afraid I can't find any more records to play. I brought three of my records along myself you know, I knew they wouldn't have them here, it's not their fault, the shops were closed.

'I brought The Mekons, "Where Were You", Phillip Glass, "Einstein on the Beach", that's mine as well and the "No New York" album.

'I'm going out to write my name on a wall now . . . OK, Ta ra.'

27 May 1979
David, back in New York, promotes 'Lodger'. Interviewed by John Avoge for WPIX, New York.

David and Joey Ramone seen at The Clash's New York Palladium concert, David left after only twenty minutes.

Other visits included Talking Heads' Greek Theater concert, a night at Madame Wong's, and a night at Hurrahs where he spurned an introduction to Joe Jackson. Another evening was in the company of David Byrne of Talking Heads at CBGB's to see a set by Nico.

June 1979
While in New York David compounds his friendship with Oona Chaplin, whom he originally met in Switzerland. This month, a charity auction was held at Sotheby's for 'Save The Children' inspired by David originally, because of a gift sent to David by Charles of the Ritz. David had received a beautiful selection of make-up from Charles of the Ritz. By way of thanks, David sent a 'Lipogram', a piece of card with his lip-print on it with the inscription, 'The lips part like

silence set for alarm – Bo. '79'. The auction also contained 'Lipograms' from many other notables, including Bette Davis, Jack Nicholson, Audrey Hepburn, Candice Bergen, James Hunt, Peter Ustinov and many more.

29 June 1979

'D.J.'/'Repetition' single released by RCA, the second single released from 'Lodger' (highest chart position No. 29). Some initial pressings were available in green vinyl and in picture sleeves. 'D.J.'/'Fantastic Voyage' single released in the US (RCA).

5 July 1979

Interviewed by Dave Herman on New York radio.

D.H. *Of course, you and Eno have worked together on many projects by now . . .*

D.B. Two or three years, something like that.

D.H. *There probably comes a time when two people who create so much, kind of, it's like two people living together, you kind of instinctually know what the other one is thinking and there is . . .*

D.B. Fortunately, that doesn't happen with Brian and I. We're still very surprised by each other, because we don't spend very much time together when we're not in the studio, and he travels as much as I do. So, he's been to Malaysia and I've been over there, and when we come back we've slightly changed our opinions about music and what we should be doing. So again, we've gone out of synch with each other, which is great for writing . . .

D.H. *Does that make for tense times in the studio?*

D.B. Smashing, yes!

D.H. *Anyone in particular comes to mind?*

D.B. Um . . . not really. I think we treat the whole thing as gentlemen, so it doesn't . . . we don't really get frayed tempers, but artistic temper sort of shows. I think the way we solve it is that one or the other will leave the studio for a couple of hours and let the other get on with it . . . follow everything through. We never throw an idea out of hand immediately without trying it out.

20 August 1979

'Look Back in Anger'/'Repetition' single released in the US (RCA).

20 August 1979

The British Phonographic Industry Ltd (BPI) make a series of carefully coordinated raids to retrieve bootleg pressings of 'The Wembley Wizard Touches the Dial', an illegal recording of one of David's May '76 Empire Pool concerts. The specially marked pressings were originally made by the BPI to trap the bootleggers. The raids on bootleg distributors which involved forty investigators is reputed to have cost about £50,000.

31 August 1979
D. A. Pennebaker's film of David's retirement concert from 1973, 'Bowie '73', premiered at the Edinburgh Film Festival. The soundtrack for the film was still poor and was later withheld by Pennebaker from general release. The film was well received at Edinburgh.

18 September 1979
A brief stop in London for video preparation of 'Alabama Song' and the revised acoustic version of 'Space Oddity'. While in London, David invites Bob Geldof to Blitz in Covent Garden. The conversation was reported for *Record Mirror* by Geldof's girlfriend Paula Yates. They spoke of Gary Numan.

'I've seen a few of Numan's videos,' said Bowie. 'To be honest, I never meant for cloning to be a part of the eighties. He's not only copied me, he's clever and he's got all my influences in too. I guess it's best of luck to him.'

Someone managed to press his way past to the table. 'Oy David, was you on speed when you made "Ziggy"?'

'No, I was completely straight.'

During this production David also recorded a mimed version of 'Space Oddity', (the '69 version) for 'American Bandstand' man Dick Clark's end of the year special.

November 1979
'John I'm Only Dancing (Again)'/'Golden Years' single released by RCA in the US (12–inch single).

'John I'm Only Dancing (1972)'/'Joe the Lion' released by RCA in the US simultaneously with its 1975 counterpart (7–inch single).

Another safari holiday in Kenya.

1 December 1979
Appeared on 'Molly's Column' an Australian TV show.

David flew back to London to do an interview for the 'Countdown' – end of the decade special, and there hangs a tale.

He insisted that the interview be conducted in London's Kew Gardens and getting in there is like trying to get an exclusive with the Queen on the lawns of Buckingham Palace.

We managed it though, after telling the attendants that we were filming a special on beautiful English gardens! Just a small white lie you might

201

say! David, by the way, posed as an expert on plants as we paid our penny to get in the gate.

Early December 1979
Filming for Kenny Everett's New Year's Eve show with David Mallet in Brixton. A remixed 'Panic in Detroit' was to be featured in the show, and the filming was to be near David's birthplace in Stansfield Road. This track was eventually substituted for a quickly prepared 'Space Oddity', the video being a spectacular update for Major Tom, the scene and idea prefacing the 'Ashes to Ashes' video released in the New Year.

7 December 1979
'John I'm Only Dancing (Again) (1975)'/'John I'm Only Dancing (1972)' single released by RCA (highest chart position No. 12). The A-side being one of the unreleased songs from the 'Young Americans' sessions. Initial release in picture sleeve and also 12–inch form.

Mid-December 1979
David travels to New York.

15 December 1979
'Saturday Night Live' appearance recorded for broadcast on 5 January 1980.

16 December 1979
'Good Afternoon' chat show interview recorded by Flo and Eddie. While in New York, David saw the Broadway production of *The Elephant Man*, unaware that the part was to be offered to him in a couple of months. David was also introduced to the play's director, Jack Hofsiss, by mutual friend Robert Boykin, co-owner of New York Hurrahs club.

25 December 1979
Christmas in New York with Zowie.

31 December 1979
Kenny Everett's New Year's Eve show broadcast featuring David's new video and the new acoustic version of 'Space Oddity'. Australian 'Countdown' interview broadcast with David on an 'End of the Decade Special'.

David also featured on 'Dick Clark's Salute to the Seventies' New Year's Eve show in a mimed video presentation of the 1969 version of 'Space Oddity' filmed in London earlier that year David was dressed as on the poster issued with 'The Alabama Song'.

1 January 1980
New Year's celebrations spent with Mick Jagger, Jerry Hall and friends at Jagger's manager's apartment near Central Park. *Melody Maker* special on the eighties published and included a short message from David about his thoughts on the new decade.

David Bowie:
All clear 1980
Personal – eyes only
Tragedy Converted
Into comedy
Indifference
Complete lack of
Task
To be 67 by 1990
To win a revolution
By ignoring everything
Else out of existence
To own personal copy of 'Eraserhead'.

January 1980
Uncut version of *The Man Who Fell to Earth* put on general release in the US, previous release having twenty minutes censored from the UK version.

5 January 1980
'Saturday Night Live' broadcast in New York including three songs from David, 'The Man Who Sold the World' which David performed encased in a solid mould body, having to be carried up to the microphone, only his arms and head being mobile.

'TVC 15' which was performed in a dress with a toy poodle at his feet with a television screen in it's mouth!

For the last number, 'Boys Keep Swinging', David adopted a puppet's body courtesy of a clever split-screen technique. A light-hearted performance for the new decade.

The show, which was recorded in December, had featured David's specially-prepared group, Blondie's Jimmy Destri and German singer/performer, Klaus Nomi.

January 1980
'1980 All Clear' promo only LP issued featuring ten tracks from as many LPs, an RCA round-up of collected works to date (RCA DJL.I–3345).

While in New York David stopped by at the Irving Platz to see Iggy's last show. Also there were Tom Verlaine and most of the Patti Smith Group. After the show, David and Iggy adjourned to Hurrahs to see James Chance and The Contortions who were playing a benefit show at the club, aided by Debbie Harry and Chris Stein.
  David flies back to Switzerland with Zowie for a short skiing break.

8 February 1980
David and Angie's divorce becomes final, David gaining custody of Joe (as Zowie had wanted to become known). Angie received a settlement of £30,000.

February 1980
David returns to New York to start work on his new LP) his follow-up to the trilogy of LPs with Eno) at New York's Power Station. It was completed in London later in the year. The LP marked the return to a more conventional style of writing as Tony Visconti had witnessed. 'He actually sat down and wrote the songs for a change, for David, this is good form.'
  During production, David was approached by director, Jack Hofsiss with the offer of the part of John Merrick, the leading role in the touring version of *The Elephant Man*.
  'The 20–20 Show', a US news magazine programme, began production on a short special about David. Early LP production filmed for the show; broadcast on US TV in 1981.

15 February 1980
'Alabama Song'/'Space Oddity' single released, the A-side receiving little airplay. The B-side was a prelude of things to come in 'Ashes to Ashes' and a stark reassessment of David's first hit in 1969. With David on acoustic guitar, the skeleton crew included Steve Bolton on lead guitar and a couple of other session men. The song was recorded in London in September '79. The A-side was recorded at the Mountain studios, Montreux. The initial release of the single by RCA came with a foldout colour poster. The 'Alabama Song' was written by Bertolt Brecht and Kurt Weill for *The Threepenny Opera* (highest chart position No. 23).

16 February 1980

David talks to fans at Hurrahs nightclub in New York. He spoke of the LP under construction and also said that he had just sold his ticket for the winter Olympics, not being able to go because of recording commitments.

March 1980

'Atomic'/'Die Young Stay Pretty', 'Heroes' 12–inch single released, ('Heroes' only available on the 12–inch edition). 'Heroes' recorded live at the Hammersmith Odeon (12 January 1980) with Robert Fripp on guitar (Chrysalis).

March 1980

Having completed the main part of the recording for 'Scary Monsters' David went to Japan to make two television commercials for Crystal Jun Rock, a Saki drink exclusive to Japan marketed by the Takar Shuzo Co. Ltd. Filming, which lasted for two weeks, was centred in a temple in Kyoto. The only lines David uttered during the commercial were, 'Crystal Jun Rock in Japan'. He made only one short interview just before he left:

Q. *Why did you agree to do the commercial?*
D.B. There are three reasons. The first one being that no one has ever asked me to do it before. And the money is a very useful thing [spoken in Japanese]. And the third, I think it's very effective that my music is on television twenty times a day. I think my music isn't for radio.
Q. *So did you write the music for the commercial?*
D.B. Yes, this is the important point and the reason I agreed to do the commercial. It's a very slow one. I didn't use bass or drums so it's very different from anything I have done before. It will be included in my next album. I don't drink while I work so I didn't drink while I wrote this one, of course.

March 1980

'Crystal Japan'/'Alabama Song' single released in Japan, the A-side taken from David's television advert. Produced by David and Tony Visconti (RCA).

27 April 1980

Iggy Pop appears at the Metropol, Nollendorf, Berlin. During the set Iggy dedicated 'China Girl' to David who was in the audience saying, 'Hi Dave, wherever you are.' David later joined Iggy on stage for a couple of numbers on keyboards and then watched the rest of the show from the side of the stage.

After the performance, David joined Iggy at the Exil restaurant in Kreuzberg, a favourite place of theirs since '77. Eventually, the large party of diners broke up and David and Iggy played billiards.

On this day in Chicago, the world's first David Bowie convention was staged. Special guests included Kenneth Pitt and Cherry Vanilla.

May 1980
Final production touches made on 'Scary Monsters' in London. 'Ashes to Ashes' video shot in Hastings. Production starting at six in the morning, featuring Steve Strange and friends from Blitz.

June 1980
Earlier part of the month spent in and around London.

David visited the museum dedicated to John Merrick (the Elephant Man) at the London Hospital to see Merrick's clothes, his stick, body moulds made after his death and the card cathedral he made in the hospital. David wanted to absorb Merrick's character for the part. David was also seen celebrating with Pete Townshend (who had just finished his section of recording on 'Scream Like a Baby'), Johnny Rotten and the group, 4 Be 2s. All of them were eventually packed off by police in separate taxis after they were found wandering around Carnaby Street, apparently drunk.

Later that week, David went to the Virgin Megastore, bought The Human League, Q-Tips, The Go-Go's, Throbbing Gristle and Elvis Costello singles and LPs. He also took in a couple of gigs. At the Venue he saw The Roches, an American group of three sisters from New Jersey. Robert Fripp and Richard Thompson accompanied David to the show. He also saw Iggy's Music Machine gig, where the support act for the show was Hazel O'Connor. As usual David's London stay was discreet. No press, radio or TV interviews were conducted.

'Madman'/'Join the Girls' single released by Cuddly Toys, A-side cowritten by David and Marc Bolan in 1977 (Fresh).

July 1980
'Ashes to Ashes'/'It's No Game' single released in the US (RCA). David went to San Francisco to see a performance of *The Elephant Man* with Phillip Anglim in the role he was soon to take over. Having seen the play a couple of times and studied the script for a few months, rehearsals for the role began in early July, the part being notoriously difficult because of Merrick's physical disabilities needing to be expressed by the actor. Rehearsals went well and David's training in mime proved useful.

While in San Francisco David was spotted leaving a shop with a batch of collector's copies of the *Eagle* comic.

29 July 1980
The Elephant Man opens at the Denver Center of Performing Arts for a week's run with Bowie in the role of John Merrick. This was his first attempt at acting on stage in a conventional role. The gamble paid off. The play was a sellout from the start, in its first week grossing $186,466, making it the biggest box-office attraction in the entire thirty-eight-year history of the Denver Center of Performing Arts. David's opening night in Denver was reported in *Variety* (6 August 80):

The acting debut on the American stage of rock singer David Bowie was greeted by a standing ovation in Denver when the singer, noted for his flamboyant musical style, took on the role of physically misshapen John Merrick, the human monster with a liking for culture.

Drawing on an early mime background and the resourceful staging of his rock shows, Bowie displays the ability to project a complex character.

Playing a man too ugly to draw a freak audience, and too human to survive within a distorted body, Bowie shows a mastery of movement and of vocal projection.

Bowie takes the stage with authority to create a stirring performance. Vocally, he is both quick and sensitive. In scene after scene he builds poignantly, crying for the chance to become civilized, though he knows he will always be a freak; pleading for a home; though he knows his presence disturbs; and questioning the rules of society; though his well being depends on their acceptance. Judging from his sensitive projection of this part, Bowie has the chance to achieve legit stardom . . .

Staff and cast for the Denver engagement included Richmond Crinkley, Elizabeth McCann, Nelle Nugent's presentation of a drama in two acts by Bernard Pomerance; staged by Jack Hofsiss; setting David Jenkins; costumes Julie Weis; lighting Beverly Emmons.

Frederick Treves, Belgian Policeman	*Ken Ruta*
Carr Gomm, Conductor	*Richard Neilson*
Ross, Bishop, Walsham How, Snork	*Thomas Toner*
John Merrick	*David Bowie*
Pinhead Manager, London Policeman, Will, Lord John	*Dennis Lipscomb*
Streetwalker, Pinhead, Miss Sandwich, Princess Alexandra	*Jeannette Landis*
Mrs Kendal, Pinhead	*Concetta Tomei*
Orderly	*Thomas Apple*
Cellist	*David Heiss*

(The American National Theatre and Academy Production)

1 August 1980
'Ashes to Ashes'/'Move On' single released, with a big budget video, codirected by David with David Mallet. The single was to herald David's return as a commercial success again and gave him his second UK No. 1 (RCA).

The first 100,000 singles released featured enclosed a series of nine stamps, four different sheets in all. All the stamps were designed by David adapting an idea by American mail-art specialist, Jerry Dreva, once of the Bon Bons Hollywood glam-art group. There were also three different single covers, each depicting David showing various reactions to a silver shoe. All featured a reference to the Hollywood artist by marking Bon Bon on one of the stamps.

The single itself, helped by the clever packaging and promotion, went gold soon after release. The video of 'Ashes to Ashes' also went to No. 1 making the first place at the MIDEM festival later in the year.

August 1980
'The Continuing Story of Major Tom' 12–inch promo-only single issued in the US. 'Space Oddity' (original version segued into 'Ashes to Ashes' – edited version)/'Ashes to Ashes' (LP version) issued by RCA. 'David Bowie – RCA radio series' promo only LP issued in the US featuring the complete 'Scary Monsters' LP and 'Space Oddity' track (RCA DJLI–3829A).

3 August 1980
Last night of *The Elephant Man* in Denver.

5 August 1980
The Elephant Man opens at the Blackstone Theater, Chicago for three weeks.

During the Chicago run, David visited a Roy Orbison gig. Orbison later attended the play.

19 August 1980
'Ashes to Ashes' reaches No. 1. David telephoned in Chicago by BBC Radio I's 'Newsbeat' reporter, Andrew Turner.

A.T. *How do you feel; No. 1 after five years?*
D.B. I see that as very exciting, what can I say? I'm very surprised. God bless the English public is what I say!
A.T. *You seem at the moment to have two successful careers. Which is the most important?*

D.B. Um, they're both intoxicating. They're both thoroughly enjoyable. I find completely different elements in both of them. It's hard to say which one I prefer, in fact.

31 August 1980
Last night of *The Elephant Man* in Chicago.

1 September 1980
Rehearsals for the Broadway run of *The Elephant Man* begun with a new cast.

3 September 1980
'Good Morning America' TV interview with David broadcast live at 7.30 a.m. on breakfast televison. David in conversation about the play and the new LP, 'Scary Monsters'.

Q. *An awful lot of performers talk about how difficult it is to deal with what the public sees them as, and do you think you're alike, do you have a problem with that because you've been so many different people?*
D.B. Not really because I don't circulate in places where there's much public . . .
Q. *You're a private person?*
D.B. It's not that as much as that I prefer travelling than sticking in cities where you're sort of immersed in the rock 'n' roll circus. So I end up in Africa or Germany or Japan. Mombassa, Berlin and Kyoto are my main ports of call.
Q. *Opening night, do you get jitters, I mean, I'm wondering about the play, but even in your concerts, are you a little nervous before you go on?*
D.B. Yes. I don't like riding in on a concert in too relaxed a state.
Q. *You like to have the adrenaline flowing then?*
D.B. Yes, very much so.
Q. *How about* Elephant Man, *did you have many jitters opening night?*
D.B. Yes, I was petrified. I didn't know what was going to happen, but once I got on stage, the supporting cast were just truly wonderful. (ABC–TV)

5 September 1980
'The Tonight Show with Johnny Carson' appearance broadcast. David featured on the show singing two songs live, 'Life on Mars' and 'Ashes to Ashes'. Interviewed pre-show by Robert Hilburn (NBC).

6 September 1980
New York *Times* interview by Robert Hilburn

'I guess I'm sort of on top of the world at the moment,' the 32-year-old Englishman said, sitting in the dressing room before an appearance Friday night on "The Tonight Show with Johnny Carson".

He's in New York for just the day, a healthy looking Bowie was relaxed and open, far different from his nervous and elusive manner of the mid-1970s when his life style seemed as troubled as the often neurotic characters in his music. Waiting for the Carson taping to begin, he chatted with friends and even signed a few autographs.

To see Bowie's first performance in two years, about twenty of the rock star's fans camped in front of NBC on Thursday night to secure tickets for the Carson show. By Friday morning, about two hundred fans were there. During the show, the fans cheered so loudly at every mention of Bowie's name that Carson finally gulped: "After all this, he'd better be good."

Speaking to Hilburn, David said, 'There is discipline involved in both rock and straight theatre, but it's a different kind of discipline. The strange thing for me was to take one character and play him with an emotional chronology from beginning to end, knowing the emotional and psychological steps he was going to take in a two-hour period. In concert, I play with the characters and evoke different kinds of emotional drive anytime I wish.'

Bowie felt comfortable in the play from the start. 'I knew after the first night that I was credible,' he said. 'I felt, "Yes, I was John Merrick tonight." That made me happy and I thought, it's a continual process. It may be imperceptible to some people, but I do find something new every night.'

12 September 1980

'Scary Monsters (and Super Creeps)' LP released by RCA, recorded in New York and London earlier that year. The record was an attempt to prove an ability to record commercially satisfying material, the LP itself supplying David with three hit singles ('Up The Hill Backwards', the fourth single release from the album reaching No. 32).

The sleeve, commissioned by David, was by photographer/designer Duffy (who designed the 'Aladdin Sane' sleeve) who in turn went via the Neal Street Gallery and thus to John Painter and Edward Bell. The nature of Bell's designs rendered Duffy's photos virtually useless for the main sleeve. Duffy was none too pleased. The mainman himself was sufficiently impressed though, to commission Bell for a further portrait from the session (which was included on the cover of the 1982 Bowie calendar and entitled 'Glamour'). The make-up for the clown/Pierrot image created for the 'Scary Monster' concept was designed by specialist Richard Sharah: 'David came to me and said he wanted a Pierrot look, and he let me design from there. Most of the time I draw up some ideas and then work with the subject around those. The preparation for David's make-up took one and a half hours.'

The clown costume was designed by Natasha Kornilof, friendly with David since his days with Lindsay Kemp. She also designed the white sailor's outfit David wore on the 1978 world tour.

12 September 1980
'Scary Monsters (and Super Creeps)' LP released in the US (RCA).

Angie Bowie's *Free Spirit* book serialized in the *Sun* for a week. It was Angie's account of life with David in the good (and bad) old days.

'Scary Monsters (and Super Creeps)' album released 12 September 1980
(RCA BOW LP 2)

Side One	*Side Two*
It's No Game (No. 1) (Bowie)	Teenage Wildlife (Bowie)
(Japanese translation – Hisahi	Scream Like a Baby (Bowie)
Miura)	Kingdom Come (Verlaine)
Up the Hill Backwards (Bowie)	Because You're Young (Bowie)
Scary Monsters (and Super Creeps)	It's No Game (No. 2) (Bowie)
(Bowie)	
Ashes to Ashes (Bowie)	
Fashion (Bowie)	

Produced by David Bowie and Tony Visconti

David Bowie (vocals, keyboards)
Carlos Alomar (guitars)
George Murray (bass)
Robert Fripp (guitar)
Dennis Davis (percussion)
Chuck Hammer (guitar)
Roy Bittan (piano)
Andy Clark (synthesizer)
Pete Townshend (guitar)
Lynn Maitland/Chris Porter (vocal backing)
Michi Hirota (Voice on 'It's No Game' (No. I))
Tony Visconti (acoustic guitar, backing vocals)

13 September 1980
'The Future Isn't What It Used To Be.' An interview with David conducted in Chicago in August by Angus Mackinnon and published in the *NME*.

David, sitting in his Blackstone Theater dressing room, explained: 'The thing is, you see, that – well, the reason why I haven't given any interviews in recent years is simply because I've become, I think, very private. Also to be honest I really don't think I've got that much to say. But why don't we just start and see how it goes?'

A.M. *Did you know anything about the Elephant Man himself before you saw the play?*

D.B. Sure. A lot of those strange freak stories appealed to me in my teens and then stayed with me – everything from hairy women to people with fifteen lips. I real all that stuff avidly and, of course, I did my homework on Merrick.

A.M. *It must have been a rather unsettling experience for you. The last time you encountered audiences as closely as you do here must have been back in the Ziggy days.*

D.B. Yes, It makes one suddenly very aware of how one's body and one's facial expressions function. It's – you do feel you're being scrutinized to an unbearable extent. It's not that pleasurable, actually.

But I think that was the first thing I had to fight. After we'd finished rehearsals and opened in Denver I was furious with myself on the first night that the thing that was preoccupying me during the performance was how people were adjusting or relating to my body movements and that I hadn't been considering the character at all. It took a good week to shake that feeling off and become interested and involved onstage with Merrick.

A.M. *Jumping around a bit, I had the impression that several of the songs on 'Station to Station' were quite strongly linked lyrically to 'The Man Who Fell to Earth': 'TVC 15' and 'Word On a Wing' and 'Golden Years'.*

D.B. 'Word On a Wing' I can talk about. There were days of such psychological terror when making the Roeg film that I nearly started to approach my reborn, born again thing. It was the first time I really seriously thought about Christ and God in any depth and 'Word On a Wing' was a protection. It did come as a complete revolt against elements that I found in the film. The passion in the song was genuine. It was also around that time that I started thinking about wearing this (fingers a small silver cross hanging on his chest) again, which is now almost a leftover from that period.

I wear it, I'm not sure why I wear it now even. But at the same time I really needed this. We're getting into heavy waters . . . but yes, the song was something I needed to produce from within myself to safeguard myself against some of the situations that I felt were happening on the film set.

A.M. *But talking about* The Man Who Fell to Earth, *I got the impression that Roeg had been very dictatorial with you, that he'd very much said it was his film, that he had a very definite idea of how he wanted you to appear in it, that he didn't really care whether you had any interesting ideas about film-making or not – those ideas could be discussed off the set but if anybody was going to channel them into the film it was going to be him.*

D.B. Absolutely correct, all the way down the line. There was no – no, very little essence of myself. I think the only freedom I was given was in choosing how the character would dress. That was it. That was the only thing I could claim at all, that I chose my wardrobe and that I put in again – I had to – that Japanese influence, something that I felt had something to do with my very weak analogy between spacemen or a spaceman and what Westerners regard the orientals as: an archetype kind of concept.

212

23 September 1980
The Elephant Man opens on Broadway at the Booth Theatre to excellent notices and is insured a good run. Celebrities who turned out for the opening night included Christopher Isherwood, David Hockney, Andy Warhol, Dianna Vreeland and Oona Chaplin, the fifty-five-year-old widow of Charlie Chaplin, who flew in from Switzerland especially. Rumours of a relationship are made in the press. Mrs Chaplin told a journalist, 'I like him very, very much indeed.' They were to form a well-publicized friendship.

Cast for the Broadway engagement:

Frederick Treves, Belgian Policeman	*Donal Donnelly*
Carr Gomm, Conductor	*Richard Clarke*
Ross, Bishop Walsham How, Snork	*I. M. Hobson*
John Merrick	*David Bowie*
Pinhead Manager, London Policeman, Will, Lord John	*Jeffrey Jones*
Streetwalker, Pinhead, Miss Sandwich, Princess Alexandra	*Judith Barcroft*
Mrs Kendal, Pinhead	*Patricia Elliot*
Orderly	*Dennis Creaghan*
Cellist	*Michael Goldschlager*
Standby for John Merrick	*Benjamin Hendrickson*

Director Jack Hofsiss
Producer Richmond Crinkley

For the run of *The Elephant Man* there were regular evening performances (except for Monday) with matinee performances each Wednesday, Saturday and Sunday.

The Booth Theater, 222 W. 45th St, New York 10036.

27 September 1980
Yves Mourousi radio interview broadcast on French radio, David interviewed on the telephone from New York.

September 1980
Howard Devoto (then of *Magazine*) interview with the *NME* published.

'It's been a long time since there have been records of the quality of something like "Low" and "The Idiot" . . . They were definitely the two, and there haven't been many records released since that are going to be worth listening to years later. I think ours will last. "The Idiot", I told the group to listen to that when we formed. You can hear that especially on "Real Life" I think.'

October 1980
Just a Gigolo released on video in the UK (VCL).

Interview with David's co-star, Patricia Elliot run, in the New York press, revealing her reaction to playing with David. 'He's real dynamite. Heavens, and so good in the role. I missed David's rock music trip though I have recently bought "Scary Monsters" and what an album. I thought, I'm in the show with a household name.'

10 October 1980
'Friday Night – Saturday Morning' TV show broadcast featuring an interview with David recorded in New York's Plaza Hotel by Tim Rice. It included extracts from the play onstage at the Booth Theater.

D.B. I've had a terrific audience that have been staunchly loyal, in the main part, to what I've done and the changes that I've taken, which as you know have been quite diverse to say the least. And there have been a sort of knotty band that have stayed with me through all of that. And so I've never tried to feel self-satisfied with what I've done which has prompted me to move in different directions. But it certainly was an incredible fulfilment for me to be able to do something, so-called 'legitimate', in fact undergo that kind of discipline and find I could withstand it and work within somebody else's very strict confines.
T.R. *Are you getting people saying, 'I enjoyed your performance but I've never heard of you before'?*
D.B. That element has crept into it, yes. There have been some regular theatre-goers who've come . . . well they had heard of me but in some sort of perverse fashion or some kind of really corrupt idea of what I was about and I suppose they've got a different impression of me now . . .
T.R. *Would you like to go back on stage in due course?*
D.B. Not particularly. I've learned an awful lot just from the few weeks that I've been doing this. I hope I can explore the part even further. If I don't then I'll be wasting a lot of time. I would like to be more adventurous with the part. Whilst all this palaver has gone on about press and opening nights and whatever, now things are relaxing more I would like to stretch out into it more. There are certain avenues that I'd like to follow that I haven't had the courage to do so, yet. But now I will probably take advantage.

The interview was recorded a week earlier during a day jammed with press and TV interviews (BBC 2).

October 1980
David sees The Psychedelic Furs at TRAX club in New York. Afterwards David went backstage to meet the group and chat with The Furs lead singer, Rhett Butler, who later said, 'He just came round afterwards and said, "Hi, I'm David," and I thought, "Christ! I know who you are. I'm Richard Butler!" What was good was the simple fact that he took the trouble to come back and tell us how much he liked the show.'

23 October 1980
Interviewed in a New York Japanese restaurant by Ian Meldrum for 'Countdown' on Australian TV.

I.M. *In 196 I interviewed you at the time of 'Space Oddity'. No one would have envisaged at that stage what David Bowie was going to do in the seventies. Did you know at that stage?*
D.B. Yes, I had a good idea because at that particular time I'd already been doing mixed-media events using poetry and mime, visual shows and whatever along with rock music. That was an attempt at just being a straightforward singer/songwriter at the time.

Later in the interview Meldrum handed Bowie a platinum record of 'Scary Monsters' which in Australia had sold 250,000 copies in about three weeks of its release and was No. 1 for five weeks.

24 October 1980
'Fashion'/'Scream Like a Baby' single released by RCA. Initial release in a picture sleeve and also 12–inch (highest chart position No. 5). *Free Spirit*, Angie Bowie's account of her life with David was published by Mushroom Publishing after legal problems. David's reaction? 'The book doesn't worry me and won't worry the fans, they expect me to be outrageous anyway.'

David approached by writer/director Herman Weigel around this time with a request to appear in *Christiane F* under production in Berlin. David was impressed and agreed to appear briefly.

Back in New York, a set was made up to represent a Berlin performance from the '78 tour, David dressed like James Dean for the part which involved a version of 'Station to Station' from the 'Stage' LP. (The concert scene in the finished production was mixed with concert footage from a Berlin AC/DC concert.)

After the work was finished, David made the most of the set and assembled a group to shoot his own video production for 'Fashion', again codirecting the piece with David Mallet.

25 November 1980

The London *Times* publish an interview with David and general feature on David's Broadway run entitled 'Bowie's Achievement on the Legitimate Stage' by Patricia Barnes.

The interview was conducted near the Booth Theater, at the same Japanese restaurant as the 'Countdown' interview. David astounded the reporter by deftly addressing the waiters in fluent Japanese.

P.B. *After several weeks in New York as an actor, is it now possible to walk down the street without being set upon by innumerable fans?*
D.B. Oh yes, I have worked out a very coherent New York lifestyle and there are two ways of walking down the street – I really buy that one. You can walk down the street wanting to be recognized and you can walk down the street not wanting to be recognized. This is especially true of New York and to a certain extent, most of America. The most you get is, 'Hi Dave, how's it going?' It's a very neighbourly. They don't get as excited at meeting you as they do in London, which is still a bit star conscious. Here you see Al Pacino walking around or Joel Grey jogging. It's quite easy to do that, it's great.

30 November 1980

The *Sunday Times* magazine feature an interview with David entitled 'Bowie Holds Court', interviewed by Gordon Burn.

5 December 1980

David interviewed for Radio I by Andy Peebles, the main topic of conversation being about the recording of 'Scary Monsters' and tragically David's work with John Lennon, who died a couple of days later. (David's interview broadcast 5 January '81.)

6 December 1980

John Lennon and Yoko Ono interviewed by Andy Peebles, Lennon's last interview. (Courtesy of BBC Publications.)

A.P. *In March 1975, as we mentioned in an earlier conversation, you teamed up with David Bowie on 'Fame'?*
J.L. I was never in the London scene in the sixties; whereas George and Paul would be going round everybody's sessions all the time, you know, and playing with everybody, I never played anywhere without The Beatles. I never jammed around with people at all.
A.P. *Loyalty. Or it just didn't interest you?*
J.L. No, shyness, insecurity and I couldn't go in a session and play like George plays, you know, a limited vocabulary on the guitar and piano. So what could I do going in with Cream, or whatever they would do in those days. So we never hung out in the clubs playing, I hung out in the discos boogying and drinking and that, but I never did that bit.

Then suddenly I was working with Elton, and Bowie was around, and we were talking and that, and he'd say come down. And I found myself doing that, you know, but he's fiddling round, he writes them in the studio now; he goes in with about four words and a few guys, and starts laying down all this stuff and he has virtually nothing – he's making it up in the studio. So I just contributed, whatever I contributed which is, you know, like backwards piano and 'Ooh' and a couple of things – a repeat of 'Fame' and then we needed a middle eight. So we took some Stevie Wonder middle eight and did it backwards, you know, and we made a record out of it, right?

So he got his first number one. I felt like, that was like a Karmic thing you know Elton gave, with me and Elton I got my first number one, so I passed it on to Bowie and he got his first and I like that track.

A.P. *Yes, remarkable.*

Y.O. It's a nice track.

J.L. Yeah I love it.

A.P. *Clever man. We mentioned* Elephant Man *earlier – which we've been to see while we've been here in New York – I must say a stunning performance from Bowie, he's a very talented gentleman.*

J.L. Amazing guy isn't he?

A.P. *I mean I was quite puzzled by that, because I thought, I wonder whether David starring in a stage play like that would encourage the wrong sort of people to turn up. The screamers may come to see Bowie and to say, to hell with the intellectual element of the play, we're just here to clock him, and it wasn't like that at all actually, it was a very sympathetic audience.*

J.L. I must say I admire him for his vast repertoire of talent the guy has, you know. I was never around when the Ziggy Stardust thing came, because I'd already left England while all that was going on, so I never really knew what he was. And meeting him doesn't give you much more of a clue, you know.

A.P. *That's very true, very true.*

J.L. Because you don't know which one you're talking to. But . . . and, you know, we all have our little personality traits, so between him and me I don't know what was going down but we seemed to have some kind of communication together, and I think he's great. The fact that he could just walk into that and do that. I could never do that.

A.P. *You did 'Across the Universe' on that album . . .*

J.L. You could never go and do *Elephant Man.*

Y.O. You can . . .

J.L. She's great, she tells me I can do everything. Make a movie, you know, because you only have to learn two lines at once.

Y.O. I'm not talking specifically about *Elephant Man* . . .

J.L. I can't even remember my own lyrics, so I couldn't go on stage and remember all that.

A.P. *Do you remember doing 'Across the Universe' with Bowie? You played guitar on that.*

J.L. Did I play on that too? Oh yeah, my God, jeeze, I did too. I didn't remember that. No, I only remember the 'Fame' session.

217

7 December 1980
'Muzikzene' broadcast on German TV, including a feature on David in *The Elephant Man* (RB).

8 December 1980
John Lennon murdered in New York.

15 December 1980
'The Best of Bowie' compilation album released, a successful package of David's most commercial work. K–Tel, who had bought the package from RCA made the most of David's success with 'Scary Monsters'. Of the sixteen tracks featured the most collectable must be the elusive 'John, I'm Only Dancing' sax version which was initially included and then taken off the 'ChangesOneBowie' LP. The record was promoted with the traditional K–Tel television advertising and was the first of David's LPs to be advertised on TV since 'David Live'. The LP got to No. 2 in the album charts, thwarted by 'Double Fantasy' by John Lennon.

25 December 1980
Christmas in New York with Zowie and David's mother, the first Christmas for seven years they had spent together. Conflict between mother and son began while David was at Bromley Tech. There were often fierce rows between the two.

Mrs Jones spoke to Charles Shaar Murray in 1975 about those early troubles. 'When he was at Bromley Technical College he started getting rebellious. He seemed to resent it if I said anything to him, and it hurt me because I'm so sensitive. I used to burst into tears.

'When I lost my husband I lost my prop. I lost somebody who understood me, someone who had a lot of tolerance. He always used to say to me, "Don't worry about David love, he's going to get on and he knows what he's doing." I don't bear David any malice. I *can't* bear him any malice because I love him too much. He was such a dear little boy, so intelligent.'

'The Best of Bowie' album released 15 December 1980 (K–Tel NE.IIII)

Side One
Space Oddity (Bowie)
Life on Mars (Bowie)
Starman (Bowie)
Rock 'N' Roll Suicide (Bowie)
John, I'm Only Dancing (Bowie)
The Jean Genie (Bowie)
Breaking Glass (Bowie, Davis,
  Murray)
Sorrow (Feldman, Goldstein,
  Gottehrer)

Side Two
Diamond Dogs (Bowie)
Young Americans (Bowie)
Fame (Bowie, Lennon, Alomar)
Golden Years (Bowie)
TVC 15 (Bowie)
Sound and Vision (Bowie)
Heroes (Bowie, Eno)
Boys Keep Swinging (Bowie, Eno)

Produced by David Bowie, Gus Dudgeon, Ken Scott, Tony Visconti and Harry Maslin.

2 January 1981
'Scary Monsters (and Super Creeps)'/'Because You're Young' single released by RCA, David's third from the LP. Original release in picture sleeve and also 12–inch (highest chart position No. 20).

With the release of this single, came the release of RCA's first cassette single with the A- and B-sides featured on both sides of the tape. The single was also accompanied by a video never broadcast in the UK.

3 January 1981
David's last night as John Merrick in *The Elephant Man* in New York. A party was held in David's honour after the show. He was presented with an Elephant Man sweatshirt and also the Elephant Man cloth backdrop featured in the show by the rest of the cast.

5 January 1981
Andy Peebles interview with David broadcast on Radio I in an hour-long feature.

10 January 1981
Record Mirror readers' poll published declaring David No. 1 male singer, No. 1 best video ('Ashes to Ashes'/'Fashion'), No. 2 LP, No. 2 single ('Ashes to Ashes') and No. 3 LP sleeve design.

January 1981

'Don't Be Fooled by the Name' – 'I'm Not Losing Sleep', 'I Dig Everything', 'Can't Help Thinking About Me'/'Do Anything You Say', 'Good Morning Girl', 'And I Say to Myself' ten-inch long-play single released. A six-track rerelease of Lower Third 1966 production (PRT) (DOW I).

February 1981

David's flat rental at 152 Hauptstrasse in Berlin expires. He hadn't lived there since the filming of *Just a Gigolo* in 1978.

February 1981

'David Bowie – Plus Five' prepared and broadcast on TV in New York. The programme, sponsored by a Reeves tele-tape company for cable broadcast, was simultaneously broadcast on FM radio and featured five of David's videos, 'Boys Keep Swinging', 'Ashes to Ashes', 'D.J.', 'Fashion' and 'Look Back in Anger'.

David was interviewed for the show by German rock critic, Karen Mechlenberg.

The programme was based on these five videos and the conversation was concerned with David's use of video.

D.B. I think video is there to be used as an art form as well as a sort of commercial device for illustration and promotion. In fact, I fell in love with video in the early seventies when I got a Sony reel to reel, black-and-white thing and videoed everything and whatever. I got a small editing machine and started playing around with that and developed some scenarios for 'Diamond Dogs'. I worked with miniature sets and cut video animation techniques which I've never seen used since. A dreadful but interesting failure.

K.M. *Do you plan to work on new video projects?*

D.B. Yes. I've got several ideas for one-hour pieces, one-hour cassettes that join visuals and music, nothing more adventurous than that at the moment. I'd like to get that done first.

'David Bowie – Plus Five' (Audio Visual Room/Reeves teletape, New York)
Directed and produced by Marcel Peragine
Video/Music tapes directed by David Bowie/David Mallet
Research and development by Karen Mechlenberg
Narration by Tom Vital
(NYC–TC31)

23 February 1981

Arrived at Heathrow from New York for a presentation ceremony.

24 February 1981
Trophy received by David at the 1981 Rock and Pop Awards ceremony at the New London Theatre for being voted No. 1 male singer in the competition arranged yearly by BBC 'Nationwide', the *Daily Mirror* and Radio I. Received his award from Lulu.

Later that week, before his return to the States David was spotted at the Virgin megastore in Oxford Street purchasing singles by Grace Jones, Tot Tatlor, Human Sexual Response, Simple Minds and The Polecats' version of 'John, I'm Only Dancing'. A long way from the time in 1967 when he used to stand in the HMV shop in Oxford Street to see what prospective customers thought of his first LP.

1 March 1981
'Bowie Friends' official fan club established in London.

20 March 1981
'Up the Hill Backwards'/'Crystal Japan' single released by RCA, the fourth A-side taken from 'Scary Monsters'. Initial release in picture sleeve and cassette single form (highest chart position No. 32).

'John I'm Only Dancing'/'Big Green Car' single released by The Polecats, A-side written by David (Mercury).

'London Boys'/'Love You Till Tuesday' single rereleased (Decca).

March 1981
'Time'/'Suffragette City', 'Ain't It Funny' single released by Hazel O'Connor.

10 May 1981
Oona Chaplin interviewed for the *Sunday People* by Chris Hutchins.

Although Lady Oona Chaplin reveres the memory of her late husband, the black veils of widowhood are not for her. Looking astonishingly younger than her years, she flies around the world, using the magnificent Chaplin mansion overlooking Lake Geneva as a base . . .

At the house which has become a shrine for devotees of Britain's most famous entertainer, she talked to me frankly about her relationship with David Bowie, who has a home nearby. 'It's a purely platonic thing, of course, although I'm crazy about him in a way. Eugene, my son who is a recording engineer, wanted to have a supper party here for David and a group of his friends, which of course was fine by me. I said I would be around for a minute before making myself scarce – I didn't want to appear rude by not looking in on them for a moment or two.

'Eugene was very impressed by him and wanted everything to be just right. He kept fussing about, saying, "David doesn't like to sit down to

221

the table to eat and he doesn't like this and he doesn't like that." I thought: "All this fuss over David Bowie." And then this very charming, very intelligent, very sensitive fellow – who came from the same part of London as Charlie, walked in here and wanted to talk. It was as simple as that.

'He couldn't have been nicer and I got very fond of him.' Fond enough, I asked, to justify the gossip stories that they were constantly together and falling in love?

'He's moved here to Switzerland, he doesn't speak French very well, he doesn't know many people round here and he is really quite lonely. So I'm his friend.'

What about reports that she had flown to America last autumn to be by his side?

'Out of the blue David called a few months ago and said, "Come to New York for the opening night of my play". I thought why not? I'm absolutely free, so I went.'

The assistant engineer on the 'Lodger' LP was Eugene Chaplin.

28 May 1981
Joe Bowie's tenth birthday.

July 1981
While in Switzerland, David visited the Mountain studios in Montreux where Queen were recording their next LP. David and Queen decided to produce a single together, the record cowritten on a 50/50 basis was 'Under Pressure'. David was also adding his vocals to the theme music for 'Cat People', with music written by Georgio Moroder.

BBC Television announce their forthcoming plays and television series in a major £34-million package. On top of the list of plays, *Baal*, a television adaptation of the play by Bertolt Brecht with David Bowie as Baal. David was reported to have taken a substantial reduction in his normal fee for such work, receiving the normal fee afforded to 'stars' in one-off BBC productions, about £1,000.

August 1981
Rehearsals and production started on *Baal* at the Television Centre, London. During filming, David was joined at the studio by Debbie Harry and Chris Stein on David's invitation. The three later spent the rest of the evening having dinner. While in London, David dropped in to see Pete Townshend, recording his solo LP in Oxford Circus Air studios. Work on *Baal* completed by the end of August.

September 1981
Interviewed for the *Radio Times* by Henry Fenwick about *Baal*. Leaves for New York.

While in New York, David attended The Rolling Stones's Madison Square Garden concert, stopping backstage before the show and afterwards going on the town with Jagger. At that time David and Jagger were kicking around ideas for a film. Jagger later elaborated during an interview, 'He has some funny ideas and we've been trying to write an original screenplay together.

'It has a real chance of happening. It will be a small-budget fun thing rather than a big Hollywood production. I also have an idea for a small musical without the band. A bit like the kind of thing Bowie used to do. Or similar to Bette Midler's show, only not so camp!'

At this time, it was announced that David had decided not to appear in Dennis Potter's *Brimstone and Treacle* film, once rejected by the BBC. The replacement for the role was Sting of The Police. Potter, though obviously disappointed that David had decided not to appear in the film, said, 'Sometimes Bowie looks as if he is dead – he's too chilling, whereas Sting has more bottled-up warmth.' David did make a curious appearance in the film, in fact during the film Sting ripped off a Bowie poster from the wall.

7 September 1981
The BBC release details of the completed production of *Baal*, producer Louis Marks commented on David's acting ability.

'Baal is someone who lives his life to the full, experiencing everything. He's rather like a rock star of today. We realized that we needed someone who was a star in his own right, a performer, a singer. We needed someone to mirror the person himself. Bowie, of course, was ideal. To our surprise he expressed interest straight away. He's a natural for the part. For one thing, he certainly knows his Brecht. He's very well read and is particularly interested in pre-First World War German drama and art. Working with him, it was apparent that he had an instinctive understanding of the character. Baal is very close to his own nature, one might say.

November 1981
Adam Ant interviewed for the *NME*.

'I envy David Bowie. He can stay right out of it all and enjoy his life, enjoy his music. I can enjoy my life like that when I've done a lot more work.'

2 November 1981
'Under Pressure'/'Soul Brother' single released by David and Queen, the first time David had shared credits on a single. It was recorded in

Switzerland and went to No. 1 two weeks after release, staying there for two weeks. Initial release in picture sleeve and 12–inch form (EMI).

19 November 1981
'Wild is the Wind'/'Golden Years' single released; two songs taken from the 1976 LP 'Station to Station'. Initial release in picture sleeve and also 12–inch (RCA).

'ChangesTwoBowie' greatest hits LP released, the second greatest hit package to be chosen by David (RCA).

With the release of 'Wild is the Wind' came a video for the song, made in London after production of *Baal* in August. At the same time a video was made for the *Baal* song, 'The Drowned Girl'. Neither has been shown in the UK. Both films featured Tony Visconti on cello.

'Changes Two Bowie' album released 19 November 1981 (RCA BOW LP3)

Side One	*Side Two*
Aladdin Sane (Bowie)	Sound and Vision (Bowie)
(On Broadway) (Weil, Mann, Leiber, Stoller)	Fashion (Bowie)
Oh, You Pretty Things (Bowie)	Wild is the Wind (Tiomkin, Washington)
Starman (Bowie)	John, I'm Only Dancing (Bowie)
1984 (Bowie)	D.J. (Bowie, Eno, Alomar)
Ashes to Ashes (Bowie)	

Produced by David Bowie, Ken Scott, Tony Visconti and Harry Maslin.

17 December 1981
Christiane F released in the UK. This was a German film made in Berlin and featuring David in a specially prepared concert sequence. *Christiane F* was the most commercially successful film ever in German cinematic history.

20 December 1981
The British television premiere of *The Man Who Fell to Earth*, broadcast on BBC 2 in a slightly-edited condition.

In 1981 David released no new LP for the first time since 1970.

8 January 1982
Bowie's thirty-fifth birthday.

30 January 1982
David voted No. 1 male singer and No. 3 songwriter in the *NME* poll
for 1981.

February 1982
More rumours, five years on from its inception, that David is still
intending to play *The Frank Sinatra Story*.
  Christiane F film released in the US.

26 February 1982
'Baal's Hymn', 'Remembering Marie A.'/'Ballad of the Adventurers',
'The Drowned Girl', 'The Dirty Song' EP released, a five-track complimentary release for the play broadcast in March. The EP was neatly
packaged in a colour gatefold rundown of the play, all songs written
by Bertolt Brecht (RCA).

1 March 1982
Work begun on *The Hunger*, David's third major film, based on the
novel by Whitley Streiber, directed by Tony Scott in his first major
film.

2 March 1982
Baal broadcast on BBC I. The Bertolt Brecht play, dramatized for TV
was David's first inroad into television acting. It was a strange work
to tackle for television and utilized split-screen techniques.

Baal by Bertolt Brecht. Translated by John Willet.
Adapted for television by John Willet and Alan Clarke

Cast

Baal	*David Bowie*
Mech	*Robert Austin*
Piller	*Russell Wootten*
Johannes	*J. Wadham*
Emile	*Juliet Hammond-Hill*
Eckhart	*Jonathan Kent*
1st Cab driver	*Wally Thomas*
2nd Cab driver	*Roy Evans*
Horgauer	*Michael Miller*
Louis	*Sylvia Brayshay*
Johanna	*Tracey Childs*
Porter's Wife	*Paola Dionisotti*

Sophie	*Zoe Wanamaker*
Soubrette	*Polly James*
Pianist	*Hugh Walters*
Mjurk	*Lean Lissek*
Lupu	*Julian Littman*
1st Policeman	*James Duggan*
2nd Policeman	*Bill Stewart*
1st Woodcutter	*Brian Coburn*
2nd Woodcutter	*P. J. Davidson*
3rd Woodcutter	*Michael Hughes*
4th Woodcutter	*Trevor Cooper*
Musical Director	*Dominic Muldowney*
Designer	*Tony Abbott*
Sound	*Mike Jones*
Script Editor	*Stuart Griffiths*
Producer	*Louis Marks*
Director	*Alan Clarke*
Lighting	*Sam Barclay*
Costume Designer	*Reg Samuel*
Make Up	*Pauline Cox*
Technical Manager	*Jeff Jeffrey*
Production Manager	*Sue Box*
Production Assistant	*Glenys Williams*
Production Floor Manager	*Laura Sims*

Radio Times magazine (27 February – 5 March edition) with feature on *Baal* and a short interview with David in New York just after the end of the play's production. Interview with Henry Fenwick:

'I've got to start writing again – I haven't written anything for over a year. Every album that I've written I've got three or four paintings to go with it as well. In Berlin they are mostly of Turks and here they're mostly of contemporaries of mine (David Byrne, William Burroughs, Phillip Glass). They are all desperate-looking people! I never show them because they are much too personal.

March 1982
General outings in London included nightclubbing at Gossips, getting drunk with three members of The Exploited punk group and Gene October and friend from the group Chelsea. The main topic of conversation was *Baal* and Berlin. Another evening was spent at Gaz, a nightclub in Soho.

11 March 1982
'Cat People (Putting Out Fire)'/'Paul's Theme (Jogging Chase)' single

released, the theme to the forthcoming film of the same name. David's vocals added in Montreux. Lyrics written by David (A-side only), music by Georgio Moroder (MCA).

Evening spent at Sadlers Wells for the premiere of the *Berlin Requiem* by the Ballet Rambert. David attended with no VIP treatment.

March 1982
General filming on *The Hunger* continued under strict security. Location work included the original setting for Bram Stoker's *Dracula* in Whitby. Also time was spent at Heaven nightclub, where David and his co-star Catherine Deneuve were shot in a scene hunting for prey, the two being modern vampires. In the scene, David was disguised with Presleyish-style quiff, jet black hair and shades as he watched a performance by Pete Murphy of Bauhaus. Production gossip leaked artificial rumours to an eager press of trouble between David and Catherine Deneuve, who evidently refused to act in a nude shower scene with David. She asked the director for a stand-in to take her place. David made a similar request. One rare on-set comment was made by David, 'It's good casting, and I'm really enjoying this film.'

May 1982
David made a brief appearance in the audience at a 'Design for Modern Living' gig at the Roebuck pub in Tottenham Court Road.

Knebworth Festival cancelled due to known headlining names refusing. David was the first artist to refuse a huge offer for a one-off performance. He also turned down an offer of £100,000 for a one-off performance at Blackbush Aerodrome.

17 June 1982
Hunger filming continued at Luton Hoo. Interviews and photographs denied by MGM officials. The filming featured David and Catherine Deneuve, both in elegant period costumes, in several eighteenth-century flashback sequences inside the building. The outside gardens were kept open to the public who were unaware of the filming.

One person who managed to talk to David was Luton Hoo public relations officer, June Hills who said, 'He was absolutely charming.'

June 1982
David with Catherine Deneuve attends a performance of the Glenda Jackson/Georgina Hale comedy *Summit Conference* at the Lyric Theatre, Shaftesbury Avenue.

David took a cut in his royalties on past album releases with RCA so that old LPs could be released (on the RCA International label) at £2.99.

Early July
Widely reported to the press that David and John McEnroe, living next door to each other in rented Belgravia flats, had tea, prompted by McEnroe disturbing David in the night with his guitar playing. David was reported to have suffered strained renditions of the Stones's 'Satisfaction' and his own 'Rebel Rebel'. He showed McEnroe the correct chords.

July 1982
Hunger information leaked from the set revealed David to be made up for a stop-frame ageing process to an age of about three hundred (give or take a few lines). Throughout production David was escorted by two bodyguards. During filming of the ageing sequence the set was closed off except for the necessary few. *Hunger* production completed in mid-July.

David spotted, looking a little younger, at London's Soul Furnace Club.

12–13 July 1982
The *Sun* and the *Star* both ran articles on David's sanity. The *Sun*'s was titled, 'I'm terrified of going mad', and the *Star*'s 'I began to doubt my own sanity'. Both pieces referred to old interviews.

Early September 1982
Production started on David's fourth feature film *Merry Christmas Mr Lawrence*, David's second film in one year.

The film, directed by controversial Japanese director, Nagisa Oshima, was the first Anglo–Japanese film to be made. It starred English actor, Tom Conti. The scriptwriter for the film, Paul Mayersberg, also wrote the screenplay *The Man Who Fell to Earth*.

The film itself was based on a short story by Laurens van der Post, 'A Bar of Shadow' from a collection of short stories in *The Seed and The Sower*. David and Conti play two prisoners who refuse to be broken by brutal Japanese guards at a camp in Java.

Osima said of David, 'He has an inner spirit that is indestructible.'

Filming was on (the Cook Islands), Auckland and Tokyo.

1 October 1982
'I Pity the Fool', 'Take My Tip' (The Manish Boys)/'You've Got a Habit of Leaving', 'Baby Loves That Way' (Davy Jones and the Lower Third) 10–inch single released (Charly). (A rerelease of the 1979 compilation EP) (CYM I).

October 1982
US release date of *The Hunger* put back until March 1983. Thus release in the UK also delayed to June.

1 October 1982
'Ziggy Stardust'/'Third Uncle' double A-sided single released by Bauhaus. A-side written by David, B-side written by Brian Eno. Also released on 12–inch containing extra tracks, 'Waiting for the Man' and 'Party of the First Part' (Beggars Banquet).

11 October 1982
Schöner Gigolo – Armer Gigolo (*Just a Gigolo*) broadcast on German TV for the first time ever (ARD). This film was recut and redubbed with new voices.

Early November 1982
Production of *Merry Christmas Mr Lawrence* completed. David went on to New York to complete preparation for a new LP. (Film premiered at the 1983 Cannes Film Festival).

5 November 1982
'Fashions' picture disc pack released containing ten of David's old singles in attractive picture-disc form:

'The Jean Genie'/'Ziggy Stardust'
'Life on Mars'/'The Man Who Sold the World'
'Drive in Saturday'/'Round and Round'
'Sorrow'/'Amsterdam'
'Golden Years'/'Can You Hear Me'
'Boys Keep Swinging'/'Fantastic Voyage'
'Ashes to Ashes'/'Move On'
'Rebel Rebel'/'Queen Bitch'
'Sound and Vision'/'A New Career in a New Town'
'Space Oddity'/'Changes', 'Velvet Goldmine'

A limited edition release of 25,000 (RCA).

18 November 1982
'Peace on Earth'/'Little Drummer Boy'/'Fantastic Voyage' single released by RCA for Christmas featuring David singing with the late Bing Crosby, recorded for Crosby's television show in December 1977 (Highest chart position No. 3).

Early December 1982
David books a three-week session at recording studios in New York.

10 December 1982
'Bowie Rare' LP released in the UK, an Italian import of single B-sides, the bonus track being 'Ragazzo Solo, Ragazza Sola – the Italian version of 'Space Oddity' released in Italy in 1970 (RCA – Italy).

17 December 1982
David's world tour for 1983 confirmed by Bewlay Bros, New York. With his contract about to expire with RCA Records, negotiations were underway with Capital, EMI's American division, headed by their chairman and chief executive, Bhaskar Menon.

1983
On Thursday 27 January David signed a five-year contract to EMI America in New York. EMI were openly jubilant: even Bowie himself was slightly taken aback by their enthusiasm. David and EMI America chairman, Bhaskar Menon appeared in front of New York pressmen to announce the signing. Afterwards David gave a number of short interviews including one for BBC 'Nationwide', broadcast the following evening.

From New York, after recording his first LP for EMI, David flew to Australia to join David Mallet to work on two new video projects to promote the LP. Promotional videos were prepared for 'Let's Dance' and 'China Girl'.

On 16 March David arrived at 5 a.m. at Heathrow after a 25-hour flight from Australia. He went to a press conference arranged by EMI to announce his new LP and tour. David was met at the airport by a handful of weary fans and a couple of photographers. After signing autographs he told them, 'I'm off to get some kip!'

The press conference of 17 March was held at Claridges Hotel. A select seventy-five members of the world press were invited and the afternoon was spent giving interviews to UK television and radio journalists.

'Let's Dance'/'Cat People' single was released on 18 March, the B-side being an updated version of the original. The single became a UK No. 1 and remained so for three weeks.

The LP 'Let's Dance' was released on 14 April and went to No. 1. EMI announced that the album was the fastest selling LP in their history since 'Sergeant Pepper'.

'Let's Dance' album EMI America AML 3029

Side One
Modern Love (Bowie)
China Girl (Bowie/Pop)
Let's Dance (Bowie)
Without You (Bowie)

Side Two
Ricochet (Bowie)
Criminal World (Godwin/Browne/ Lyons)
Cat People (Putting Out Fire) (Moroder/Bowie)
Shake It (Bowie)

Produced by David Bowie and Nile Rodgers

David Bowie (vocals)
Nile Rodgers (guitar)
Stevie Ray Vaughn (lead guitar)
Carmine Rojas/Bernard Edwards (bass)
Omar Hakim/Tony Thompson (drums)
Rob Sabino (keyboards)
Mac Gollehon (trumpet)
Robert Arron/Stan Harrison (tenor, flute)
Steve Elson (baritone, flute)
Sammy Figueroa (percussion)
Frank Simms/George Simms/David Spinner (backing vocals)

David Bowie's 1983 UK tour opened in London at the Wembley Arena on 2 June, the start of three sell-out shows. The tour moved on to Birmingham and to three open-air shows at Milton Keynes Bowl on 1, 2 and 3 July and another in Scotland.

Every show was sold out within a day of announcement. The promoter, Harvey Goldsmith, said later that it was easily the biggest response to any shows he had previously handled, even outselling The Rolling Stones's shows of the previous year.

After an absence from the public eye of nearly three years, Bowie had once again proved his ability to return in a big way. Ten years on from his initial 'superstar' status, it seems as if he never went away.

Appendix One

Filmography

Love You Till Tuesday

Produced and backed by Kenneth Pitt.
(For full reference see February 1969.)
English/German.

The Virgin Soldiers
(1968) Columbia Pictures

David featured briefly in a barroom fight
as an extra. David cast in the film by
Ned Sherrin. *The Virgin Soldiers* was
adapted from the novel by Leslie
Thomas and starred Hywel Bennet.

The Image
(1969) A Negus–Fancey Production

Produced by Negus–Fancey
Directed by Michael Armstrong
Screenplay by Michael Armstrong
Director of Photography – Ousama Rawi
Editor – Julian Hindson
Music by Noel Janus
Production Company – Negus–Fancey
Distribution Company – Border Films

Featuring:
David Bowie The Boy
Michael Armstrong The Artist

(Running Time: 15 mins) (Black and
White)

Bowie '73' (filmed July 3rd 1973)
D. A. Pennebaker Productions

Produced and Directed by Richard
Pennebaker
Filmed by Jim Desmond
Mike Davis
Randy Franken
D. A. Pennebaker
Assistants – Steve Lysohir
– Phillip Mesure
Unit Manager – Stacy Pennebaker
Music Mix – Mike Moran
Editor – Lorry Whitehead
Associate Producer for Pennebaker, Inc.
– Edith Van Slyck
Concert Sound – Ground Control
Concert Recording – RCA Mobile
Filmed and Recorded – The
Hammersmith Odeon, London

Featuring:
David Bowie
Jeff Beck
with Mick Ronson
Trevor Bolder
Woody Woodmansey
Additional Musicians:
Ken Fordham
Brian Wilshaw
Geoffrey MacCormack
John Hutchinson
Mike Garson

(Also released as *A London Show* in
Europe)
(Running time: varies from 1–2 hours)

The Man Who Fell to Earth (1976) British Lion Films

Produced by Michael Deeley
      Barry Spikings
Directed by Nicolas Roeg
Screenplay by Paul Mayersberg
Written by Walter Trevis
Musical Director – John Phillips
Camera Operator – Gordon Hayman
Editor – Graeme Clifford
Executive Producer – Si Litvinoff

Featuring:
Thomas Jerome Newton   *David Bowie*
Nathan Bryce   *Rip Torn*
Mary-Lou   *Candy Clark*
Oliver Farnsworth   *Buck Henry*
Peters   *Bernie Casey*
Professor Canutti   *Jackson D. Kane*
Trevor   *Rick Riccardo*
Arthur   *Tony Mascia*
Elaine   *Linda Hutton*
Jill   *Hilary Holland*
Helen   *Adrienne Larussa*
Jewellery Store Owner   *Lilybelle Crawford*
Receptionist   *Richard Breeding*
Waiter   *Albert Nelson*
Peter's Associate   *Peter Prouse*
Capt. James Lovell   *Himself*
Preacher and Congregation of Presbyterian Church, Artesia, N. M. *Themselves* (Running Time: 140 mins (UK); 120 mins (US).

Schöner Gigolo – Armer Gigolo (Just a Gigolo) (1978) Leguan Films

Produced by Rolf Thiele
Directed by David Hemmings
Screenplay – Ennio De Conan
      Joshua Sinclair
Musical Director – Jack Fishman
Editor – Maxine Julius
Assistant Director – Eva-Maria Sconecker
Production Manager – Lutz Winter
Art Director – Peter Rothe
Director of Photography – Charley Steinberger
Costume Design – Ingrid Zoré

Make-up and hair for David Bowie, Sydne Rome, Marlene Dietrich – Anthony Clavet

Featuring:
Paul Von Przygodsky   *David Bowie*
Cilly   *Sydne Rome*
Helgar   *Kim Novak*
Captain Herman Kraft   *David Hemmings*
Mutti   *Maria Schell*
Prince   *Kurt Jurgens*
Baroness Van Semering   *Marlene Dietrich*
Eva   *Erica Pluhar*
Gustav, Paul's Father   *Rudolf Schündler*
Aunt Hilda   *Hilde Weissner*
Otto   *Werner Pochath*
Von Lipzig   *Bela Erny*
Major Von Muller   *Freidhelm Lehmann*
Lothar   *Rainer Hunold*
Frau Aeckerle   *Evelyn Künneke*
Frau Uexkull   *Karin Hardt*
Frau Von Putzdorf   *Gudrun Genest*
Greta   *Ursula Heyer*
Gilda   *Christiane Maybach*
Director   *Martin Hirthe*
Max, Cilly's Agent   *Rene Kolldehoff*
Drunken Worker   *Gunter Meisner*
1st Man in Bath   Peter Schlesinger

Filmed entirely on location in Berlin
World Sales – ICM Paris
(Running time: 147 mins)

**Wir Kinder Vom Bahnhof Zoo
(Christiane F.)
Solaris Film Productions**

Produced by Bernd Eichinger
             Hans Weth
Directed by Ulrich Edel
Screenplay – Herman Weigel
Based on the Der Stern book
Christiane F
Transcribed and edited from tape
recordings by
   Kai Herman
   Horst Rieck

Featuring:
Christian F.   *Natja Brunckhorst*
Peter   Thomas Haustein
Special guest appearance
David Bowie   *Himself*

*(German Dialogue – English Subtitles/
English Language Version)*
(Running Time: 120 mins)

The Hunger (1983) MGM

Produced by Richard Shepherd
Directed by Tony Scott
Screenplay – James Costigan
Costumes – Milena Canonero
Based on the novel by Whitely Strieber

Featuring:
David Bowie
Catherine Deneuve
Susan Sarandon
Beth Ehlers
Graham Jarvis
Zoe Wanamaker
Pete Murphy

**Merry Christmas, Mr Lawrence
(1983) (Anglo–Japanese Production)**

Directed by Nagisa Oshima
Screenplay by Paul Mayersberg
Adapted from the short story, 'A Bar of
     Shadow' by Laurens Van Der Post

Featuring:
Jack 'Straffer' Celliers   *David Bowie*
John Lawrence   *Tom Conti*
Hicksley   *Jack Thompson*

Appendix Two
Single releases and catalogue numbers

June 1964 – November 1972

'Liza Jane'/'Louie Louie Go Home' (Vocallion Pop V. 9221)
'You're Holding Me Down'/'I've Gotta' (Coral 62492) The King Bees
'Restless'/'Take My Tip' (Stateside SS405) Kenny Miller
'I Pity the Fool'/'Take My Tip' (Parlophone R 5250)
'You've Got a Habit of Leaving'/'Baby Loves That Way' (Parlophone R 5315)
'Do Anything You Say'/'Good Morning Girl' (Pye 7N. 17079)
'Can't Help Thinking About Me'/'And I Say to Myself' (Pye 7N.17020)
'Can't Help Thinking About Me'/'And I Say to Myself' (Warner Brothers WB 5815) US
'I Dig Everything'/'I'm Not Losing Sleep' (Pye 7N.17157)
'Rubber Band'/'The London Boys' (Deram DM. 107)
'Rubber Band'/'There is a Happy Land' (Deram 85009) US
'Over the Wall We Go'/'Everyday of My Life' (Reaction 591012) Oscar
'The Laughing Gnome'/'The Gospel According to Tony Day' (Deram DM. 123)
'The Laughing Gnome'/'If I Were a Rich Man' (HMV Pop 1600) Ronny Hilton
'Love You Till Tuesday'/'Did You Ever Have a Dream' (Deram DM. 135)
'Love You Till Tuesday'/'Did You Ever Have a Dream' (Deram 85016) US
'Love is Always'/'Love is Always' (Palette PB 25.579) Dee Dee, Belgium
'Silver Treetop School for Boys'/'I've Lost a Friend and Found a Lover' (Polydor 56189) The Slender Plenty
'Silver Treetop School for Boys'/'Sugar Chocolate Machine' (CBS 3105) The Beatstalkers
'Silly Boy Blue'/'One Minute Women' (Parlophone) Billy Fury
'Silly Boy Blue'/'One Minute Women' (Malma Records M 12018) Billy Fury, US
'Deborah'/'Child Star' (Regal Zonophone 3008) Tyrannosaurus Rex
'Rain Coloured Roses'/'Everything is You' (CBS 3557) The Beatstalkers
'Little Boy'/'When I'm Five' (CBS 3936) The Beatstalkers

'Space Oddity'/'Wild Eyed Boy from Freecloud' (Philips BF 1801)
'Space Oddity'/'Wild Eyed Boy from Freecloud' (Mercury 72949) US
'The Prettiest Star'/'Conversation Piece' (Mercury MF 1135)
'Memory of a Free Festival Pt I'/'Memory of a Free Festival Pt 2' (Mercury 6052 026)
'Memory of a Free Festival Pt I'/'Memory of a Free Festival Pt 2' (Mercury 73075) US
'Ragazzo Solo, Ragazza Sola'/'Wild Eyed Boy from Freecloud' (Philips BW704 208) Italian
'Ragazzo Solo, Ragazza Sola'/'Sheila') (Numero Uno ZN 50016) The Computers, Italian
'All the Madmen'/'All the Madmen' (Mercury 73173) US
'Holy Holy'/'Black Country Rock' (Mercury 6052 049)
'Oh, You Pretty Things'/'Together Forever' (RAK 114) Peter Noone
'Oh, You Pretty Things'/'Together Forever' (Bell 45131) Peter Noone
'Hang Onto Yourself'/'Moonage Daydream' (B & C CB. 149) Arnold Corns
'Eight Line Poem'/'Bombers' RCA (no matrix) US promo only
'Walnut Whirl'/'Right on Mother' (RAK 121) Peter Noone
'Changes'/'Andy Warhol' (RCA 2160)
'Changes'/'Andy Warhol' (RCA 74–0605) US
'Starman'/'Suffragette City' (RCA 2199)
'Starman'/'Suffragette City' (RCA 74–0719) US
'All the Young Dudes'/'One of the Boys' (CBS S.8271) Mott the Hoople
'All the Young Dudes'/'One of the Boys' (Columbia 4–45673) Mott the Hoople, US
'All the Young Dudes'/'One of the Boys' (CBS S.3963) Mott the Hoople
'Hang onto Yourself'/'Man in the Middle' (B & C CB.189) Arnold Corns
'John, I'm Only Dancing'/'Hang Onto Yourself' (RCA 2263)
'Do Anything You Say', 'I Dig Everything'/'Can't Help Thinking About Me', 'I'm Not Losing Sleep' (Pye/EP 7NX.8002)
'The Jean Genie'/'Ziggy Stardust' (RCA 2302)
'The Jean Genie'/'Ziggy Stardust' (RCS 74–0838) US
'Walk on the Wild Side'/'Perfect Day' (RCA 2303) Lou Reed
'Walk on the Wild Side'/'Vicious' (RCA PB. 2303) US Lou Reed
'Space Oddity', 'Moonage Daydream'/'Life on Mars', 'It Ain't Easy' (RCA EP 45–103) promo only
'Space Oddity'/'The Man Who Sold the World' (RCA 74–08761) US

US and UK promotional singles are issued for all of David's single releases, some in a similar form to the publicly-available releases, some in mono/ stereo version of only the A-side.

April 1973 – November 1982

'Drive In Saturday'/'Round and Round' (RCA 2352)
'Time'/'The Prettiest Star' (RCA APBO.0001) US
'Life on Mars'/'The Man Who Sold the World' (RCA 2316)
'The Prettiest Star'/'Love Around' (UK 44) Simon Turner

'Let's Spend the Night Together'/'Lady Grinning Soul' (RCA APBO.0028) US
'The Laughing Gnome'/'The Gospel According to Tony Day' (Deram DM123)
'Sorrow'/'Amsterdam' (RCA 2424)
'Sorrow'/'Amsterdam' (RCA APBO. 0160) US
'The Man Who Sold the World'/'Watch that Man' (Polydor 2001 490) Lulu
'Slaugher on 10th Avenue', 'Growing Up and I'm Fine'/'All Cut Up On
    You', 'Andy Warhol' (RCA DJEO 0259) US promo only
'Rebel Rebel'/'Queen Bitch' (RCA LPBO. 5009)
'Rebel Rebel'/'Lady Grinning Soul' (RCA APBO.0278) US
'Rock 'N' Roll Suicide'/'Quicksand' (RCA LPB05021)
'Diamond Dogs'/'Holy Holy' (RCA APBO.0293)
'Diamond Dogs'/'Holy Holy' (RCA APBO.0293) US
'1984'/'Queen Bitch' (RCA APBO. 10026) US
'Andy Warhol'/'Dizzy Heights' (RCA 2446) Dana Gillespie
'Rock 'N' Roll With Me'/'The Divine Daze of Deathless Delight' (Epic EPC
    2661) Donovan
'Knock on Wood'/'Panic in Detroit' (RCA 2466)
'Rock 'N' Roll With Me'/'Panic in Detroit' (RCA PB.10105) US
'Young Americans'/'Suffragette City' (RCA 2523)
'Young Americans'/'Knock on Wood' (RCA PB. 10152) US
'London Boys'/'Love You Till Tuesday' (Decca F. 13579)
'Life on Mars'/'Down by the Stream' (EMI 2305) The King's Singers
'Fame'/'Right' (RCA 2579)
'Fame'/'Right' (RCA PB.10320) US
'Space Oddity'/'Changes', 'Velvet Goldmine' (RCA 2593)
'Golden Years'/'Can You Hear Me' (RCA 2640)
'Golden Years'/'Can You Hear Me' (RCA PB. 10441) US
'TVC 15'/'We are the Dead' (RCA 2682)
'TVC 15'/'We are the Dead' (RCA PB.10664) US
'Suffragette City'/'Stay' (RCA 2726)
'Stay'/'Word on a Wing' (RCA PB.10736) US
'Fascination'/'We Just Want to Play For You' (WMOT K 11002) Fat Larry's
    Band
'Sound and Vision'/'A New Career in a New Town' (RCA PB.0905)
'Sound and Vision'/'A New Career in a New Town' (RCA PB.10905) US
'China Girl'/'Baby' (RCA PB 9093) Iggy Pop
'Be My Wife'/'Speed of Life' (RCA PB.1017)
'Be My Wife'/'Speed of Life' (RCA PB.11017) US
'I Got a Right'/'Gimme Some Skin' Holland–Siamese (PM 001) Iggy Pop/
    James Williamson
'Heroes'/'V–2 Schneider' (RCA PB.1121)
'Heroes'/'V–2 Schneider' (RCA PB.11121) US
'Heroes'/'V–2 Schneider' (RCA PB.9167) French
'Helden'/V–2 Schneider' (RCA PB.9168) German
'Success'/'The Passenger' (RCA PB 9160) Iggy Pop
'Beauty and the Beast'/'Sense of Doubt' (RCA PB.1190)
'Beauty and the Beast'/'Sense of Doubt' (RCA PB.11190) US

'Over the Wall We Go'/'Beauty Queen' (RSO 2090 270)
'I Got a Right'/'Sixteen' (RCA PB.9213) Iggy Pop
'Liza Jane'/'Louie Louie Go Home' (Decca FL3807)
'Breaking Glass'/'Art Decade', 'Ziggy Stardust' (RCA BOW I)
'David Bowie's Revolutionary Song'/'Charmaine' (MA–185–V) Japan
'I Pity the Fool', 'Take My Tip'/'You've Got a Habit of Leaving', 'Baby
   Loves That Way' (EMI NUT EP) (EMI.2925)
'Boys Keep Swinging'/'Fantastic Voyage' (RCA BOW 2)
'D.J.'/'Repetition' (RCA BOW 3)
'D.J.'/'Fantastic Voyage' (RCA PB.11661) US
'Look Back in Anger'/'Repetition' (RCA PB.11724) US
'John, I'm Only Dancing (Again) (1975)'/'John, I'm Only Dancing (1972)'
   (RCA BOW 4)
'John, I'm Only Dancing (Again) (1975)'/'Golden Years' (RCA PD.11886)
   US
'John, I'm Only Dancing (1972)'/'Joe the Lion' (RCA PB.11887) US
'Alabama Song'/'Space Oddity' (RCA BOW 5)
'Madman'/'Join the Girls' (Fresh Purl 7/10) Cuddly Toys
'Crystal Japan'/'Alabama Song' (RCA SS.3270) Japan
'Ashes to Ashes'/'Move On' (RCA BOW 6)
'Ashes to Ashes'/'It's No Game' (RCA PB.12078) US
'Space Oddity – Ashes to Ashes'/'Ashes to Ashes' (RCA DJLI–3795) US
   Promo only
'Fashion'/'Scream Like a Baby' (RCA BOW T.7)
'Fashion'/'Scream Like a Baby' (RCA PB.12134) US
'Scary Monsters (and Super Creeps)'/'Because You're Young' (RCA BOW 8)
'Up the Hill Backwards'/'Crystal Japan' (RCA BOW 9)
'John, I'm Only Dancing'/'Big Green Car' The Polecats
'Under Pressure'/'Soul Brother' (EMI 5250) Queen and David Bowie
'Under Pressure'/'Soul Brother' (EMI 52501) US
'Wild is the Wind'/'Golden Years' (RCA BOW 10)
'Baal's Hymn', 'Remembering Marie A.'/'Ballad of the Adventurers', 'The
   Drowned Girl', 'The Dirty Song' (RCA BOW II)
'Cat People (Putting Out Fire)'/'Paul's Theme (Jogging Chase)' (MCA 770)
'Ziggy Stardust'/'Third Uncle' (BEG 83T) Bauhaus
'Fashions' – Collection of ten picture-disc singles
'Space Oddity'/'Changes', 'Velvet Goldmine' (RCA BOWP 101)
'Life On Mars'/'The Man Who Sold the World' (RCA BOWP 102)
'The Jean Genie'/'Ziggy Stardust' (RCA BOWP 103)
'Rebel Rebel'/'Queen Bitch' (RCA BOWP 104)
'Sound and Vision'/'A New Career in a New Town' (RCA BOWP 105)
'Drive In Saturday'/'Round and Round' (RCA BOWP 106)
'Sorrow/'Amsterdam' (RCA BOWP 107)
'Golden Years'/'Can You Hear Me' (RCA BOW 108)
'Boys Keep Swinging'/'Fantastic Voyage' (RCA BOW 109)
'Ashes to Ashes'/'Move On' (RCA BOWP 110)
'Peace On Earth'/'Little Drummer Boy'/'Fantastic Voyage' (RCA BOW 12)

Appendix Three

US album catalogue numbers
April 1967 – December 1982

'David Bowie' (Deram DES. 18003)
'Man of Words, Man of Music' (Mercury SR. 61246)
'The Man Who Sold the World' (Mercury 61325)
'Hunky Dory' (RCA LSP.4623)
'The Rise and Fall of Ziggy Stardust and The Spiders from Mars' (RCA
    LSP.4702)
'Space Oddity' (RCA LSP.4813)
'The Man Who Sold the World' (RCA LSP.4816)
'Images 1966 – 1967' (London BP. 61829)
'Aladdin Sane' (RCA LSP.4852)
'Pin-Ups' (RCA APL.I.0291)
'Diamond Dogs' (RCA APL.I.0576)
'David Live' (RCA CPL.2.0771)
'Young Americans' (RCA APL.I.0998)
'Station to Station' (RCA APL.I.1327)
'ChangesOneBowie' (RCA APL.I.1732)
'Low' (RCA APL.I.2030)
'Heroes' (RCA AFL.I.2522)
'David Bowie with Eugene Ormandy & The Philadelphia Orchestra/Peter
and the Wolf' (RCA Red Seal ARL.I.2743)
'Stage' (RCA CPL.2.2913)
'Lodger' (RCA AQL.I.3254)
'Scary Monsters (and Super Creeps)' (RCA AQL.I.3647)
'ChangesTwoBowie' (RCA BOW LP 3)

Further Reading

Carr, Roy and Shaar Murray, Charles, *Bowie – An Illustrated Record*, Eel
  Pie, 1981
Bowie, Angie, *Free Spirit*, Mushroom, 1981
Colin, *David Bowie – Discography*, Subterraneans, 1978
Douglas, David, *Presenting David Bowie*, Pinnacle Books, 1975
Fletcher, David Jeffrey, *The Discography of a Generalist*, 1979
Kelleher, Ed, *David Bowie – A Biography in Words and Pictures*, Sire
Hunter, Ian, *Diary of a Rock 'n' Roll Star*, Panther, 1974
Miles, Barry, *David Bowie's Black Book*, Omnibus Press, 1980
Miles, Barry, *Bowie in His Own Words*, Omnibus Press, 1980
Reed, Rex, *Valentines and Vitriol*, US, 1975
Tremlett, George, *The David Bowie Story*, Futura, 1974
Various contributors, *David Bowie – A Portrait*, Wise Publications, 1974